Working Together:
Native Americans
and Archaeologists

Edited by
Kurt E. Dongoske, Mark Aldenderfer, and Karen Doehner

SOCIETY FOR AMERICAN ARCHAEOLOGY

The Society for American Archaeology, Washington, D.C. 20002
Copyright ©2000 by the Society for American Archaeology
All rights reserved. Published 2000
Printed in the United States of America

Photo credit: cover—Tarran Panamarioff and Mikaela Provost participating in the Alutiiq Museum's Community Archaeology Program, at the Outlet Site, Kodiak Island, Alaska. Photo by Amy Steffian. Reproduced by permission of the Alutiiq Museum.

Library of Congress Catalog Card No: 00-101173
ISBN No. 0-932839-18-5

Table of Contents

Acknowledgments .... *iii*

Foreword
Alison Wylie .... *v*

Reflections on the Beginnings of "Working Together"
Mark Aldenderfer .... *xi*

I. Native American Perspectives on Archaeology 1
    Exploring Ancient Worlds
    Roger C. Echo-Hawk 3
    From Specimens to SAA Speakers: Evolution by Federal Mandate
    Gary White Deer 9
    A Navajo Student's Perception: Anthropology and the Navajo
    Nation Archaeology Department Student Training Program
    Davina TwoBears 15

II. Transforming the Archaeological Model 23
    NHPA: Changing the Role of Native Americans in the Archaeological Study of the Past
    T. J. Ferguson 25
    Painting a "New" Face on CRM: Integrating Traditional Culture and Archaeology
    Janet Cohen and Nina Swidler 37
    Hopi Oral History and Archaeology
    *T. J. Ferguson, Kurt E. Dongoske, Mike Yeatts,
    and Leigh J. Kuwanwisiwma* 45
    Native American Oral Traditions and Archaeology
    Roger Anyon, T. J. Ferguson, Loretta Jackson, and Lillie Lane 61
    The White Mountain Apache Tribe Heritage Program:
    Origins, Operations, and Challenges
    John R. Welch 67
    NAGPRA, the Conflict between Science and Religion, and the
    Political Consequences
    G. A. Clark 85
    Native Americans, Western Science, and NAGPRA
    Joe Watkins 91
    Native Americans and Archaeology: A Vital Partnership
    Robert Kelly 97
    International Implications of the Impact of Repatriation
    in Nevada Museums
    Amy Dansie 103
    Repatriation's Silver Lining
    Thomas W. Killion and Paula Molloy 111

III. Native Peoples and Archaeologists Working Together: Case Studies 119

The Archaeological Field School in the 1990s:
Collaboration in Research and Training
Barbara J. Mills 121

Involving the Caddo Tribe during Archaeological Field Schools in
Texas: A Cross-Cultural Sharing
*James E. Bruseth, James E. Corbin, Cecile E. Carter,
and Bonnie McKee* 129

Collaboration at *Inyan Ceyaka Atonwan* (Village at the Rapids)
Janet D. Spector 133

The Integration of Traditional and Scientific Knowledge on Leech
Lake Reservation, Cass Lake, Minnesota
Rose Kluth 139

Archaeology and Alutiiq Cultural Identity on Kodiak Island
Rick Knecht 147

Archaeology, Education, and the Secwepemc
George P. Nicholas 155

Time, Trust, and the Measure of Success: The Nevada Test Site
Cultural Resources Program
Colleen Beck, M. Nieves Zedeño, and Robert Furlow 165

IV. Native Peoples and Archaeologists Working Together beyond the Borders 173

Working Together on the Border
Randall H. McGuire 175

Making History in Xaltocan
Elizabeth M. Brumfiel 181

Archaeology in the Middle of Political Conflict in
Yautepec, Mexico
Michael E. Smith 191

The New Role of the Ancient Lovers of Sumpa
Karen E. Stothert 199

Working Together—Archaeological Research and Community
Participation
Charles Stanish and Chapurukha M. Kusimba 209

Afterword: Who was Arthur C. Parker, Anyway?
David Hurst Thomas 213

References Cited 225

Contributors 235

Acknowledgments

Many individuals contributed to the preparation and production of this book and we wish to recognize them here. First and foremost, we want to thank all of the contributing authors who cared enough to take the time to reflect on the changing relationship between archaeologists and indigenous peoples and share their experiences with us. We are encouraged that through a continuing constructive dialogue, like the ones presented here, a more holistic discipline of archaeology will emerge that is responsive to the multiple narratives of the past. Special thanks are extended to Keith Kintigh, president of the Society for American Archaeology, the SAA Board of Directors, and the Publications Committee for their approval and support of this publication as its first in the new SAA monograph series. We also would like to particularly recognize Tobi Brimsek, SAA executive director, for her support and assistance in the publication of this volume, and to Elizabeth Foxwell, SAA publications manager, for her diligent efforts in copy editing the manuscript and guiding it through production. Lastly, but by no means least, we would like to extend our gratitude to George Nicholas and Roger Anyon, who during a conversation prior to an SAA-sponsored session on the impacts of repatriation in Seattle, suggested a collective publication of articles from the Working Together column in the *SAA Bulletin*.

Kurt E. Dongoske
Mark Aldenderfer
Karen Doehner

Foreword

Alison Wylie

In 1973, in a brief article published in *American Antiquity*, Elden Johnson urged the Society for American Archaeology to make "responsibilities to American Indians" a central and defining commitment of professional archaeological practice (Johnson 1973:130); he identified disrespectful treatment of burials, and lack of consultation and communication as areas of particular concern to Native Americans. In the event, other calls to action took precedence. The defining slogan of North American archaeology—that "archaeology is anthropology or it is nothing" (Binford 1962; Willey and Phillips 1958)—took on new significance. It was imperative, argued a generation of ambitious New Archaeologists, to do archaeology so it matters. This was, most immediately, a commitment to make a difference to a particular kind of scientific anthropology, to use archaeological data as the basis for establishing an explanatory understanding of large-scale, long-term cultural systems and processes. The subject of inquiry was to be, not the "Indian behind the artifact," but "the system behind both the Indian and the artifact" (Flannery 1967:120). Entangled with the now infamous rhetoric of positivism and eco-system functionalism was a strong conviction that this kind of understanding could make a difference in the world. Although never a dominant theme in the published literature, I remember intense and hopeful discussions in the 1970s about ways in which a more systematically scientific archaeology might be our most effective tool for challenging racist and imperialist presuppositions about ancestors, antecedents, and first peoples (see Kelly this volume 1998:25), for illuminating a wider range of human capability and cultural forms than we can come to understand through any other means and, more generally, for learning from the past very much in the spirit articulated by the Hopi tribal chairman, Vernon Masayesva: "you never know where you are going unless you understand where you have been" (Ferguson et al. 1995:13). But just as "the Indian" was to be read out of explanatory account, so too were particular descendent communities, living contexts, and local interests read out of political accounts. The Enlightenment vision at work here is one in which systematic scientific inquiry, properly conducted, could be expected to yield an understanding of humanity (past and present) that transcends all specific contexts of action or understanding, and in this serves us all, society as a whole. The history of anthropology as a whole is structured by the inherent tension between these ambitions and a long tradition of resistance to all forms of cultural context-stripping; archaeology is one particularly volatile site at which this legacy is being played out.

In the 30 years since North American archaeologists declared a renewed commitment to "anthropological archaeology," conceived in these terms, strong arguments have been made to restore agency, intention, and lifeworld to the archaeological subject; cultural process is very often inscrutable when abstracted from the localized histories and contexts through which it operates. And the underlying political vision, never so clearly articulated as when under threat, has faced sustained and profound challenges, intellectual, political, and legal. One after another of the archaeological contributors to *Working Together* remark that their training did little to prepare them to deal effectively with the complex political, cultural dynamics of the contexts in which they now work (Welch), to communicate effectively across lines of ethnic, class, and national differences (Brumfiel), much less to develop strong working relationships with those whose heritage they study (Spector). I remember a graduate classmate explaining why he had transferred from a specialization in sociocultural anthropology to archaeology: He didn't much like dealing with living subjects; he was uncomfortable enlisting them as subjects; the dead ones didn't give you so much trouble, he said, wryly. No doubt this was a minority view, even in the mid-1970s, but it is striking in retrospect. Despite being trained in departments of anthropology (or perhaps, through some oppositional logic, because of this), archaeologists inherit a long tradition in which their subject domain is conceived of as safely distant from any of the living cultures their ethnographic colleagues study, and that they themselves negotiate in the process of pursuing their research. There is much in this that reflects a lingering tradition of "imperial archaeology" (Echo-Hawk, citing Riding In, 1993:5). As Spector describes one of the central messages she internalized as a graduate student, archaeological cultures are largely presumed to be dead, literally (by annihilation) or figuratively (by assimilation, displacement, or transformation). It is this taken-for-granted attitude that has been decisively challenged by descendent communities, especially the First Nations, in the last 30 years, culminating in NAGPRA legislation but originating in demands for repatriation and control over cultural heritage that date back at least a century (see Spector 1994, and Welch 1997–1998, rewritten 1999). Native America, and indigenous peoples around the world, are a vital force, now in a position to insist upon and, increasingly, to enforce a heritage interest in many of the landscapes, sites, and artifacts that archaeologists have studied in the name of anthropological science (see Yellowhorn 1996). Under these conditions, there are increasingly few areas in which archaeology can offer a refuge for anthropologists interested in culture—cultural systems and processes—but not in the people whose lives are shaped in diverse ways by particular cultural histories and dynamics.

In some areas archaeologists can draw on long-standing traditions of consultation and collaboration; the process of "quietly working together" (Schwab 1993) has been under way for years. But as often as not the challenge archaeologists face is that of inventing new forms of practice from the ground up. Taken together, these Working Together columns represent an impressive body of innovative practice, rising "beneath our feet like an unexpected continent" (Echo-Hawk, *postscript*). Several quite different models of practice emerge here. Those that leave the archaeology largely as it stands take the form of formal, arm's length consultation, but even this can prove transformative in ways participants say they hadn't expected. In several cases, simply keeping tribal groups apprized and arranging for site visits, meeting NAGPRA reporting requirements, or setting up a framework for site management, draws attention to unexpected points of convergence in interest and understanding, opening opportunities for more sustained collaboration. Beck et al. describe a sustained 20-year process of developing an effective "broad spectrum" management program for the Nevada nuclear test site; the key, they say, is to secure the long-term participation of tribal and pan-tribal representatives, a point reiterated by a number of contributors who insist that "working together" is an on-going process. But when tribal elders and cultural specialists serve as advisers to archaeological projects and tribal monitors are routinely present in the field, when native communities get directly involved in the doing of archaeology–when native students join field projects and pursue training in archaeology (e.g., Mills, TwoBears, Welch), and when 75 tribal councils hire archaeologists and another 18 take over SHPO functions (Ferguson 1996:36, *postscript*)—this initially consultative relationship often takes a dynamic turn. Indeed, that it should become a "two-way street" (Cameron 1993:12) seems to be a precondition for sustained and productive interaction.

Time and again contributors report that "an exchange that began as professional etiquette became a mainstay in research" (Knecht 1994:8). They find their thinking about the cultural past reoriented in subtle and profound ways. Some develop the creative double-vision of culture brokers. Many report that these interactions raise new questions and enrich their understanding of the cultural significance of archaeological sites and artifacts; they come to an appreciation of what Echo-Hawk calls "the historicity of oral traditions" (1993:6), both as a much neglected resource for archaeological inquiry and as divergent traditions for understanding the cultural past. Knecht describes an evolving partnership with the Alutiiq on Kodiak Island that is emblematic of much that is most inspiring in the contributions to *Working Together*: "As we puzzled over the past together, it became clear to both archaeologists and the native community that neither had a monopoly on knowledge; we needed each other to truly understand the culture history of the island" (1994:8). His vision of a long-term collaborative relationship is one in which joint projects take on a life of their own, and in which Native Americans play a pivotal role—indeed, a central and controlling role—in the archaeological articulation of their history. Examples drawn from his work on Kodiak Island and that of other contributors include programs of cultural documentation and preservation that incorporate oral history and ethnography as well as regional survey and archaeology (Ferguson 1999; Kluth 1996; Schwab 1993); exhibits and reports designed specifically for local communities (Brockoff n.d.; Brumfiel 1994;); permanent community cultural centers and regional museums (Stothert 1998); managed cultural tourism (Welch 1997, rewritten 1999); the rejuvenation of traditional cultural practices (Bruseth et.al.); and educational programs tailored to the needs and interests of descendant communities (see also Nicholas 1997). In all cases, the collaborative enterprise is much more than a matter of "simply adding the voices of so-called 'others'"; as Spector makes the case, it requires a fundamental commitment to "sharing the power and privilege of setting archaeological priorities and standards" (1994:10).

Not all the accounts of "working together" are as positive as these. Some contributors describe situations in which deep-rooted mistrust and fundamental differences in interest and sensibility are all but impossible to overcome (Dansie 1999:31). Others describe local contexts structured by intractable local conflicts (Smith 1997), or by conflicts between local and regional or national governments (McGuire 1996), in which they find themselves co-opted, misrepresented, and manipulated. But in the cases where collaboration seems to work, I note three persistent themes that bear consideration.

The first is a willingness, on the part of the archaeologists involved, to consider that there are other ways of knowing—other epistemic goals and grounds for understanding the cultural past—than those embodied in established archaeological practice. This is not a matter of abandoning the constitutive goals and values of scientific archaeology *tout court*, or of treating all systems of knowledge and belief as equivalent, in purpose or in credibility. Rather, it is a matter of recognizing that archaeology, as it has been defined and practiced in North America, reflects a highly specific set of cultural, institutional interests which should, by their own lights, be treated as negotiable, open-ended, and evolving. In fact, scientific traditions animated by Enlightenment ideals have always been highly opportunistic about their goals and standards, methods and sources of evidence; it is a hallmark of this profoundly pragmatic enterprise that its advocates and practitioners stand ready to consider possibilities and exploit opportunities ruled out by its own internal *status quo*, as much as by that of the larger society and its institutions. To presume that we know clearly and finally what constitutes properly "scientific" modes of practice—in archaeology or in any other research context—is to betray the very commitment to resist dogmatism in all its forms, to hold everything open to revision in light of experience, that is the creative force central to the traditions of scientific practice that have inspired so many archaeologists. Under the circumstances, it is not just impolitic but inimical to the spirit of this enterprise to reject out of hand the questions, approaches to inquiry, and perspectives on the past brought in to play by engagement with descent communities.

Within the space created by this openness to innovation, two other persistent themes emerge. One is a commitment to cultivate a reciprocity of exchange: accountability in both an intellectual and political sense. As articulated by many of the contributors to *Working Together* this requires, first of all, of giving up any presumption that archaeological interests (*qua* scientific) trump all other interests in archaeological sites and material, that archaeologists can claim "incontestable rights of inquiry" (Dansie 1999:31). This is a matter, crucially, of maintaining an open negotiating stance, recognizing the claims of others and, as White Deer puts the point, leaving "ample room for reconciliation" in position statements (1998:8). Beyond this, it is a matter of looking for ways to give back to those whose cultural heritage is under study (TwoBears 1995:4), of asking what archaeology has to offer, not so much to society as a whole—humanity as an abstraction—but to specific others who have an interest in or are affected by archaeological research.

By extension of this last principle, a third theme is a commitment to build project-specific coalitions, recognizing differences but emphasizing delimited areas of common interest. Contributors identify a great many points of convergent interest in understanding the cultural past where strategic collaboration has proven fruitful for all involved; this is a point that has been made even by as formidable a critic of anthropological archaeology as Vine Deloria (1992). But in addition, both Native American and archaeological contributors cite the ethic of conservation that has taken hold in archaeology since the mid-1970s (Lipe 1974) as an area where, despite differences in what this is understood to involve, archaeologists and Native Americans are in a position to make common cause. There is much to be gained by joining forces in opposition, for example, to looters and pot hunters (White Deer 1998:8), in advocating for stronger heritage legislation and in supporting the programs for protecting cultural heritage that already exist. The initiatives that embody these principles will certainly transform archaeology; they realign fundamental assumptions about the goals and identity of archaeology as a discipline. But as Spector puts the point, the future of the discipline depends on it (Spector 1994:10).

Reflections on the Beginnings of Working Together

Mark Aldenderfer

I don't consider myself much of an innovator, but one thing I am very proud of is the success of the Working Together column in the *SAA Bulletin*. While I cannot take full credit for its origins, I do think I have had some positive influence on how the column has evolved into what it is today: a serious vehicle for the exploration of how relationships between native peoples and archaeologists can be improved. Very few archaeologists working today in any part of the world would question the need for such improvement. Some are motivated by a genuine desire to correct past injustices inflicted upon native peoples by archaeologists, while others may work to improve these relationships out of simple self-preservation so as to retain a promising research career or lucrative contract. The sincerity of our motives matters little, however, if in fact our professional and personal behavior reflects an awareness that we must respect the native peoples with whom we work. The pages of the Working Together columns are filled with examples of that respect. In some instances, respect may imply little more than tolerance of diversity and difference. Elsewhere, it may involve the development of truly collaborative research, training, and publication efforts with native peoples that are in great part decided by their interests, and not solely those inspired by the dictates of a scientific archaeology. Working together, then, has become foundational to modern archaeology, and this professional responsibility should rank as highly as does the conservation ethic within our field.

Some History

I assumed editorship of *SAA Bulletin* in early 1993. My publication priorities in the March 1993 Editor's Corner (Aldenderfer 1993) proposed a column designed to foster greater communication and cooperation between Americanist archaeologists and their Latin American colleagues. This proposal shortly became Dialogues—Interamerican Exchanges, a venue for authors to detail the problems and prospects for archaeology in their countries. This column fit with my ideas of making the *Bulletin* more inclusive, but at the time, I was thinking only about archaeologists.

People with other agendas began offering proposals and publication ideas. One of these early innovators was Philip DeBarrios, who sent me an unsolicited paper on the efforts of the Society for California Archaeology (SCA) to find ways to develop better relationships with California's native peoples. This paper was published (DeBarrios 1993), and in one sense, it can be considered as the first paper in the Working Together series. The title of the paper even features the words "working together," and probably stimulated the title of the column that was soon to follow. In the same issue, a short piece also appeared on Arizona's attempts to facilitate interaction between native peoples and archaeologists. Without having a formal place in the pages of the *Bulletin*, these issues were already finding their way into print.

The credit for formalizing the Working Together column goes to Tristine Lee Smart, then a graduate student of anthropology and archaeology at the University of Michigan. In late March, Smart sent me an email with an outline of her proposal:

> Over the last few years, I have become increasingly concerned about finding ways to improve communication and cooperation between archaeologists and Native American communities. From talking to people, I have learned that there are many archaeologists who have been involved on some level in activities aimed at improving communication, mutual understanding, and cooperation with the people whose past they study. However, it is hard to find out who these people are and what they have been doing. Currently, there is no appropriate venue for people to write about these kinds of activities. I was wondering whether it would be possible to have a column in the *SAA Bulletin* that is devoted to brief descriptions of these kinds of activities written by archaeologists or members of the concerned communities. This would not only provide a way for archaeologists to learn about the kinds of activities that have or have not worked, it would also be a concrete demonstration of SAA's commitment to improving communication and mutual understanding between archaeologists and members of concerned communities (Smart to Aldenderfer, March 28, 1993).

This note helped me to solidify my own thinking on these relationships. I asked Smart to develop a more specific proposal and to contact Roger Anyon, a member of SAA's Board of Directors and the SAA Task Force on Native American/SAA Relations; and Joe Watkins, chair of that task force, to get a sense of the climate for such a column. Both strongly endorsed the idea, and Anyon suggested that Native Americans write at least some of the columns. They also encouraged her to contact Robert Kelly, vice-chair of the task force, and Kurt Dongoske, who had discussed a similar idea for a column with Anyon.

Following this series of conversations, Smart's proposal for the column arrived in May 1993, and included a list of nine potential contributions.

During the development of the column, an important issue arose:

> If we ask someone to write a paper for this column, are you prepared to publish it even if it is critical of SAA? Personally, I think we must be willing to listen to and publish critical comments if we are serious about improving communication with concerned communities (Smart to Aldenderfer, July 1, 1993).

The answer, of course, had to be "yes." I was aware of many legitimate grievances held by native peoples, and if the column was to be taken seriously, we had to be ready to weather complaint and criticism. However, as editor I also had to consider my audience, and it was clear that most of my colleagues would not listen to the most strident and insulting voices writing about archaeology, regardless of the message. I suggested the following guidelines:

> I have no problem with criticism of SAA under a few fairly general conditions: The tone cannot be abusive or condescending and there cannot be *ad hominem* remarks of any kind. If we are in fact trying to foster a spirit of cooperation and build a basis of mutual respect and trust, extreme positions on either side of the divide have no place. (Aldenderfer to Smart, July 2, 1993).

We have published columns critical of archaeologists and SAA, but I think that in every instance, such comments have been written with the spirit intended—to find a basis for mutual respect despite strong and sometimes very negative differences.

Roger Echo-Hawk, a historian and member of the Pawnee tribe, launched the series with his piece, "Exploring Ancient Worlds" (Echo-Hawk 1993). He eloquently stated the problem ("The American archaeological community has proven beyond a doubt that it can study Indian history in North America without involving any living Native Americans . . .") and summed up the reaction to this state of affairs by native peoples ("Under these conditions, it is easy for some Indians to reject archaeology as an unacceptable form of inquiry"). Although he offered no simple palliative to this situation, he made one request:

> It is time for SAA to explore in earnest the frontiers of cooperative archaeology. These explorations will ultimately help to shape the character of American archaeology as a new generation of archaeologists enters the twenty-first century.

Echo-Hawk described clearly, but without rancor, the central issue dividing archaeologists and native peoples, and urged SAA members to work to change the situation.

Reaction to Echo-Hawk's column was prompt. Two positive letters were published in the next issue of the *SAA Bulletin* [11(5)], followed by two more in the 12(1) issue. Unsolicited manuscripts began to arrive, and together with five of those requested by Smart, formed the core of the column through 1994 and into 1995. During this period, the first non-U. S. column was published, a paper by Elizabeth Brumfiel describing her experiences with native peoples and outreach programs in Mexico (Brumfiel 1994).

After this initial rush of comment, we received more public feedback in early 1995, when Kurt Dongoske sent us a letter to the editor for publication. The letter, although laudatory, offered a trenchant criticism:

> Yet, as I review the past year and a half of articles I am struck by the fact that only one of the many articles presented a Native American's critical perspective of archaeology. . . . The majority of these articles tend to illustrate the working relationship between Native Americans and archaeologists as "warm and fuzzy" (Dongoske 1995:7).

He went on to remind us that plenty of negative sentiment regarding archaeologists still existed on the part of Native Americans, and urged that the column become truly diverse, rather than simply self-serving and self-congratulatory. He then offered concrete recommendations on how to broaden the scope and diversity of columns.

I took his comments seriously. To ensure a properly balanced column, I then invited Dongoske to serve as associate editor for the column. After his initial surprise, wondering how he had been cornered into an extra volunteer job, he graciously accepted the challenge. He has enthusiastically supervised the column ever since, editing 23 columns to date. Although many of these have described positive interactions, others have been quite critical of archaeologists, such as Gary White Deer's (1998) strong critique of those who resist the Native Graves Protection and Repatriation Act (NAGPRA). Dongoske also has provided a forum for those who challenge NAGPRA, best exemplified in the exchange between Geoff Clark (1998) and Joe Watkins (1998). Judging from the spate of letters to the editor, it is clear that SAA members have been paying close attention.

Working Together has been a wonderful success. Many of the articles are reproduced in this volume. Of these, four were written by Native Americans and four have dealt with Latin American contexts. We have generated interest in building bridges and forging respect, and although there is much work to be done, I believe the column has been important in training that new generation of archaeologists that Echo-Hawk envisioned in 1993.

Some Reflections

The editorial process for Working Together has made me reflect on my own career, including my training and approach to teaching my students about archaeology. Although in my more cynical moods my crankiness increases when I read of yet another scholar's epiphany who now regrets the course of his or her career path but now knows the truth. I must admit that through reading the columns and comparing the experiences of others to my own, I can see that some of my long-standing beliefs and consequent field practices were not terribly sensitive to the native peoples with whom I worked. In retrospect, while I have no direct knowledge that these practices were harmful to anyone or anything, they nevertheless can be seen to perpetuate an attitude that I now see is ripe for adjustment. The beliefs to which I refer are those commonly associated with science's conceptualization of the world. Before you tune me out, let me state clearly and forthrightly that I am wholly committed to using a scientific perspective in my research. I believe that science is a powerful way of knowing the world, and that compared to most other ways of knowing, it has obvious advantages to any scholarly discipline.

Having said that, I've not slept through the past 25 years, either. I have read the critiques of science, and accept some of them. Although I have little sympathy for post-modern ways of knowing, I grant that there is much to be learned from such critiques, and have made an honest effort to incorporate the best of it into my work. I consider myself to be an "enlightened processualist" who sees real possibilities for the useful accommodation of science with postprocessual theories and perspectives (Aldenderfer 1998:58).

Where, then, is the problem with science? The problem lies with people who have an incomplete understanding of putting science to proper use. The term "scientism" perhaps captures best the essence of what I mean here. Kaplan (1964:405) defines it as the "pernicious exaggeration of both the status and function of science in relation to our values." He goes on to note that scientism often takes on a air of omnipotence, and that with it, science becomes an end in itself—indeed, the only worthwhile end to be considered. What I find interesting is Kaplan's definition is his use of the term "values." Values, of course, define the contexts within which we work. Although many of us may feel that values are not part of the scientific enterprise, this belief is mistaken. Science is not detached from the world, as many would have it be, but in fact, the scientific temperament "is marked by judiciousness and caution, care and conscientiousness." (Kaplan 1964:380). In other words, true scientific practice is informed by values and does not seek to eliminate them. Science does seek to eliminate bias, which is something that "is believed or not according to whether our values would be better served if it were true than if it were false." (Kaplan 1964:373).

Scientism, in contrast, seems to promote few values, or perhaps better stated, biased values. Scientism promotes the idea that the objects of our studies are simply that—objects, and that we may deal with them as we like because we are doing science, which is superior to all other ways of knowing. Scientism, then, acts to disconnect us from values that remind us of our humanity, and that our actions have consequences we must consider before acting.

It's quite easy to see how scientism has affected archaeological practice. As a graduate student, I was well trained in scientific method, and in a sense, cut my scientific teeth on Kaplan's book. But I consulted my course notes and syllabus and found that the chapter on values was not part of that, or any other, course. In this sense, I was taught scientism, and believe that many of my generation were likewise instructed.

What is so odd about this situation, of course, is that most of us also were trained as anthropologists, a fact pointed out by one of the early letter writers to the *SAA Bulletin* who commented on Echo-Hawk's column:

> It is ironic that almost all American archaeologists should be trained in anthropology, yet so many seem to lack a sensitivity to issues of race and culture. Further, it is unlikely that we will be able to raise our own consciousness without the counsel of others. It is heartening, therefore, that the *SAA Bulletin* has taken the lead with its Working Together series (Noble 1993:4).

Clearly, for many of us, scientism trumped anthropology and the sense of values it could have provided, and thus we find ourselves in a valueless vacuum, challenged from many directions.

Although archaeology must acknowledge its shortcomings, some responsibility for this situation lies squarely with native peoples and their biased rejection of anything that resembles a Western perspective on their origins. Although I can understand this rejection from an emotional perspective, I find it very difficult to accept from an intellectual one. Echo-Hawk's inaugural column speaks eloquently of the dangers that native peoples' bias creates: the rejection by "a committee of leading Colorado Indians" of Echo-Hawk's depiction of what mainstream archaeology thinks is the most likely hypothesis on Native American origins in North America is a chilling reminder that religion can be a powerfully negative force laden with bias against nonbelievers. While the initiative for working together lies squarely with the archaeological community, our compromises must insist that native peoples actively seek to identify and eliminate their personal biases when dealing with us.

Final Thoughts

I have now begun archaeological research in Tibet, and among other things, I am engaged in the study of Tibetan Buddhist temples and monastic institutions. I've learned about Buddhism in this process and of relevance to this discussion is the notion of karma, which is literally defined as "action" (Samuel 1993:378). Karma in Buddhist societies often is used as an explanation for one's place in life, for actions in past lives create the conditions for future lives. One should avoid morally bad actions because of their adverse effects on future lives, and thus one should promote good actions so as to ensure a better rebirth. Although I didn't see it that way at the time, I consider the development of the Working Together column as one of those good actions that I hope will balance my scientism.

There are numerous ways in which one can modify one's archaeological karma if guilty of scientism: One of the most important routes is to reintroduce a consideration of values and ethics in courses for both undergraduate and graduate students. Become accountable (Watkins et al. 1995) and seek to be sensitive to issues of cultural difference no matter what the workplace. We will be better archaeologists (and people) for it, and perhaps our cumulative good actions will lead to a much more positive rebirth of archaeology than its many detractors have predicted.

I.
Native American Perspectives on Archaeology

Exploring Ancient Worlds

Roger C. Echo-Hawk

When Vine Deloria Jr. characterized the Society for American Archaeology as "anti-Indian" in a 1989 issue of the Native American Rights Fund (NARF) *Legal Review*, the chair of SAA's Public Relations Committee demanded a retraction. But noting SAA's opposition to Indian-supported repatriation legislation, NARF promised instead to keep a vigilant eye on SAA. This incident highlights the state of relations between Indians and archaeologists in the United States—relations shaped by a powerful legacy of what historian James Riding In has aptly termed "imperial archaeology." For SAA members who do not see themselves as anti-Indian or as conqueror anthropologists, it is important to develop appropriate forums for reviewing relations between Indians and archaeologists, and for discussing projects which have brought both communities together as partners rather than as opponents.

The American archaeological community has proven beyond doubt that it can study Indian history in North America without involving any living Native Americans, and Indian historians have managed to preserve a vast array of oral traditions about the past without any assistance from archaeology. But what would happen if archaeologists, as a matter of course, began to work in full partnership with Indians? This is a question which SAA *must* investigate if it is uncomfortable being viewed as "anti-Indian" by Indian intellectuals. Substantial areas of disagreement exist between archaeologists and Indians, and while many disputes will not be easy to address or resolve, this should not deter our quest to understand the past, and it should not prohibit the development of better relations between Indians and archaeologists.

Even though archaeologists ought to work in partnership with Native Americans, not all Indians want to make friends with "arkies" and "anthros." American archaeologists have not typically sought to cultivate good relations with Indian tribes, and many archaeologists have felt justified in purposefully ignoring Indian sensibilities in conducting archaeological research, particularly in the treatment of Indian graves and human remains. University anthropology departments have shown little interest in recruiting Native American archaeology students (or professors), and consequently, very few Indians have become professional archaeologists in this country. Under these conditions, it is easy for some Indians to reject archaeology as an unacceptable form of inquiry. For those few Indians who may develop a serious interest in the profession, the barriers are considerable.

The term "prehistory" conveys to all people the deliberate impression that Indian historians have failed to create and hand down any form of legitimate record about human events dating back more than three or four centuries. From the perspective of popular attitudes, this has contributed to the devaluation of Native American intellectual traditions, and archaeologists have happily displaced Indian historians as experts on the ancient past. Physical anthropologists—close colleagues of archaeologists—have exacerbated this situation by devoting great energy (up to World War II) in an embarrassing quest to develop scientific proof for Indian intellectual inferiority. This racist history cannot be ignored by Native Americans.

Examining archaeological journals, Indian authors are rare—even as coauthors—and it would be surprising to find a major journal which has had a Native American editor during its life span. In the *Plains Anthropologist*, for example, one finds that during the 1980s at least 80 percent of the papers concerned Native America as a primary focus of study, but substantially less than 1 percent of the authors were Indians, and far more dead Indians appeared in the pages of this journal than living Indians. It would be fair to observe that the journal's audience has had more opportunity to learn about Native Americans from Indian skeletons than from Indian historians and Indian archaeologists.

In spite of these conditions, many Native Americans are curious about archaeology, and a growing number of archaeologists have worked in partnership with tribal historians. The reconciliation of archaeology and Indian oral traditions could bring important changes to our understanding of the past, and perhaps "prehistory" can some day be replaced with "ancient Indian history." For Indians and archaeologists who believe that archaeology *and* oral traditions ought to be acknowledged as necessary components of ancient Indian history, it is vital that SAA provide real leadership in encouraging its members to develop meaningful dialogue and mutually rewarding interaction with Indian tribes. It is time for SAA to explore in earnest the frontiers of cooperative archaeology. These explorations will ultimately help to shape the character of American archaeology as a new generation of archaeologists enters the twenty-first century.

Some archaeologists may wonder: What exactly can Indians offer to the study of the "prehistoric" past? This question can never be answered until both Indians and archaeologists cultivate a sense of mutual respect for the unique contributions of each group. The entire academic community displays little regard for the historicity of oral traditions as a class, whether told by Indians, Norse chroniclers, or any other group of people. Archaeologists who specialize in the study of Indian origins, for example, do not typically consult Indian creation stories, though Native American historians have preserved and handed down such traditions as historical documents. Many Indians, for their part, refuse to embrace archaeologically-based explanations for Indian origins.

A committee of leading Colorado Indians expressed some reluctance to accept my "Ancient Worlds" (presented in full below) as a contribution to a Denver art project honoring the history of Native Americans associated with the state. They objected to my reliance on anthropology, and I withdrew the essay after they suggested that all the discussion of archaeology and science by removed from the text. It seems doubtful that "Ancient Worlds" would have met with greater approval from a committee of archaeologists—but the objections would have centered on my use of oral literature. Until a new climate is introduced into relations between Indians and archaeologists, the integrative approach featured in "Ancient Worlds" will find little acceptance anywhere, and the various stories told about Indian origins can never be reconciled, and we can never share a common history. What role will SAA play in bringing us all together as partners in exploring the past?

Ancient Worlds

The first people dwelt in a land of lingering darkness. In some Native American origin stories, humans emerged from this region to witness the sun's creation or the ordering of night and day. Thousands of years later, many Indians said that their ancestors entered the world from a dark place located underground. Other oral traditions, however—told in both Asia and America—describe the creation of earth from a watery world, and these stories do not typically associate darkness with the first people.

Many archaeologist believe that humans from Asia entered North America more than 11,000 years ago. As Ice Age glaciers absorbed water, sea levels fell hundreds of feet and "Beringia" appeared in the far north, linking Asia to Alaska. Some of the oldest human sites in eastern Beringia can be found above the Arctic Circle, where darkness lingers over the earth. Other scholars believe that humans followed the coastlines of Beringia by boat into the Americas—a route which does not pass through the Arctic Circle.

Climatologists believe that the Ice Ages were swept by windstorms of much greater power than present-day hurricanes and tornadoes, and in one Indian tradition, the first people were created in the heavens and placed on earth by tornadoes. Other Indian stories say that the climate underwent a swift change when the animals (who reigned over the earth) caused summer to appear. Paleoclimatologists have found that a very sudden global warming event may have occurred 11,700 years ago at the end of the Ice Age. This date coincides with the earliest accepted archaeological evidence for the presence of humans in Alaska.

Many Native American oral traditions refer to the existence of dangerous "monsters" and giant animals in ancient times, and other stories are set in a period when animals and birds ruled the world. Paleontologists describe Ice Age America as a realm dominated by giant animals, or "megafauna." Mammoths, mastodons, and giant sloths towered over human hunters; and fearsome short-faced bears, great cats, and other creatures could have made the New World a dangerous place for unwary people.

In many Indian traditions, a great flood covered the earth in ancient times, and some stories associate this event with the end of the age of monsters. Traditions of a mighty deluge can be found in oral and written literatures from around the world. The end of the most recent Ice Age, some 12,000 years ago, could have involved cataclysmic flooding. As the glaciers slowly melted, for example, the sudden release of a massive ice sheet into the ocean would have brought worldwide flooding. The end of the Ice Age also coincides with the extinction of many species of megafauna around the world.

The first Americans made artifacts and left sites which archaeologists can study for insights into the distant past. The ancient ancestors of modern Native Americans also created verbal documents about their experiences, and successive generations of Indians heard these stories as accounts of actual, not fictional, historical events. If Native American origin traditions shed light on the life ways of people who settled in North America during the last Ice Age, then Indian literature preserves a remarkable legacy of documents about ancient human history in the New World.

SAA Bulletin, September 1993

Postscript
Discovering a Partnership Ecology

Uneasy coexistence seemed the best that one could hope for in relations between Native Americans and archaeologists during the 1980s and early 1990s. The politics of polarization tended to define the character of engagement between these communities, and it endures as a real means of gathering and exercising the power to shape the surfaces of our world. In this confrontational environment, however, a vast interfacing of mutual interests has arisen beneath our feet like an unsuspected continent, a new ecology of relationships. But many Indians and archaeologists still have little interest in knowing what this land holds.

For Indians who once bonded with one another through a shared suspicion of culturally insensitive anthropologists, the second coming of Kennewick Man signifies confirmation of their continuing fears that the academic world bristles with plots to undermine an empowered Native America. For anthropologists who once bonded with one another through a shared suspicion of academically insensitive Indians, the second coming of Kennewick Man signifies confirmation of their continuing fears that Indian country bristles with plots to replace science with religion. For anthrophobic Indians and NAGPRAphobic scholars, the world is, naturally enough, a polarized spot in the universe.

For the rest of us, the ends of the political earth offer fascinating places to visit and read about, but the growth of a new partnership ecology during the 1990s has led us to discover a map of the world that features a vast geography floating somewhere between the poles. In this place, we can share the intellectual journeys of such persons as Roger Anyon et al. (1997), William Arbogast, Forrest D. Tierson, and Alden Naranjo (1996), Robert L. Hall (1997), Steve Holen and John Peterson (1995), Barbara Mann and Jerry Fields (1997), Janet Spector (1993), Lynn Teague (1993), and many others who have contributed to the creation of a world in which Indians and archaeologists can interact in interesting, constructive ways.

American archaeology has changed greatly in only a few short years, primarily because most archaeologists simply have never seen themselves as anti-Indian, and most Indians really are curious about archaeology. As for the twenty-first century, I am willing to forecast that the continuing presence of nay-sayers to partnership will become more a reflection of tolerable intellectual diversity than an indication of intolerant intellectual apartheid. The stormy climate of the 1980s can truly be said to have moved during the 1990s toward a kinder, gentler rain upon the world—a rain that promises to sustain us all in the next millennium.

From Specimens to SAA Speakers: Evolution by Federal Mandate

Gary White Deer

> *History says, Don't hope*
> *On this side of the grave.*
> *But then, once in a lifetime*
> *The longed for tidal wave*
> *Of justice can rise up,*
> *And hope and history rhyme.*
>
> *So hope for a great sea-change*
> *On the far side of revenge.*
> *Believe that a future shore*
> *Is reachable from here.*
> *Believe in miracles*
> *And cures and healing wells.*
>
> Seamus Heaney
Nobel Laureate

The year 1966 unfurled like a Vaudeville landscape, a backdrop lowered behind an American performing center stage, flush with post-war boom. It was an America that was dutifully paving over itself, engaged in an incredible make-over that demolished its own cultural markers, and asphalted its own short-term and tenuous immigrant history. While America alternately bulldozed and tap danced, a small, intent group bearing field notes and calipers waited in the theater wings to observe the curtain rise on another special act, one of new federal policy. Then, as now, this particular act played to its own select box of professional devotees. As the curtain rose, and while more general audiences snored, academics and lawyers broke into what has amounted to a 30-year-plus round of sustained applause.

If the National Historic Preservation Act of 1966 left the collective attention span of its general American audience wandering toward the exits, Native America wasn't even allowed in the theater. There were a few of us perhaps outside, just around the corner from the ticket booth, who probably heard the scattered but determined applause, urban newcomers caught in the prelude of a government relocation program. Most of us though were still well out of town, in Indian Country, or Native Hawaii, or in Native

Alaskan areas, places where those writing and staging federal policy hadn't considered playing to yet.

That was too bad. Aside from the obvious entertainment value of pitting "bone jockeys" against their potential specimens, Native America has always appreciated, in cultural terms, the concept of historic preservation, and we have our own methodologies concerning its application. Instead, that slow, contentious process leading to mutual understanding would be further delayed, until in this decade another federal enactment would mandate that Native America be allowed into the Big Top. Now that we have, so to speak, arrived, we are noticing that the applause has lessened a bit. Those most likely to be clapping now seem to be lawyers.

On the eve of the National Historic Preservation Act, Native America was without its own voice. General American society had, over the years and through various government policies and practices, effectively muzzled tribal nations. These policies and practices were not just effective political intimidation; more than this, they served as an aggregate of rationalizations that documented a pervasively abusive relationship between an immensely powerful perpetrator and its victims.

In 1966 Native Americans were still generally treated as wards of the federal government. With limited exception, we were considered to be inarticulate, backward, and given over to superstition. We were mostly regarded as a colorful but nevertheless benighted people, whose one redemptive opportunity consisted of assimilating into the lower and middle ranks of the American hierarchy. To this end, Indian children in appalling numbers were routinely transported hundreds of miles from their families and tribal communities to serve out their primary and secondary school years in boarding schools run by the Bureau of Indian Affairs. In most cases, native religious life survived underground, concealed as far as was possible from the inquisitive zeal of Christian mission boards. As might be expected, the free exercise of tribal sovereignty was severely restricted as well. Among the Oklahoma Choctaw, for example, elections were banned by federal policy. Instead, a federally appointed "Principal Chief" was allowed to preside over the ongoing dismantling of tribal lands and resources. Decades of this special kind of care and attention had not failed to achieve special results; American Indians during this recent period attained the lowest life expectancy rates and the highest infant mortality rates in the country.

Most frequently, the federal government acted as both policymaker and public spokesman for tribal affairs. The abuser had effectively stilled the voice of the abused, and within a long, enforced silence, declared itself to be both guardian and benefactor. The civil rights protests of the late 1960s and early 1970s shattered that prolonged silence. Native America, like the rest of the country, found itself caught up in the rising tide of anti-establishment sentiment that engaged all levels of American society. Perhaps ironically, the numbers of white American youth in beads and headbands were often seen by us as a sort of sign or turning point. Activist protests at Alcatraz and Cass Lake quickly crescendoed into intertribal solidarity, a common Indian cause embodied by the motto of the American Indian Movement—Sovereignty, Land, and Culture—variations of which frequently surface as Indian conference themes today.

This period of challenge and confrontation engendered a widespread backlash against the natives-as-specimens mentality of Western empiricism. Initially, this backlash was directed at cultural anthropologists, perhaps because these folks were more obvious targets to communities where they had ticked everyone off with so many insensitive questions. It could be assumed perhaps that while the "anthros" (as these folks were called by militants) were being duly castigated, archaeologists sporting field notes and callipers, cheered by the distraction, quietly continued their methodical livelihood, which included digging up the militants' antecedents; testing, photographing, cataloging, and with the impassivity of coroners; and recording their most lively presumptions in technical journals. It would only be a bit later when Native America, in its turn, would begin to question the propriety of such practices.

In 1973 United States forces surrounded an essentially unarmed group of Indian civil rights activists at Wounded Knee, South Dakota. The army lobbed high caliber rounds at will into the tiny hamlet, restrained only by the presence of world media attention. The siege would prove to be the watershed incident of Indian protest for the 1970s.

The venue that the American Indian Movement (AIM) picked was a poor tactical location, but rich in symbolism as the site of the infamous Wounded Knee Massacre, fewer than 100 years earlier. Many Indian communities can still easily recall the AIM caravans heading toward South Dakota, and the friends and relatives who joined them. When it was all over, of course, a prolonged civil rights protest had proven no match for the greatest military power in the world. Closure on social justice issues would elude the Disco Decade, as it had eluded America for almost 200 years.

In spite of this lack of closure, or perhaps because of it, Native America remained imbued with its new sense of solidarity. This renewed combination of sovereignty and social activism, diffused through emerging ranks of Native American professionals and proactive traditionalists, would help to provide the impetus for the passage of Public Law 101-601, the Native American Graves Protection and Repatriation Act, or NAGPRA.

While Indian nationalist leaders paled overall in comparison to their more illustrious and eloquent historical predecessors and while they often succeeded in alienating much of their own perceived constituency, their protests were nevertheless courageous, legitimate, and long overdue. Native America found its voice, and began to speak in economic, political, education, medical, and preservationist terms, engendering commitments in these areas that would become the basis for the current infrastructure of tribal governments.

As the doctrine of tribal sovereignty began to slowly reassert itself, economic development programs, fueled by an infusion of federal monies, followed. The Mississippi Choctaw first contracted an archaeologist in 1976 to survey the site of an industrial park. Other tribal nations, relatively early on, began to see the advantages of developing their own cultural resource programs to counterpoise incursions by federal and state agencies and began relationships with contract archaeologists as well.

The decade of the 1980s was one marked by steady economic growth and a consolidation of power, of tribal employment, of an explosive reinterpretation of the American dream. Under tribal scrutiny, Indian Health Service hospitals began to modernize, no longer viewed simply as dispensers of topical medicine or places to die. Native Americans were graduating from high schools and then colleges in record numbers. Although far from the national standards, Native American per-capita income increased substantially during this period of more amicable assimilation.

Traditional Native American religious beliefs, for the most part however, remained relatively unchanged. Most traditional communities were still unaware that their ancestors were being unearthed and studied with regularity. The enormous collections of human remains housed in universities and other institutions were not generally known. Tribal members who knew of these desecrations ascribed it to the usual basic lack of respect and understanding of things spiritual by Western science and were unable to pursue their concerns further.

Meanwhile, Yuchis continued to wash their hair with spicewood after funerals, Shawnees continued to fire rifles at grave side to startle the spirit into departing, Choctaws continued to observe poled pulling ceremonies during proscribed mourning periods, and Seminoles continued to place items with their burials. Such trait continuation throughout the whole of Native America ensured that original understandings between the seen and unseen worlds were maintained.

In sum perhaps, the most significant development to occur during this 25-year era was the rise of tribal governments. These political entities are required by federal law to adhere to a European American form of contentious democracy, in exchange for federal recognition. While stopping short of fielding armies and navies, tribal governments nevertheless are now the repositories of semi-autonomy. They are empowered as limited participants in the articulation of current federal law. The re-emergence of tribal sovereignty, albeit in limited form, is the real reason why Native Americans are now sought as conference speakers and not merely as specimens by archaeology. Like it or not, Western science now has to consult with us, to regard us, and tribal governments are now the licensed intermediaries of that mandated exchange.

NAGPRA was the landmark legislation that created the unique space Native America and archaeology occupy today. It is, to be sure, evolution by federal mandate, an ongoing process that has changed forever how the occupants of this new landscape may regard one another. So, with these general observations loosely in tow, where are we going, generally speaking, with all these cranio-metrics-based assumptions about Kennewick Man? Bill Lipe, past president of SAA, has been quoted as saying, "Genes don't get transmitted in tribal sized packages. Our view is that the relationship is so remote that repatriation of the skeleton would not reflect what congress intended in the law" (Mauro 1997).

This argument in and of itself is easily answerable, at least in the short term. Whether or not the Kennewick skeleton is truly Caucasoid is a moot point. It would be an argument from ignorance to suggest that simply because no known data exists to directly connect this skeleton to Native America that there is, in fact, no direct connection.

Beyond any of this, however, what I really wanted to hear Lipe say was something like "We appreciate Native America's cultural and racial connection to these issues and support their doctrine of tribal sovereignty in these matters. However, because of the unprecedented potential for data retrieval which we believe will contribute to a common understanding, we also support a compromise agreement with those tribal nations now involved in the repatriation of Kennewick Man, and SAA looks forward to assisting in a dialogue toward this end." Something not that wordy perhaps, but certainly words to that effect.

Aside from the obvious merits of either position on the Kennewick issue, larger questions present themselves. How effective are we at communicating really, when going to federal court is perceived as a first option? Where are all those resources of mediation like the NAGRPA Review Committee or the Repatriation Coalition, and why aren't they being utilized?

In this regard, SAA is to be congratulated for continuing the dialogue with Native America begun in New Orleans in 1996. I suggest that this communication continue, because frequent communication can lead to effective communication. On these issues, ongoing communication between all parties is essential.

Although SAA may not always find itself in agreement with portions of the Native American position on issues like repatriation, there should always remain in any of your public positions ample room for reconciliation. We have far more in common with each other than we may now realize, and it will always be to our mutual advantage to pursue common ends.

Are tribal governments doing enough to enhance a reconciliatory relationship? On the tribal side, it must be realized, science has been embraced as a tool. In fact, there are now archaeologists who owe their incomes to tribal governments. Now, let me ask in relation to this fact, how many Native American traditionalists are there in the pay of archaeology as consultants, and at what comparable salaries and benefits?

Is this relationship as important to Native America as it is to archaeology? Archaeology, if it plays its cards right, far from damaging its livelihood, can help to effect a new paradigm within which it may dine at the NAGPRA table for years to come. (This may not always be so for tribal governments, which have no comparable empirical institutions, and whose mission must also include economic development and the overall quality of life of its citizens.) With regard to any proposed amendments to NAGPRA, I would like to propose an amendment to SAA that I assure you Native America will fully support.

Nashville, Tennessee, the site of the 1997 SAA Annual Meeting, is a major conduit for the trafficking of Native American grave goods. Virtually the whole of the South and Southwest has become pockmarked with the efforts of pot hunters. Particularly in the south, pot hunting is a major growth industry. Mussel shell boats now park over submerged burial grounds in the middle of the Tennessee River, as their occupants loot graves underwater. At recreational bends of our great waterways traffickers in Indian grave goods pass out business cards to tourists. Flea markets abound in grave trophies, as locals with metal detectors comb remote sites, and clandestine organizations of grave robbers like the Rebel Club reckon their membership in the thousands. Burial sites are under wholesale attack by industrial development as well.

It's time to take a stand both on principle and on policy. As NAGPRA does not currently address private land issues, I propose the Society for American Archaeology consider giving its support to an amendment that will in strong measure prohibit the looting and desecration of burials and objects of cultural patrimony now on private lands. While this proposed amendment will not stem the hemorrhaging of remains and artifacts from public lands, it will make a critical difference on property where the interests of the common good should proclaim these objects to be American cultural patrimony. Such a proposed amendment would achieve a measure of solidarity between archaeology and Native America that could serve as a framework within which all pending issues might be reconciled.

The day for proactive archaeology has arrived. It is now time to join with tribal nations to forge a common agenda, to create a common ground within this space that federal policy has mandated us.

Native America has struggled and achieved much since passage of NAGPRA. We have faced down congressional bullies, stood up for our civil liberties, revitalized our traditions, and witnessed a rebirth of our tribal institutions against all conceivable odds. Perhaps it has been our destiny to achieve this. We do know that our hard-won victories are linked to the common destiny of all who witness injustice and try to right it, who feel our reverence for our kindred dead and try to respect it, and who understand the sacredness of life and then try to live in a sacred manner. We invite the esteemed SAA again to continue with us in a spirit of reconciliation and in common cause. It is in this spirit that I leave you.

SAA Bulletin, May 1998

A Navajo Student's Perception: Anthropology and the Navajo Nation Archaeology Department Student Training Program

Davina TwoBears

My maternal clan is *Todich'ii'nii,* Bitter Water clan, and I am born for *Tachii'nii,* Red Running into the Water clan. My maternal grandfather is *Tabaahi,* Edge Water clan, and my maternal grandfather is also *Todich'ii'nii.* My mother's family is from the community of Bird Springs, Arizona, on the Navajo reservation. My parents are Tom and Anita Ryan. Currently, I'm pursuing a master's degree in sociocultural anthropology at Northern Arizona University. Because I don't want to offend anyone, it has been very difficult for me to write this. I am very young and am still learning, but in this piece, I'll share with you how I became interested in the field of anthropology, my ideas and goals, and my involvement with the Navajo Nation Archaeology Department-Northern Arizona University (NNAD-NAU) student training program.

Because I am a Navajo, many people ask how I became interested in anthropology—I majored and became interested in anthropology because it was *only* anthropology courses in college that allowed me to learn about Native Americans in an academic setting for the first time in my entire education. Many times, Native Americans are only acknowledged at Thanksgiving, or in more progressive schools, on Native American day, week, or month. Thus, it is not surprising that I chose anthropology as a major in college. I took courses on Native American policy, as well as law, literature, prehistory, history, and Mesoamerican archaeology. It was wonderful to absorb all of this new information by learning from Native American professors and students. I experienced a kind of renaissance by working with the native professors, but I also had a rude awakening as I learned about the ways in which some anthropologists obtained their data. As I progressed in my major, I discovered that anthropologists have a bad reputation in Indian country.

As most of us are aware, not many Native Americans enter the field of anthropology because of negative experiences between tribes and anthropologists. Our profession is oftentimes considered impractical (as it is not economically beneficial), disrespectful, and misleading or incorrect by most Native Americans. I'll be honest in admitting that I feel the same about anthropology, even though I am an anthropologist myself.

It is hard, as a Native American, to be the object of study. At anthropology conferences, I often feel like a walking specimen to be photographed, documented, measured, and dissected. It's a strange feeling to think that so many non-Native American scientists find us Indians interesting objects of study, and that they would go so far as to write books about us, and then as "experts," talk about us to other scientists at conferences. It makes one feel as though a Native American is not even a person or human, but just a very complex, interesting thing.

However, I obviously think that anthropology is useful. Why would I continue to pursue a degree in this field otherwise? I see anthropology not just as a study of human cultures, both in the past and present, but as a means to an end, or a beginning. I see anthropology as a way to "help" people. Many anthropologists balk or become angry at the idea of "getting involved," or collaborating and consulting with Native Americans. However, with native peoples working with anthropologists and becoming anthropologists themselves, just imagine how much richer and fuller our profession, not to mention our lives, can be. Whether we like it or not, our profession is changing to include Native Americans, so why not just go with the flow and make the best of it? I see our profession only improving with Native American involvement. I heard an anthropologist say that our profession will improve if only we learn the language of the people whom we are studying. I think this would be great, but this is a very limited goal. I think that our profession will only improve with increased participation of the people whom we study, and by giving something back to them. If we as anthropologists want to rid ourselves of our bad reputation, then we will need to work on this. I am not saying that all anthropologists and their research is bad, but instead, I am only challenging our profession to involve Native Americans more, and to give something back to them. It is up to you to realize the way in which this will be accomplished.

Personally, I believe that Native American anthropologists are important at several levels. Native Americans who become anthropologists and archaeologists can only benefit our tribes and Native Americans in general. We can determine what is appropriate to publish, and what is not. We can determine how and what is to be exhibited in museums. We can determine what gets studied, photographed, recorded, and what should be left alone. We can determine what should get excavated, if at all, and how it should be done. I only point this out because as Native Americans, our input has been and is for the most part left out. As professional Native American anthropologists, however, we will not be so easy to ignore. People may say that science has no limits, but I disagree, since I advocate for more respect and communication from our profession. This is not an outrageous or an impossible request. People also will say that Native Americans should not or cannot study their own culture because it's not objective or scientific, but no one is totally objective. Perhaps these people are just threatened by a growing pool of minority scientists—I don't know. If we do study our own cultures, at least our research, books, and lectures will be more valuable, interesting, and useful to us.

More immediate tangible goals for Native American anthropologists are:

(1) We could publish culturally appropriate textbooks, which native educators know are in high demand for our Native American youth and the wider public. For example, I read a sample from a soon-to-be published book that compared the traditional Navajo and western scientific viewpoints of astronomy. A Navajo medicine man was consulted by the Navajo author of this book, which will provide Navajo students with a more open-minded education, but most significantly, a traditional Navajo perspective. This perspective is too often left out of a Navajo child's education in school;

(2) Native anthropologists could serve as teachers and/or professors of Native American culture, history, traditions, and language;

(3) Native American anthropologists can be valuable resources in devising programs for culture and language preservation, since many tribes face a decrease in speakers of their particular language;

(4) With the passage of laws such as the Native American Graves Protection and Repatriation Act (NAGPRA), Native American anthropologists are needed to work with this law, as well as to care for the sacred/ceremonial objects and human remains once they are repatriated. I believe Native American anthropologists will do and are doing much to benefit our particular tribes, Native people in general, and the wider public. We just need to continue to use our imaginations and remain motivated. I am looking forward to being a Navajo anthropologist in this time of great restructuring. I take pride in my chosen profession, and I, as a Native American, have to put up with being mocked and teased for being an anthropologist.

One example of how Native Americans can be trained to become anthropologists is the Navajo Nation Archaeology Department-Northern Arizona University student training program (NNAD-NAU), an initiative to do something about the lack of credentialed Navajo anthropologists. Many of the higher positions in the NNAD and the Navajo Nation Historic Preservation Department (NNHPD) are not held by Navajos, including the director's position. An agreement was set up with Northern Arizona University in 1988, whereby Navajo and/or Native American students majoring in anthropology are eligible to be employed and trained by the NNAD. Our office primarily works with contract archaeology on the Navajo reservation, which involves recording and mapping historic/prehistoric sites, and traditional cultural properties or TCPs (sacred/ceremonial, plant/herb gathering areas, and burials), in the way of development on the Navajo reservation.

I remember my grandmother yelling at me once because I found some black-on-white pottery sherds and brought them to her as a gift. "No! No! No! Go take those back where you found them! You're not supposed to bother those! Don't play with that!" I don't remember everything she said, but I know she was mad! I think that my grandmother was trying to tell me that if I used something that once belonged to a dead person, their ghost will cause me harm. But since the purpose of our surveys is to identify, record, and protect prehistoric/historic archaeological sites, as well as TCPs, I am comfortable with working with these materials.

During my time at NNAD-NAU, I worked on various projects, including archaeological surveys on the Navajo reservation. This required cultural and artifact identification skills, ethnographic interviewing skills in Navajo and English, and a familiarity with federal and tribal laws and policies. It is a really difficult job. We as archaeologists are required to determine what should be protected, why this is the case, how to record it, and then, if necessary, to reroute a project so that it will not disturb the significant area in question. We must learn to think and work fast without wasting precious time. Time is money in this business. Our work requires a great deal of maturity, responsibility, accountability, and credibility. If we make mistakes it is the Navajo people who will suffer from delayed roads, water electricity, or other service. Clearly, we are under a lot of pressure. But when I am driving on the "res," it's nice to see the places where I conducted archaeological surveys, now developed with homes, electricity, and/or water. I know that I helped make it happen for my people.

I am also under stress since I can't communicate with my people. I am a walking anomaly, a freak. I look Navajo, I am Navajo, but I don't speak Navajo. It's really embarrassing and difficult for me to talk to my own people when I can't even communicate with them in my own language. But, I manage, even though it is hard. I do want to learn my language, and the only way is to speak it. So my job gives me an opportunity to practice.

The report writing is a learning experience in and of itself. The technical reports we are required to write demand a grasp of the English language and grammar. I know my writing skills improved with this experience. At NNAD-NAU, I learned on the latest word-processing and graphic design computer software and hardware. We use the graphic software to draw beautiful maps, which were once done with pen and ink and double-stick tape, a very messy, time-consuming process. On the computer, it does not take long to produce much better quality maps once you become familiar with all of the short cuts. Also, we may use the computers and laser printers to write our college and graduate papers after work hours.

Recently, I hooked up to the Internet, which I can also access through a NNAD-NAU computer. Now I receive mail from different lists concerning anthropology, archaeology, NAGPRA, Native Americans in general, museums, and feminism. This is an excellent source of education, information, and opportunity for me as a Native American anthropologist and student.

Many other opportunities for training are available to students, one of which is the N16 Navajo Mountain Road Project. A road needs to be built in the Navajo Mountain community, but before the road is built, archaeological sites that will be destroyed must be recorded, collected, and analyzed. Employees from our office are responsible for the excavation, collection, and curation of artifacts (mostly ceramic sherds, lithics, and ground stones). During this past summer, several students spent two weeks out at Navajo Mountain gaining excavation experience. One student, interested in ancient stone tool production on the Navajo reservation, assisted with the analysis of lithic flakes and tools from this project. Another student, interested in ceramics because he is a potter himself, experimented with clays and paints so as to identify those used by the Anasazi, and worked closely with the ceramic analyst. Since I am interested in working in a museum someday, I received experience in artifact storage and organization by acting as the lab manager for a short period of time.

In addition to such experiences, students are encouraged to attend conferences and workshops within the field of anthropology. In 1992 I traveled to the National Indian Education Association conference in Albuquerque, New Mexico, to set up an information booth regarding our program. I also participated in NAGPRA training during the past year. In addition, we students seek out conferences on the reservations, including the Navajo Studies Conference, as well as those sponsored by Navajo Community College. I believe conferences are important sources of communication and education. At a Navajo weaving conference at Arizona State University, I recently met a Navajo anthropology student who gave an excellent paper on Navajo male weavers. Role models are hard to come by, and I was extremely grateful to make his acquaintance.

Students also take advantage of other internships during the summer to supplement their training. For example, since I am very interested in working in the museum field, this past summer I was a Native American intern at the Museum of Northern Arizona and worked with the summer shows of Zuni, Hopi, and Navajo art. Another student was interested in communicating and learning from the Navajo elderly. He was able to work within the ethnographic interviewing program at NNHPD with other Navajo "cultural specialists," who conduct ethnographic interviewing to help identify and protect TCPs before roads are built on the reservation. Currently, I am involved with student recruitment. Last year our department applied for and received a grant from the National Park Service. In it, I will be responsible for recruiting students from local Navajo high schools, as well as universities in Arizona and New Mexico to join our training program. In October, I organized an open house at NAU, which many Navajo and Native American students attended. The staff and students at NNAD-NAU were essential to the success of the open house. Soon I will continue to recruit for our student training program. During these trips, I hope to entice more Native American students into the field of anthropology, and introduce them to job opportunities and current issues such as repatriation and reburial, museum collaboration, NAGPRA, the National Museum of the American Indian, and more.

The NNAD-NAU student training program does not force students to do anything they do not want to do. For example, I am not forced to conduct excavation with which I am uncomfortable. In essence, we students are given the chance to pursue our own anthropological interests within and outside of NNAD-NAU.

My experiences here at NNAD-NAU will remain dear to me. I hope that this program will continue to grow and prosper. One way I would like to see our program expand would be to include more Navajo teachings. This of course boils down to money or funding and dedication/interest from staff and students. Some may say it is the individual's responsibility to learn more about their language/culture, which is true, but why can't we learn in an environment such as the student training program as well? Programs such as ours will need to wrestle with their departmental goals and how to realize them. Armed with an M.A. in sociocultural anthropology and NNAD-NAU job experience/training, I hope to make positive changes for the Navajo people and/or other Native American tribes. I think that having a program such as ours is valuable and educational. I don't know how I would have made it through graduate school without the support of the NNAD-NAU student training program. I would like to thank the Navajo Nation—thank you. This is a good idea, and I hope other tribes will follow and improve upon the example set by the NNAD-NAU.

SAA Bulletin, January 1995

Postscript

I have been living in Tomah, Wisconsin, for the past four years, but this past spring, I worked again for the Navajo Nation Archaeology Department (NNAD) in Arizona. This was a great opportunity to observe how the NNAD Student Training Program has progressed since 1995, the year I left. I am happy to report that student training program continued to grow, not only in the physical space, but in the number of Navajo/Native American students employed. In fact, there are so many students now that space has become a problem, as desks and computers vie for every available nook and cranny. I was impressed with the work being done, which included the same type of work that I had done as a student. However, other ventures in archaeology are now underway, such as archaeological fieldwork in Australia's outback with a Native Aborigine archaeologist. Students were, and still are, taking advantage of every opportunity to learn and discover new and different types of archaeological and anthropological work and educational experiences, with continued NNAD support. I was very pleased with the success that I viewed and experienced firsthand.

However, in the face of such apparent success and growth was the reality of budget cuts. Despite the continuous growth in the student training program and the number of student participants, the budget continues to decrease. In 1999, the Navajo Nation suggested elimination of the budget for the NNAD Student Training Program for the first time. Thankfully, the problem was immediately brought to the new president of the Navajo Nation, who was on the Northern Arizona University (NAU) campus at the time. In his presentation to NAU students, he made it known that he desired to see more mutually beneficial relationships between the Navajo Nation and NAU. (Ironically, on that same day, the student supervisor of the NNAD-NAU Student Training Program was meeting with tribal officials in Window Rock, Arizona, and discussing the budget).

"How could the Navajo Nation be eliminating the budget for such an apparently successful program?" I wondered—a program that employs Navajo and other Native American students while they are obtaining their anthropology and archaeology degrees. Students learn to support themselves in the real world while gaining invaluable anthropological and archaeological experience. They learn responsibility to contractors and the local Navajo people, as they must deal with both in their archaeological work. They conduct their own archaeological surveys, write their own reports, as well as draft their own field maps on computers. In short, Navajo students are providing a necessary service to their own tribe's needs for archaeological clearance for any development on the Navajo reservation. Students must become familiar with southwestern archeology and the traditional cultural places on the Navajo Reservation. Navajo students who don't speak Navajo fluently are placed in situations where they must try to speak their native tongue, which helps them to learn more of their own language. The list of benefits go on and on. These benefits were pointed out to the Navajo Nation president. Impressed, he suggested the students write letters to him and explain what the NNAD-NAU Student

Training Program means to them. With the combined efforts of the student supervisor and the students, the program was funded again this year.

The NNAD Student Training Program at NAU is exactly the type of program that the Navajo Nation president is encouraging between the Navajo Nation and NAU. Yet, its funding was on the butcher's block. This case points to the importance of communication and the necessity to inform the Navajo Nation government of the value of programs such as this one.

The NNAD Student Training Program is realizing its goals of producing professional, educated Navajo and Native American anthropologists/archaeologists, who are definitely in the minority in the professional world. The NNAD Student Training Program, and others like it, deserve to be continually supported. I respectfully encourage tribal officials to be aware of the types of programs they approve for funding, and ask that they accept invitations by students to tour their programs. In this way, tribal officials may see for themselves the success of such programs. In turn, the students in these types of programs should take time to make a connection with tribal governmental officials in creative ways. These steps take time and energy, but I believe they are necessary, because budget cuts are a reality that we all must deal with.

During my time in Arizona in spring 1999, it was great to see more published works by Native Americans. This is a definite, long-overdue improvement. I wish these sources had been available to me as a student. A lot of spectacular joint ventures between Native American and non-Native American anthropologists and archaeologists are now being done and should continue to be encouraged. I noticed, however, that some of these joint ventures are being presented at professional meetings where Native Americans are not well represented. I would respectfully ask that the professional Native and non-Native anthropologists and/or archaeologists remember the people from whom their research came from and include them in the sharing of such valuable research. This can be accomplished by publishing in the tribal newspaper, presenting a paper at the tribe's community college, or sponsoring a symposium at the local college or university attended by a high percentage of Native American students. Since this information is coming from a certain tribe or Native group, it should be shared with that group in some way out of respect for them. I am sure members of the tribe would appreciate such knowledge.

As we enter the year 2000, great levels of communication and understanding have occurred between the world of anthropology, which includes archaeology, and the world of Native peoples. Native peoples are now using anthropology to their advantage and are becoming more involved in the field. I am sure that I am not the only one to feel this growth, and feel that it is good. May we all keep up the good work.

II.
Transforming the Archaeological Model

NHPA: Changing the Role of Native Americans in the Archaeological Study of the Past

T. J. Ferguson

The relationship between Native Americans and archaeologists in the United States has changed substantially since the passage of the National Historic Preservation Act (NHPA) of 1966. In the last 30 years, under the impetus of the NHPA, Native Americans have implemented numerous initiatives to increase their involvement in archaeological research and strengthen their control over the management of their heritage resources. This column reviews the economic, political, social, and intellectual aspects of these initiatives, and then assesses the current status and future prospects for incorporation of Native American perspectives in archaeological method and theory.

The Role of Native Americans in Archaeology before the NHPA

Native American involvement in archaeology did not begin with the NHPA. Native Americans have a long history of contributing to archaeological research. The first generation of archaeologists in the Southwest used Native Americans as laborers, field archaeologists, and sources of the ethnographic analogies used to interpret the archaeological record. From 1882 to 1920, Native American field archaeologists employed by scholars, such as Frank Hamilton Cushing, Jesse Walter Fewkes, and Frederick Webb Hodge, worked with the archaeological record and provided important clues on how it should be interpreted.

As the focus of archaeological method and theory changed to time-space systematics and processual approaches, the intellectual involvement of Native Americans in archaeology waned. This is not to say that there were no important Native American archaeologists in the twentieth century. Arthur C. Parker, the Seneca Indian and New York State archaeologist who served as the first president of SAA, and Edmund J. Ladd, a Zuni Indian who served as Pacific archaeologist for the National Park Service (NPS), provide two examples of Native Americans who made significant contributions to our discipline during this period.

It was not until the passage of the NHPA in 1966, however, that Indian tribes, as well as individual Native Americans, became directly involved in conducting and regulating archaeological research. The growing number of tribes involved in archaeology in the last 30 years has greatly increased the numbers of both Native Americans employed as archaeologists and archaeologists employed by Native Americans. These trends are helping to restructure the intellectual growth of our discipline.

Impacts of the NHPA

The NHPA has had three important impacts on Native American involvement in archaeology. The first was to increase the number of Indian tribes sponsoring archaeological research. Passage of the NHPA spawned the rapid development of cultural resources management as a source of employment and research opportunities. Many, if not most, U.S. archaeologists are now involved at some point in their career with the identification and evaluation of historic properties uner the edict of the NHPA, in the mitigation of adverse impacts to these sites through mandated data recovery programs, or in the management of these activities.

The increase in the number of archaeologists working on Indian lands, as well as the need to get "archaeological clearance" prior to development of land modifying projects, were both of interest to tribal leaders in the 1970s. Within five years of passing the NHPA, for instance, the governor of Zuni Pueblo, Robert E. Lewis, began a program in association with the Arizona State Museum to train tribal members to undertake work mandated by the NHPA. From the outset, Lewis' goals were to provide employment, keep money circulating within the Zuni economy, and provide the rapid delivery of necessary archaeological services to the Zuni Indian Reservation. This effort led to the establishment of a tribal archaeology program in 1975, which now includes a regulatory office (the Zuni Heritage and Historic Preservation Office) and a contract business (the Zuni Cultural Resources Enterprise).

Similarly, the Navajo Nation responded to the NHPA in the early 1970s by expanding its museum-based archaeology program to include a contract business. With roots in litigation work for the Indian Claims Commission, the Navajo program eventually grew to include the Navajo Archaeology Department (providing archaeological services under contract) and the Navajo Nation Historic Preservation Department (fulfilling a regulatory function).

Reaping the financial benefits of the NHPA was an early part of the rationale for tribal sponsorship of archaeological research and remains important today. During the last two decades, both the Zuni and Navajo programs have provided major sources of employment for tribal members, and many of the wages paid to the non-Indian archaeologists employed by these programs are spent on the reservation, helping the tribal economy.

The other two important impacts of the NHPA are related to the 1992 amendments of the act. One of these amendments officially recognized that traditional cultural and religious sites—"traditional cultural properties"—are historic properties that may be eligible for the National Register of Historic Places, and therefore must be considered during the review process to ensure compliance with Section 106 of the NHPA. Section 106 requires federal agencies to consider the effect of their undertakings on historic properties before permits are issued or funds are expended.

Traditional cultural properties in the national historic preservation program are required to be inventoried and evaluated in a manner similar to archaeological sites. In fact, many traditional cultural properties are archaeological sites—introducing an ethnographic component into historic preservation activities. Many tribes prefer to undertake their own ethnographic research using tribal employees or consultants rather than employ outsiders for the studies. Tribal research of traditional cultural properties engages tribes in the implementation of the NHPA, and, more often than not, increases tribal involvement with archaeology in general.

The third impact of the NHPA has been to foster a tribal role in the management of heritage resources, including the regulation of archaeological research. Once tribes began to provide professional survey and excavation services for federal compliance with Section 106, many also decided to become more involved in the regulation of that research on their reservations. This involvement led to the establishment of many tribal historic and cultural preservation offices, allowing tribal assumption of functions formerly fulfilled by State Historic Preservation Officers (SHPOs). Between 1992 and 1997, 15 tribes assumed SHPO responsibilities for their reservation (Table 1). The functions assumed by Tribal Historic Preservation Officers (THPOs) include inventorying resources, determining the eligibility of places for the National Register, education, and planning and compliance review pursuant to Section 106 of the NHPA. While the revised NHPA encourages tribes to embrace professional standards and guidelines in historic preservation activities, it also mandates that tribal

Table 1. Tribes Assuming SHPO Functions.

Tribe	State
Confederate Salish and Kootenai Tribes of the Flathead Nation	Montana
Confederated Tribes of the Colville Reservation	Washington
Confederated Tribes of the Umatilla Reservation	Oregon
Confederated Tribes of the Warm Springs Reservation	Oregon
Hualapai Tribe	Arizona
Lac du Flambeau Band of Lake Superior Chippewa Indians	Wisconsin
Leech Lake Band of Chippewa Indians	Minnesota
Mille Lacs Band of Ojibwe Indians	Minnesota
Narragansett Tribe	Rhode Island
Navajo Nation	Arizona, New Mexico, Utah
Spokane Tribe of Indians	Washington
Standing Rock Sioux	North Dakota, South Dakota
Tunica-Biloxi Tribe	Louisiana
White Mountain Apache Tribe	Arizona
Yurok Tribe	California

values be taken into account. This means that each tribe can fashion a program to meet its particular needs. Because these new THPO programs are still in development, their full impact on archaeology cannot yet be assessed. It is clear, however, that they will have a major effect on the practice of archaeology on Indian lands by structuring research questions that are relevant to tribes and regulating the methods by which those questions are investigated.

Number of Tribes Participating in Archaeology

One way to measure the participation of Native Americans in archaeology is by counting the number of tribes that have received federal grants to undertake archaeological research or develop historic preservation programs. The NPS has taken the lead in providing historic preservation funding for tribes. Information distributed by the Tribal Preservation Program of the NPS documents that between 1990 and 1997, 249 Historic Preservation Fund grants totaling $9 million were awarded to 170 tribes. Not all grants deal with archaeology per se; many involve cultural research, ethnobotany, rehabilitation of historic buildings, cultural camps, and other activities representing the breadth of Native American priorities for historic preservation. A review of NPS grants made in 1995 and 1996, however, indicates that 32 of the 75 grants were for archaeological research, the development of tribal ordinances governing historic preservation, or other historic preservation regulatory activities. These 32 grants totaled $1,671,900—almost half of the total funds awarded.

By combining data on NPS grants gleaned from *CRM* and the *SAA Bulletin*, I compiled a list of 57 tribes actively involved in tribally-based archaeological research and historic preservation programs (Table 2). These tribes are located in 21 states over a wide geographical area. This is undoubtedly a conservative list; there are probably additional tribes engaged in archaeological research that were not represented in the consulted sources. However, these 57 tribes constitute almost 10 percent of all tribes in the United States—a cogent testimony to the effectiveness of the NHPA in increasing Native American participation in archaeology. These tribal archaeology and historic preservation programs increase the tribal

Table 2. Tribes Engaged in Archaeological Research and Historic Preservation Programs.

Tribe	State
Afognak Native Corporation	Alaska
Bannock-Shoshone Tribe	Idaho
Caddo Tribe	Oklahoma
Camp Verde Apache Tribe	Arizona
Catawba Tribe	South Carolina
Chugach Community	Alaska

Table 2 *continued*

Tribe	State
Confederated Salish and Kootenai Tribes of the Flathead Nation	Montana
Confederated Tribes of the Colville Reservation	Washington
Confederated Tribes of the Umatillaans	Oregon
Confederated Tribes of the Warm Springs Reservation	Oregon
Coquille Indian Tribe	Oregon
Dakota Tribe	Minnesota
Eastern Shoshone Tribe	Wyoming
Gay Head Wampanoag	Massachussetts
Gila River Indian Community	Arizona
Hopi Tribe	Arizona
Houlton Band of Maliseet Indians	Maine
Hualapai Tribe	Arizona
Iowa Tribe	Oklahoma
Jemez Pueblo	New Mexico
Klamath Tribe	Oregon
Kodiak Area Native Association	Alaska
Lac du Flambeau Band of Lake Superior Chippewa Indians	Wisconsin
Leech Lake Band of Chippewa Indians	Minnesota
Little Traverse Bay Band of Odawa Indians	Michigan
Lower Sioux Indian Community	Minnesota
Mashantucket Pequot Tribe	Connecticut
Me-Wuk Indians	California
Mescalero Apache Tribe	New Mexico
Mille Lacs Band of Chippewa Indians	Minnesota
Mille Lacs Band of Ojibwe Indians	Minnesota
Mohegan Nation	Connecticut
Narragansett Tribe	Rhode Island
Navajo Nation	Arizona, New Mexico, Utah
Northern Cheyenne and Crow	Montana
Pokagon Potawatomi Nation	Michigan
Port Gamble S'Klallam Tribes	Washington
Port Graham Corporation	Alaska
Quileute Tribe	Washington
Salt River Pima-Maricopa Indian Community	Arizona
San Carlos Apache Tribe	Arizona
Seminole Tribe	Florida
Seneca Nation	New York
Sokaogon Chippewa Community	Wisconsin
Spokane Tribe of Indians	Washington
Squaxin Island Tribe	Washington
Standing Rock Sioux Tribe	North Dakota
Suquamish Indian Tribe	Washington
Tunica-Biloxi Tribe	Louisiana
Turtle Mountain Band of Chippewa Indians	North Dakota
Wampanoag Tribe of Gay Head Indians	Massachussetts
White Mountain Apache Tribe	Arizona
Wichita and Affiliated Tribes	Oklahoma
Yavapai Apache Tribe	Arizona
Yurok Tribe	California
Zuni Pueblo	New Mexico, Arizona

control in establishing the archaeological agenda on tribal lands, thus helping to make archaeological research more relevant to Native Americans.

Economic Considerations

Tribal archaeology and historic preservation programs have positive financial benefits for tribes (Table 3), as can be seen by examining the FY1996 historic preservation budgets for five tribes in Arizona and New Mexico. By any standard, the $4 million budget and 67 employees of the Navajo Nation Historic Preservation Department are impressive. In fact, the Navajo program is the largest historic preservation office in the nation, larger than any state or federal office. The Navajo Nation Archaeology Department combined with the Navajo Historic Preservation Department, spends more than $7 million and employs more than 150 people in historic preservation and archaeological research. With control of this funding, the Navajo Nation has become the leading agency governing the archaeological research conducted on the Navajo Indian Reservation.

The Navajo Nation budget is much larger than any other tribal program and almost four times the size of the operating budget for the State of Arizona, excluding Heritage Fund Grants funded by the Arizona Lottery (Figure 1). While the annual budgets and staffs of other tribal programs are smaller, they are still significant when compared to the population of the tribes or the size of their reservations. For instance, the 2,000-member Hualapai Tribe actually spends the most preservation dollars per capita—$190 per tribal member (Figure 2). The Hopi Tribe spends about $48 per capita, while the other tribes spend around $20 to $25 per capita.

Another way to measure preservation budgets is to look at the available funds in relation to the size of landbase (Figure 3). In this perspective, Zuni Pueblo spends the most money—$147 per km^2. The other tribes spend between $34 and $90 per km^2. All of the tribes spend more per km^2 than the State of Arizona.

Table 3. Comparative Data for Historic Preservation Programs.

	Typical Budget	Number of Employees	Population	Landbase (km^2)	Funding Per Capita	Funding (Per km^2)
Navajo Nation	$4,000,000	67	200,000	44,504	$20.00	$89.88
Zuni Pueblo	$250,000	4	10,000	1,707	$25.00	$146.46
Hopi Tribe	$478,000	12	10,000	6,242	$47.80	$76.51
Hualapai Tribe	$379,000	7	2,000	4,048	$189.50	$93.63
WM Apache	$230,000	5	12,000	6,734	$19.17	$34.16
State of Arizona	$1,263,753*	11	4,710,650	295,260	$0.27	$4.28

* Arizona funding includes $510,699 from the Historic Preservation Fund and $753,054 in matching funds from the Arizona Department of Transportation used to support archaeological highway projects. SHPO grants distributed from the Arizona Heritage Fund are not included in this table.

Figure 1

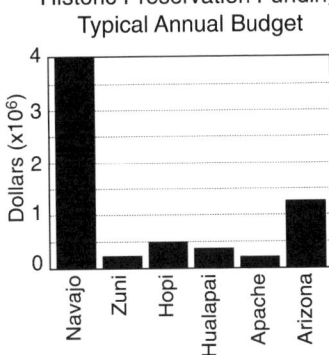

Figure 2

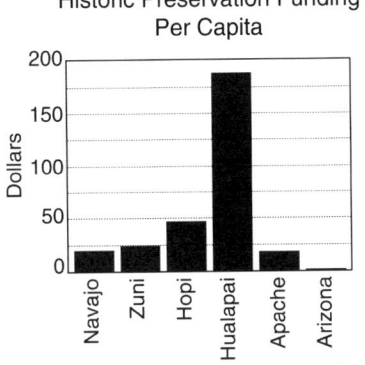

When examining these charts, it is evident that all of the tribes have significantly more financial resources per capita and per km² of land than the Arizona State Historic Preservation Office. This is partly due to economies of scale because certain functions must be provided regardless of landbase or population size. However, this discrepancy also is due to a much broader range of research and preservation activities undertaken by tribes to fulfill cultural preservation mandates.

Figure 3

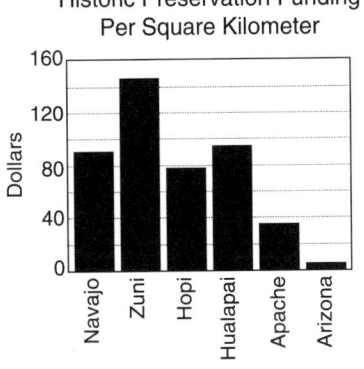

Ultimately, the success of THPOs depends on long-term programmatic funding. SHPOs are funded from allocations from the U.S. Historic Preservation Fund using revenues from offshore mineral leases. A similar permanent arrangement needs to be made for tribes in a manner that ensures that tribes and SHPOs are not competing for the same limited funding sources. The continued success of the NHPA requires that THPOs and SHPOs both have the funding necessary to carry out their mandates.

Native American Archaeology in a Social and Political Context

The tribes that have become directly involved in archaeological research have sought to redefine professional ethics and sponsor archaeology that is conducted in ways acceptable to Native American values. *Native Americans and Archaeologists, Stepping Stones to Common Ground*, (Swidler et al. 1997), offers stimulating personal views about social and political factors involved in making archaeological research and heritage management acceptable to contemporary Native Americans.

There are many reasons why Native Americans in the United States allow archaeologists to work on their land or do archaeology themselves. These include the management of cultural resources using tribal values, a genuine interest in tribal history, the litigation of land claims, attainment of intellectual parity with non-Indian researchers, facilitation of development, retention of financial benefits, and maintenance of political sovereignty. For many tribes, the tribal assumption of SHPO responsibilities has become a meaningful way to assert tribal sovereignty because it replaces a regulatory process led by a state official with a tribal process led by a tribal official.

As tribes have become major employers of archaeologists, many non-Indian archaeologists now have regular, face-to-face interaction with Native Americans. To some degree, this interaction entails a process of socialization whereby archaeologists come to understand and accommodate Native American values, even if they do not personally subscribe to those values. This new understanding can have a profound effect on how these archaeologists choose to do archaeology. I know of few archaeologists who have worked for Indian tribes for any length of time who have not come to reevaluate their thoughts about archaeological excavation and the study of human remains.

Many archaeologists employed by tribes find themselves in the role of a "cultural broker," explaining the reasons and methods of archaeology to Native Americans, and, simultaneously explaining to non-Indians why Native Americans want certain approaches to archaeology. This is difficult work, fraught with the potential for misunderstandings on both sides.

Intellectual Aspects of Collaboration with Native Americans in Archaeological Research

In explaining archaeology to Native Americans, archaeologists routinely examine the epistemological basis of their discipline. Recognizing that Native Americans view the past in fundamentally different ways than non-Indians, these archaeologists often will incorporate cultural relativism and multidisciplinary approaches in their research without relinquishing their commitment to collect archaeological data scientifically. Further, they explore ways to report their results without precluding alternative interpretations by Native Americans. Science and traditional history complement rather than compete with each other in this approach.

Many archaeologists working with Native American traditional cultural properties find their research blurs the boundaries between archaeology and ethnography. In dealing with cultural landmarks and landscapes, these subdisciplinary distinctions often have little relevance to Native Americans. Many of the places that have cultural importance to contemporary native peoples have archaeological manifestations, yet these can only be fully understood and evaluated using knowledge derived from traditional history and cultural practice. This new and still emerging body of work is a new form of ethnoarchaeology, which, unlike earlier formulations of ethnoarchaeology designed primarily to improve archaeological method and theory, is oriented towards managerial and interpretive goals.

Unresolved Ethical Issues

As should be expected, the current developments in Native American archaeology entail a number of unresolved and sometimes contentious issues: the confidentiality of privileged information, use and publication of scholarly results, and the place of the traditional structure and use of esoteric knowledge vs. the scholarly freedom to pursue academic research. Determining what information should remain confidential and how this can be accomplished is a difficult task. The archaeological ethic of sharing work with peers through publication often conflicts with tribal ethics to keep certain types of cultural information esoteric and private. These unresolved issues provide a dynamic tension in the daily work of both Indian and non-Indian archaeologists working for or with tribes, and will result in a new code of ethics that will foster archaeology as an acceptable discipline for Native peoples.

Prospects for a Native American Archaeology

Following and using the archaeological report series produced by tribes in the Southwest for the last 20 years, I have seen the Navajo Nation and the Zuni Pueblo produce hundreds of reports, all meeting high professional standards. The more recently established programs operated by the Gila River Indian Community and the Hopi Tribe have begun to contribute to the professional archaeological literature generated by tribal organizations. These reports are subjected to the same review process as other archaeological reports and must meet the same standards.

Most of the principal investigators and project directors employed by tribes are non-Indian and have been successful in making the research questions and archaeological method and theory guiding tribal archaeological research meet the standards of the profession. This is important because it has given tribal programs the credibility they need.

While tribes produce solid archaeological reports, these rarely contain Native American perspectives interpreting the archaeological record. The question, then, is: If tribes are doing solid, conventional archaeology, what are the prospects for the development of uniquely Native American perspectives in archaeological research? Ultimately, the answer depends on our success in providing the academic preparation needed by Native Americans to fill high-level archaeological positions. The challenge here is to provide Native Americans with the rigorous scholarly standards for scientifically-valid work without forcing them into normative paths of non-Indian thinking—a far from easy task, but not an unattainable one either.

Several years ago I attended an ethnobiology conference in Albuquerque where a distinguished panel of scholars discussed ethnotaxonomy, using the Linnaean classification as a frame of reference. After hearing these papers, Joe Zunie, a Zuni colleague attending the conference, said he thought the papers implied the Linnaean system was based on some ultimate truth that the folk classifications lacked. He turned to another archaeologist and asked, "Don't these people know that the Linnaean system is just one more folk classification?" This was an insightful observation, and it is upon such insights that a Native American perspective will ultimately be developed.

At present, we can only glimpse what such a Native American archaeology might entail. Carlos Condori, an Aymara from Bolivia, and Roger Echo-Hawk, a Pawnee from the United States, have both published on the historiographic basis for historical interpretation provided by Native American oral traditions and how they can be used in reconstructing archaeological culture history. The use of Native American traditional histories in archaeological research has great potential but its success will be contingent upon the participation of tribal members in all aspects of the research, from research design through fieldwork to report preparation.

Condori (1989) also suggests that Native American archaeology can be developed using Native concepts of time and space. Archaeologists already use multiple temporal frames of reference, including calendrical time, radiocarbon time, and relative time based on archaeological phases. There is no reason why Native concepts of time cannot also be arrayed alongside these other frames of reference.

Traditional Native American knowledge about the past is sometimes embedded in a conceptual framework that is spatial rather than temporal. For instance, the Páez Indians of Colombia transmit historical knowledge in fragments of oral narratives that allow listeners to construct a history based on their spatial knowledge of geographical referents. There is, therefore, not one history but multiple histories. It should be possible to use these and other similar principles to structure archaeological research but Native peoples will have to take the lead in accomplishing this task. When they do so, our profession will be enhanced with important new ways of understanding the past.

Conclusion

The NHPA has increased participation of Native Americans in archaeology, and the control of tribes over archaeological research and the management of heritage resources. The increasing number of Native Americans working as professional archaeologists is beginning to change the paradigmatic basis of our discipline in new and exciting ways. This is an invigorating prospect for archaeology, and we can further the process by continuing to work together. Non-Indian and Indian archaeologists need to continue collaboration in research, and both groups need to continue working with traditional Native peoples in the study of the past. In so doing, the archaeological research being conducted for and by Native Americans under the auspices of the NHPA will help to restructure our discipline and enrich our intellectual understanding of the archaeological record.

SAA Bulletin, January 1999

Postscript

Since this article was written in 1997, changes in the administration of the NHPA have continued to strengthen the role of Native Americans in historic preservation. In 1999, the Advisory Council on Historic Preservation revised 36 CFR 800, the regulations implementing Section 106 of the NHPA. The revised regulations emphasize consultation with Indian tribes and Native Hawaiian organizations. Consultation with Indian tribes must respect tribal sovereignty and the government-to-government relationship between the federal government and Indian tribes. Even tribes that have not elected to assume SHPO responsibilities on their lands must be consulted about undertakings on or affecting their lands on the same basis and in addition to the SHPO. The principle is that Indian tribes should have the same extent of involvement when actions occur on tribal lands as the SHPO does for actions within the state. Off tribal lands, federal agencies must consult the appropriate tribe or Native Hawaiian organization.

Three additional tribes have assumed SHPO responsibilities for their lands: Poarch Band of Creek Indians (Alabama), Cheyenne River Sioux Tribe (South Dakota), and Mescalero Apache Tribe (New Mexico). With the addition of these tribes, a total of 18 tribes have now assumed the role of SHPO on their lands. Several additional tribes have set up tribal historic preservation offices but have not assumed SHPO responsibilities.

In 1997 and 1999, the National Park Service (NPS) funded 23 tribal archaeological and historic preservation projects, with grants totaling $861,300. Additional NPS projects in 1997 and 1999 funded oral history projects, botanical and ethnographic research, and other cultural preservation projects that did not focus on archaeology per se. With funding from the NPS, 18 new tribes became engaged in archaeological research or historic preservation: Ak Chin (Arizona), Bridgeport Indian Colony (California), Lower Elwa Klallam Tribe (Washington), Native Village of St. Michaels (Alaska), Native Village of Venetie (Alaska), Newhalen Tribal Council (Alaska), Nez Perce (Idaho), Passamaquoddy of Indian Township (Maine), Passamaquoddy of Pleasant Point (Maine), Poarch Band of Creek Indians (Alabama), Pueblo of Acoma (New Mexico), Rosebud Sioux

(South Dakota), Round Valley (California), Sealaska Corporation (Alaska), Timbisha Shoshone (California), Tuolumna Band of Me-Wuk (California), White Earth Nation (Chippewa, Minnesota), and Wrangell Corporation (Alaska). This brings the total number of tribes directly involved in archaeological activities to 75.

Thus the trend of Native Americans becoming more directly involved in archaeological research and cultural resources management has continued since 1997 and shows no sign of abatement. As this trend continues in the future, we can expect profound changes in the way that archaeology is conducted on Indian land. The future holds exciting prospects for an archaeology that is congruent with Native American values and interests.

Painting a "New" Face on CRM: Integrating Traditional Culture and Archaeology

Janet Cohen and Nina Swidler

For several years now, the Navajo Nation Historic Preservation Department's (HPD) Roads Planning Program has combined the expertise of archaeologists, Navajo cultural specialists, and ethnographers for an interdisciplinary, integrated approach to cultural resource management (CRM) investigations. The purpose of these investigations has been to identify, protect, and manage prehistoric and historic sites, including traditional cultural places, sacred sites, in-use sites, and burials, situated along Navajo Nation road improvement projects. Funding for these projects derives from the Federal Highway Administration and is passed through the Bureau of Indian Affairs (BIA) to HPD under an Indian Self-Determination and Education Assistance Act contract (known as the 638 contract). Investigations are accomplished by both in-house field service staff and third-party contractors to comply with Section 106 of the National Historic Preservation Act and the Navajo Nation Cultural Resource Protection Act. The following discussion will focus on the evolution of our programmatic procedures that enables researchers to work together using a multidisciplinary approach.

At the time of the Roads Planning Program's inception in 1989, all of the program staff and many in HPD had a strong archaeological orientation toward CRM. Before the ethnographic component was added to the program, archaeologists primarily focused on intensive field surveys to identify prehistoric and historic resources. Although they occasionally conducted interviews to collect additional information, this aspect of the archaeological investigations was, at best, unstructured. Since the practice of archaeology precludes the identification of places without material remains, a wide range of what we now refer to as traditional cultural properties (TCPs), such as prayer offering places, herb or mineral gathering areas, and landscape features, were unintentionally overlooked.

The publication of *National Register Bulletin 38* (guidelines for identifying and evaluating TCPs) in 1990 and a predicted threefold increase in road construction funding levels for the Navajo Nation in 1991 spurred the Roads Program to build a CRM program that included both archaeological and traditional culture components. Using ethnographic methods to identify places of traditional importance is not new to Navajoland, even in the context of CRM. For over a decade, discussions of consultation with tribal members to identify these types of properties have appeared in the literature. For example, in his 1982 *American Antiquity* article, Dave Doyel promoted a way in which places of concern to local Navajo communities could be recognized through consultation with medicine men.

By late 1992 the cultural specialists and ethnographers, interacting as a team, were conducting ethnographic assessments of our linear project areas. These assessments involved the research of documentary sources and the interview of community residents and tribal officials to identify TCPs and burial locations. From this information, the team developed protection or other management strategies for places that might be directly or indirectly impacted by construction activities. What had previously been an informal and inconsistently applied protocol for interviewing by archaeologists working alone developed into a structured and systematic procedure for conducting CRM ethnography.

This team approach allowed for complementary areas of expertise to be utilized for the common goal of protecting traditional and historical sites. Cultural specialists provided the framework for identifying places important to Navajo people. Educated in their traditions by elders, they came to the job well versed in Navajo language and culture. They not only provided language interpretation, but, of equal importance, they provided the cultural interpretation of the information gathered during interviews. The cultural specialists knew *how* to ask questions correctly to elicit information required for management purposes. Their knowledge of traditional "etiquette" allowed them to establish rapport even in the most difficult and sensitive of situations. Steeped in the most fundamental social rules, they enjoyed access to traditional medicine people and the elderly, both crucial sources for identifying traditional and sacred places. The cultural specialists also maintained connections within family, clan, and community networks and could rely on the wisdom of Navajo spiritual leaders and traditional practitioners to provide guidance regarding management recommendations.

On the other hand, formally trained ethnographers provided guidance on interview methodologies. While the collection of information is essential, the ability to successfully communicate that information to the intended audience is also critical. Thus, the ethnographers' skills in technical writing and computer applications were a welcome addition. Their experiences and education also allowed them to adapt more easily to a bureaucracy based on the legislative mandate of Section 106 than could the cultural specialists. This background guided the more formal structure of interviews, field notes, and reports.

While the team approach worked well for the cultural specialists and ethnographers, it unfortunately excluded a crucial component: archaeology. Little collaboration between the archaeologists and the ethnographic team took place; fieldwork efforts were not coordinated, and separate reports were produced. This inevitably led to inconsistent and incomplete project management recommendations.

The basic problems in coordinating the ethnographic and archaeological components of CRM assessments unfolded for several identifiable reasons, most notably the different theoretical perspectives and methodologies that the archaeologists, ethnographers, and cultural specialists brought to the job. Program archaeologists had been doing CRM work for compliance with Section 106 for many years while the ethnographers and cultural specialists had little or no practical experience in that arena. Further exacerbating these differences was the perspective held by the cultural specialists, ethnographers, and other CRM professionals that the Section 106 framework was, and is not, an adequate mechanism for protecting and managing traditional places. Making the necessary cognitive shift from a traditional perspective to the 106 framework, and then acting on it for practical management purposes, was particularly difficult in light of this perspective, especially for the cultural specialists.

Another problem was of a more pragmatic nature. The level of effort necessary to complete an ethnographic assessment was greater and more time intensive than a standard Class III archaeological survey. While the archaeologists had to identify, record, and make management recommendations of sites in the assessment phase, the ethnographic team did this, plus developed and implemented mitigation or treatment measures. This difference caused scheduling conflicts for the initiation and completion of projects.

Since our in-house fieldwork procedures served as a model for the way contractors performed assessments, similar problems developed on projects contracted to third parties. These difficulties can be traced to the organization of the earliest contracts that combined archaeological and ethnographic methodologies. In these contracts, archaeology and ethnography were presented as separate but equal contract components. Appearing as such in the scope of work, these documents did little to promote either an integrated field strategy or reporting structure. Consequently, on contracted projects, archaeologists and the ethnographic teams tended to conduct the fieldwork independently from one another. Again, this resulted in inconsistent and incomplete management recommendations at the reporting phase, particularly with regard to evaluation and management recommendations made for TCPs. A primary cause was the ideological differences archaeologists and ethnographers maintained for the management of archaeological resources vs. places of traditional cultural importance. Resulting reports were often so fragmented that they were next to impossible to review for technical and compliance purposes. The Road Program's lack of guidance on a range of complicated issues including contract structure, informed consent, site mapping, reburial of human remains, and consultation with interested parties, combined with the acute philosophical differences, exacerbated the purely logistical problems experienced by researchers.

Although it was difficult to accept that the old way of organizing our work was not working, this realization has helped effect positive change. Great strides have been made in the past year or so resolving earlier problems. Today, project work on both in-house and contracted projects reflects a truly integrated approach. In-house, we reorganized our technical staff into two nondisciplinary subsections: field services and contract administration. The field services section now consists of archaeologists, cultural specialists, and ethnographers. In-house cross training has provided a better appreciation for the respective disciplines, while ongoing formal training has led to a better understanding of Section 106 requirements. Fieldwork efforts are now dovetailed, and as a team, staff are collaborating on forms and maps and producing integrated reports.

Such collaborations help archaeologists gain a more complete understanding of historical sites with traditional components. For example, the cultural specialists contribute a literal (Navajo) interpretation of the material remains of ceremonial sites and features. Similarly, with prior knowledge that a given ceremony was held in a specific place, a cultural specialist can identify the material remains of spatially discrete ceremonial components for the archaeologists. They also provide an interpretive link between and among historical sites that are spatially and temporally associated. Archaeologists, on the other hand, have taught the ethnographic team more precise approaches for descriptive recording and mapping of identified resources. Changes in data collection such as these and a developing respect of one another's' strengths have resolved many of the earlier problems. As their knowledge and experience increased, the cultural specialists have taken on the primary responsibility for in-house ethnographic work from the fieldwork stage through report production, working closely with the archaeologists. At the same time, the ethnographers are gradually moving away from in-house fieldwork into contract administration.

Similar changes have been incorporated into our contracts. The directions furnished to contractors have been revised to achieve greater integration of both investigation techniques and report presentation. For example, the emphasis on separate application and presentation of archaeological and ethnographic methodologies is gone. Scopes-of-work have been completely overhauled to reflect one set of goals, one set of project specific objectives, one set of reporting requirements, and one set of deadlines. We now receive integrated reports that indicate that researchers are coordinating their efforts and presenting data with a unified voice.

Although numerous problems still exist, the majority no longer emanate from program procedures but from a number of larger issues that still need to be addressed. Of paramount importance is the development of a tribal historic preservation plan that will enable research to be conducted that is relevant to both the Navajo people and the national preservation program. Along with this is the need to develop and regularly update policies for issues such as the treatment of human remains, consultation with interested parties, informed consent, and curation.

Ideally, with a preservation plan in place, the next challenge is to develop a methodology that will allow us to adopt a less piecemeal, more ecological strategy for cultural preservation. Currently, in the context of road development, cultural resource investigations are conducted *after* project scoping and planning are completed. A preferred approach is to have preservation specialists involved in the earliest stages of project planning. This would allow for the incorporation of information regarding cultural landscapes and regional preservation concerns into the decision-making process that selects alternative project designs. Information concerning specific sites could then be gathered during the Section 106 assessment process.

Another problem to be addressed is that many federal laws, regulations, and policies conflict with one another. For example, Federal Highway Administration policy states that highway funds *cannot* be used to investigate cultural resources outside of proposed construction zones. On the other hand, the regulations of the National Historic Preservation Act specifically direct us to identify and evaluate all historic properties located within the area of potential effect of an undertaking. In the case of many cultural resources, and particularly TCPs, the area of potential effect extends far beyond the construction zone! Resolution of these contradictions is essential.

Finally, it is our opinion that the entire project planning and design process should reside within one organization. Currently, a significant problem is the fragmentation of project planning, design, consent, and construction responsibilities. Different programs within the tribe are responsible for developing the seven-year priority construction schedule, for conducting the cultural resource inventories, and for performing the project review to ensure all necessary consents and permits are in place. BIA contracts the environmental assessments to a third party and retains full control of project design and construction. This division of responsibilities without a central coordinating entity does not facilitate the exchange of relevant information or promote cooperative efforts. This contest for control emanates from a lack of trust that BIA and the tribe have for one another and is not an issue that is easily solved or overcome. For example, in an effort to coordinate the environmental requirements of road projects, the tribe attempted to expand our contract with BIA to provide the necessary services for preparation of environmental documents. Unfortunately, BIA rejected this proposal. We hope that at some point in the future, the Navajo Nation will be able to minimally assume this responsibility. In the long run, this would enable the Navajo Nation to take a more holistic approach to economic and community development while addressing Navajo preservation concerns.

Note: The Navajo Nation Historic Preservation Department is acknowledged for giving us the opportunity to write and update this article. The opinions expressed here are solely those of the authors. Thanks, too, to Mike Yeatts for his valuable comments on the draft and Kurt Dongoske for encouraging us to publish our thoughts. Previous versions of this article were presented at the 1995 Annual Meeting of the Society for Applied Anthropology and the 1995 Navajo Studies Conference.

SAA Bulletin, January 1997

Postscript

Since this column was originally published, the Roads Program has progressed in several areas. We've maintained or gained ground in a most important arena—enhancing Navajo participation in preservation decision making. Other issues remain partially or wholly unresolved but direct future efforts. We previously described how the program approached both in-house and contracted projects. Operating much as described, the in-house field services and contract administration units are autonomous. While this independence has fostered intellectual and methodological freedom, it also resulted in decreased coordination. We have recognized this problem and are working toward restoring a greater level of integration by improving communication.

The program has made significant progress in furthering our long-term commitment to integrate both Navajo and other tribal voices into compliance-driven cultural resources investigations. This begins in our field services unit, with Navajo staff seeking input from local communities. It continues and is often expanded in our contracted data recovery projects where researchers more fully explore alternative explanations and interpretations offered by tribes regarding their connections to project areas. To this end, we have instituted firm guidelines for consulting with interested parties and follow standardized procedures for obtaining informed consent.

The program and Bureau of Indian Affairs (BIA) have worked cooperatively to integrate cultural resources information into various stages of project design. For example, the BIA now includes us in project field reconnaissance meetings at the beginning of a project and final plan-in-hand review meetings before construction. The BIA also has helped mediate conflicts such as the controversy between the Federal Highway Administration's policy limiting assessment to the construction zone and an agency's legal responsibility to identify potential impacts to the area. The BIA accomplished this by revising its policy to allow us to conduct assessments within a wider right-of-way corridor. This strategy delineates a larger buffer zone and enables the agency to avoid or reduce impacts to resources through project redesign.

On another level, the tribe has developed and updated many policies important for the management of cultural resources and human remains. For example, the policy for the disposition of human remains has been updated and a curation policy is undergoing final review. However, some issues still need to be addressed. The development of a tribal historic preservation plan remains of paramount importance, yet cannot move forward without the passage of the yet-undefined tribal resource management plan. Nevertheless, efforts have been initiated on a programmatic level to develop a research design that will guide future investigations related to road development. We anticipate that these results will become an integral part of the overall preservation plan.

Another significant problem that is beyond our control is the lack of a central coordinating entity. The fragmentation of responsibilities for project planning, design, consent, and construction still exists with no resolution in sight. The tribe and the BIA are continuing discussions to resolve this dilemma. Despite these circumstances, our program maintains the financial support of the federal government and the quality of CRM on the Navajo Nation will continue to improve. With persistent effort, the remaining problems will eventually be resolved.

Hopi Oral History and Archaeology

*T. J. Ferguson, Kurt E. Dongoske, Mike Yeatts,
and Leigh J. Kuwanwisiwma*

Haliksa'i! Listen! The Hopi emerged into this, the Fourth World, from the *Sipapuni* in the Grand Canyon. Emerging, they encountered *Ma'saw,* guardian of the Fourth World, and made a spiritual pact with him, wherein the Hopi would act as stewards of the earth, vowing to place their footprints throughout the Fourth World as they migrated in a spiritual quest to find their destiny at the center of the universe. Hopi clans embarked on a long series of migrations throughout the Southwest and beyond, settling in various places, until, after many generations, they arrived at their rightful place on the Hopi mesas.

During the migration period, the Hopi clans established themselves throughout the land by cultivating and caring for the earth. As directed by *Ma'saw,* the setting of Hopi "footprints" included establishment of ritual springs, pilgrimage trails, shrines, and petroglyphs. As they migrated they left behind the graves of their ancestors, ruins, potsherds, grinding stones, and other artifacts to pay the mother earth for use of the area, and as evidence that they had vested the land with their spiritual stewardship, fulfilling their pact with *Ma'saw.* These archaeological sites today constitute monuments by which Hopi verify clan histories and religious beliefs, and provide physical proof that they have valid claims to a wide region. Yes, this is the way it is. *Ta'a, yanhaqam.*

Introduction

Through acts and omissions of the United States, many aboriginal lands claimed and used by the Hopi Indians have been taken from them. As a result, the Hopi today are concerned not only with preservation of sacred areas, ancestral graves, and cultural sites on their own reservation, but also in other developing areas where they have no jurisdiction. In response to this, the Hopi Tribe's Cultural Preservation Office (CPO) has attempted to use existing historic preservation legislation as a means of input to management decisions made for historic properties in Arizona, New Mexico, Colorado, and Utah.

Today, the Hopi, with a population of about 8,500, occupy 12 villages on three mesas on a reservation in northern Arizona. The Hopi Tribe is also concerned about sites in adjoining areas that were occupied by Hopi ancestors during the clan migrations.

Hopi efforts to participate in the decision-making process that affects their ancestral sites coincide with a burgeoning movement in the historic preservation field to consider traditional cultural properties as historic sites, and with federal and state agencies' efforts to implement the Native American Graves Protection and Repatriation Act (NAGPRA), and related state legislation. Implementation of NAGPRA and the National Historic Preservation Act as amended on October 30, 1992, requires consultation with Indian tribes and traditional religious leaders whose resources are subject to impact. The Hopi Tribe takes the opportunity and responsibility to consult seriously. Additionally, the CPO believes that a true inventory and consideration of a proposed project's effects on cultural resources cannot be obtained without ethnographic and ethnohistoric research to complement a standard archaeological inventory. Genuine consultation with the Hopi Tribe requires more than simply written notification of a proposed impact from a land management agency, with a 30-day period for comment.

In this paper we (1) describe how the consultation process works, (2) discuss the Hopi perspectives of how and why archaeological sites constitute traditional cultural properties, and (3) examine cultural preservation goals in relation to archaeological and ethnohistorical research, with the objective of describing the need and importance of the consultation process.

The Hopi Cultural Preservation Office

The Hopi CPO was established as a tribal program in the Department of Natural Resources in 1988. It currently has a full-time staff of 11: a director, a tribal archaeologist, three project archaeologists, a media specialist, three Hopi research specialists, an administrative assistant, a transcriber, and several secretaries. The CPO is dedicated to preserving the spiritual and cultural essence of the Hopi, encompassing various concerns: archaeology, ethnology, recovery of stolen sacred artifacts, farming, and preservation of the Hopi language. The program is supported directly by the Hopi Tribe, with supplemental funding from project sponsors who require its professional services. With respect to archaeology and ethnology, the CPO is challenged to develop an appropriate means for the Hopi villages, clans, and religious societies to participate in program activities by contributing the esoteric, highly guarded information needed for management purposes.

Much of this esoteric information is embedded in clan history or the ceremonial knowledge of Hopi religious societies. Clan history is ritual knowledge, rarely shared legitimately with other clans, and much less so with non-Indians. Past anthropological research has occasionally violated researcher–informant confidentiality, resulting in the guarded context of current research. The Hopi have objected to much of the past research, but had no way to control it. This legacy has left many Hopi suspicious of scholarly research, bringing about a cautious attitude that affects the CPO in its own research activities. The CPO decided that direct involvement of Hopi elders would make current research more acceptable to the Hopi people.

The Hopi Cultural Resources Advisory Task Team

A Hopi Cultural Resources Advisory Task Team was established in 1991 to guide and assist the CPO research activities. Assembling this team has been a significant accomplishment. This Advisory Team currently consists of 18 men, representing all of the Hopi villages, and a number of prominent clans, priesthoods, and religious societies. Importantly, it also includes representatives from autonomous villages that decline to send representatives to the Hopi Tribal Council and which do not otherwise participate in the centralized Hopi tribal government.

The advisory team holds monthly meetings, but also calls special meetings to consult on specific issues. Field trips are made as necessary to inspect project areas and to evaluate sites, providing an important way to contextualize project impacts on resources and the opportunity to identify traditional cultural properties that archaeologists may have overlooked or not recognized during surveys. When more intensive field investigations are required, a subset of the advisory team is appointed.

Advisory team members hold distinguished positions of authority within the traditional village social structure, but their committee participation is a secular activity separate from their regular religious responsibilities. Since advisory team activities take these men away from farming and other productive activities, tribal policy provides an honorarium for time spent on CPO consultation. Funding is provided by both the tribe and project sponsors.

The CPO considers advisory team members to be experts in Hopi culture, possessing important information for management of cultural resources. The CPO values their contributions, as it would the contribution of any specialist or expert. Unfortunately, many bureaucrats and archaeologists don't value traditional learning as much as they do western education, as is demonstrated by the double standard commonly applied in ethnohistoric research. "Informants," those who actually have the knowledge, are the least likely to be viewed as "educated," and therefore, are the least likely to be compensated for their knowledge. Anthropologists and historians who use this information are the ones compensated for that "knowledge," gained indirectly. This stems from several historical prejudices: (1) the traditional view that Native Americans are the subject of research, not active participants as cultural experts in their own right (this view objectifies people and reduces them to "data," and some anthropologists refuse to pay for data); (2) the tendency to value formal western education more than traditional learning; and (3) the belief that cultural properties are of greatest concern to Native Americans and, therefore, their time and knowledge should be volunteered to protect them. This would be valid if an undertaking impacted a resource controlled by Native Americans, but a Native American group would rarely propose an action that would knowingly destroy a resource of cultural value. Impacts are more often related to federal, state, and private agencies pursuing their own agendas for development. In this context, a request for volunteer information, because it is in the "best interest" to protect resources valued by the tribe, is extortion.

The CPO considers this situation analogous to that of archaeologists who are also interested in cultural resource protection. Archaeologists are no longer asked to donate their time to locate and evaluate cultural resources in developing areas, or to mitigate impacts on those resources. Professional archaeologists established the need to be paid for this work three decades ago. The Hopi Tribe thinks the emerging federal and state requirements for consultation with cultural advisors and tribal elders needs similar funding.

Hopi accounts of clan migrations relate that the ancestors, the *Hisatsinom,* passed through many areas of the Southwest before the gathering of clans on the Hopi mesas. Each clan followed its unique route and established its own history. The Hopi know that the area occupied by the *Hisatsinom* transcends the geographic constraints of the culture areas defined by archaeologists. Although these cultural constructs play an important role in contemporary archaeological theory, they constitute foreign concepts in the Hopi's understanding of the past. The knowledge and history obtained during migration is specific to each clan and constitutes esoteric information that is not shared between clans. Consequently, the process of compiling information for legal and management purposes is complex and time consuming, requiring consultation with many people. The consultation process should be initiated early during project planning to allow sufficient flexibility for the CPO to compile information from the advisory team and input from other Hopi people. Consultation should be initiated through a letter addressed to the tribal chairman, presenting relevant information for the proposed development, and requesting information about concerns the Hopi Tribe may have. Federal and state agencies should not assume that consultation will consist of a single exchange of letters, or that a lack of response within a 30-day period constitutes tribal concurrence.

Consultation with Sponsors, Regulatory Agencies, and Other Tribes

The Hopi CPO has developed a protocol for combining archaeological and ethnohistorical research with participation and review by the advisory team on two large projects: the Glen Canyon Environment Studies (GCES) sponsored by the Bureau of Reclamation, which studied the environmental impacts relating to the Glen Canyon Dam operation; and the Salt River Project's (SRP) Fence Lake Mine and Transportation Corridor Project, in New Mexico and Arizona.

The CPO and advisory team have benefited from numerous meetings with regulatory agencies where state and federal responsibilities in the compliance process were explained. For people who have not been inculcated into the sometimes arcane rules and regulations of historic preservation, the compliance process can be bewildering and confusing. Effective consultation depends on the advisory team understanding exactly what they are consulting about. For the Fence Lake Mine project, a series of informative meetings were held with SRP, representatives of the Arizona and New Mexico state historic preservation officers, and the Bureau of Land Management. The CPO held additional meetings with the various Hopi villages and other local groups to share project information and to seek advice on how to proceed. A total of 27 meetings were held. Similar meetings were held for the Glen Canyon Environmental Studies project with the Bureau of Reclamation and the National Park Service.

Presumably these meetings have laid the groundwork for future projects. However, the dynamic nature of historic preservation and cultural resources management may require continuing education as new laws are passed, and as new ways are developed to implement existing rules and regulations.

In formal consultation for NAGPRA and the National Historic Preservation Act, the Hopi tribe has explicitly stated that its participation in the compliance process does not imply endorsement or support of a particular development or project. Its interest is in protecting as many sites as possible, not in facilitating their destruction through new development.

Archaeological Sites as Traditional Cultural Properties

For the implementation of the 1966 National Historic Preservation Act, traditional cultural properties are defined by P. L. Parker and T. F. King as historic sites that are important because of "their association with cultural practices or beliefs of a living community that (1) are rooted in the community's history and (2) are important in maintaining the continuing cultural identity of the community." To qualify for inclusion in the National Register of Historic Places, traditional cultural properties must exhibit four attributes: an age greater than 50 years; existence as a tangible property; integrity in relation to the transmission and retention of cultural beliefs or the performance of ceremonial practices; and integrity of condition wherein their traditional cultural significance has not been reduced through alteration of location, setting, design, or materials. Consultation to identify and evaluate traditional cultural properties should play a key role in the historic preservation compliance process. If state and federal regulators determine traditional cultural properties to be eligible for the National Register, the project impact on these sites must be considered and this process provides an opportunity to protect the site.

For management purposes, all Hopi traditional cultural properties can be reduced to historic sites, although this is not an entirely satisfying procedure. The real significance of many of these sites is as sacred sites, and under existing law, sacred sites have less protection than historic sites. Since all Hopi shrines and religious practices were established in ancient times, and are integral in the transmission and retention of Hopi culture, these sacred sites meet the criteria for classification as traditional cultural properties. The conceptual and legal reduction of sacred sites to historic sites is pragmatic management, but is nonetheless emotionally difficult for tribal elders.

The Hopi have many different types of traditional cultural properties: shrines, sacred sites, springs, resource collection areas, and geographical landforms with place names that commemorate prehistoric or historic events. In the Hopi perspective, every ancestral archaeological site is also a traditional cultural property, because they are tangible monuments validating Hopi culture, history, and the Hopi's covenant with *Ma'saw*. As such, archaeological sites play a central role in the transmission and retention of Hopi culture. Moreover, every prehistoric Hopi village also has an associated village shrine that retains contemporary religious significance.

The Hopi tribe's definition of ancestral archaeological sites as traditional cultural properties was derived from consultation with the advisory team. The standard definition was read and discussed in the context of a specific set of archaeological sites in the SRP Fence Lake Mine project area. Eligibility of these sites for inclusion in the National Register of Historic Places was reviewed, and Hopi advisors decided that archaeological sites were eligible in that they were associated with events that have made a significant contribution to the broad patterns of Hopi history (i.e., clan migrations), they are associated with the lives of persons significant in our past (i.e., Hopi ancestors), they are a portion of a larger entity that is significant (i.e., clan migrations), and they have yielded or have the potential to yield information pertinent in prehistory and history.

Regulatory agency archaeologists stated at the outset of consultation with the Hopi tribe that they did not think the definition of traditional cultural properties was intended to be so broadly applied to all sites. In their view, the concept of traditional cultural properties had targeted a different set of cultural sites not usually recorded by archaeologists. In the absence of any other means of management, the Hopi are glad to see these other cultural sites managed as historic properties. However, taking the Parker and King definition of traditional cultural property at face value, tribal members decided that "cultural property" also applies to all ancestral archaeological sites—an example of one special interest group interpreting the same language in very different ways. Archaeologists should realize that their interpretation of the language in federal guidelines, rules, and regulations is not necessarily the only or even the best interpretation. The CPO has been successful in convincing some parties to the consultation process that its definition of archaeological sites as traditional cultural properties is valid. This definition means, of course, that the Hopi now expect to be consulted about the mitigation plan for archaeological sites suffering adverse impacts.

Conventional archaeological culture history has focused on the Hopi's relations to archaeological sites on or near the Hopi Indian Reservation, although, as discussed previously, Hopi concerns for *Hisatsinom* archaeological sites extend over a much wider region. Hopi CPO staff archaeologists play an important role in identifying *Hisatsinom* archaeological sites.

On the Hopi Reservation, the professional CPO staff conducts archaeological inventories and prepares reports that meet cultural resource management standards. In a recent survey of 24.4 miles along State Highway 264, conducted for the Arizona Department of Transportation, 48 archaeological sites and 19 traditional cultural properties were located. Ethnographic interviews and archival research identified four additional cultural properties destroyed during prior road construction. Potential impacts to orchards and farming areas of cultural importance to the Hopi were also identified.

This survey exemplified the difficulty in classifying and managing archaeological sites and traditional cultural properties. These categories are not mutually exclusive and one site may exhibit characteristics that allow its classification in both categories, creating a management dilemma. Many "archaeological sites" also meet National Register of Historic Places eligibility criteria for traditional cultural properties. Similarly, many "traditional cultural properties" also have archaeological manifestations. This dual classification can be problematical. For instance, the Hopi tribe simultaneously wants to enter archaeological site data into the archives maintained by the Arizona State Museum *but* not reveal the location of certain traditional cultural properties. The description and location of archaeological sites in site forms and technical reports may inadvertently reveal information about an associated traditional cultural property, even if specific information is withheld. Classification as only an archaeological site eligible for the National Register under criterion *d* may result in a determination of mitigation through data recovery. However, if this site is also a traditional cultural property, such as a shrine, there can be no mitigation, and its destruction may have a deleterious effect on Hopi culture. This illustrates the importance of accurately assessing site qualities, and is something the Hopi tribe still seeks to resolve.

For projects conducted by agencies outside the Hopi Reservation, CPO archaeologists review survey reports to collate and summarize data for review by the advisory team, composed of tribal elders. For instance, a recent National Park Service survey of 255 miles along the Colorado River through the Grand Canyon documented a total of 475 sites, of which 235 were deemed to be *Hisatsinom* sites. Surveys of the SRP Fence Lake Mine and Transportation Corridor Project identified about 600 sites, the majority of which are prehistoric pueblo sites deemed *Hisatsinom*. Professional archaeologists have been essential in sorting through the voluminous information presented in technical reports, helping the CPO avoid information overload.

Some archaeologists believe that Indians may be interested in preserving sites but that they are not interested in archaeology per se, i.e., the discipline that scientifically studies material culture. The Hopi, however, *are* interested in archaeology. Hopi elders want to know what types of data archaeologists collect and how these data are used to reach conclusions. Many compare archaeological findings to their own system of knowledge. Points of congruence between the two systems of knowledge are often explained in terms of Hopi ritual knowledge. For instance, Hopi prophecy forecasts a time when even the ashes left by the ancestors will be used to prove their claims. Hopi cultural advisors make the connection between this prophecy and flotation analyses of hearth contents for macrobotanical studies.

In general, archaeologists have inconsistently used Hopi knowledge in the interpretation of the archaeological record. Archaeologists have posed the questions of "what happened to the Anasazi?" "where did they go?" The Hopi know where the "Anasazi" went—to the Hopi mesas, among other places. Many archaeologists use the Hopi in an ethnographic analogy to interpret architectural function and to label archaeological features; the terms and concepts used by archaeologists derive from the Hopi lifeway, e.g., kiva and Katsina. Archaeology would benefit if theorists would consistently research and more rigorously use Hopi understanding of the prehistoric cultures of the Southwest.

When development threatens ancestral sites, the Hopi CPO always recommends preservation and protection. A Hopi would never recommend the destruction of an ancestral site. However, the Hopi tribe recognizes that consultation allows it a role in the decision-making process, though not in a final management decision. While the Hopi tribe does not condone the destruction of ancestral archaeological sites, it will recommend mitigation through scientific study for sites that others have decided to destroy. Many Hopi think a written record is better than no record at all, providing documentation of Hopi monuments, so that memory of them will not be entirely lost once their physical manifestation is gone.

Osteology and Reburial of Human Remains

The remains of ancestors buried in archaeological sites are of special concern to the Hopi because of religious significance. From the Hopi perspective, the only proper disposition of disturbed or excavated ancestral human remains and their associated funerary objects is respect and reburial.

Implementation of NAGPRA necessitates consultation with Native American groups claiming cultural affinity to the buried human remains. NAGPRA regulatory procedures are still being developed, but clearly, the required research and consultation substantially overlaps with that required for the National Historic Preservation Act since both federal laws often pertain to the same sites.

The issue of cultural affinity as defined in NAGPRA raises questions about how affinity is determined—it is one thing to claim cultural affinity and another to prove affinity objectively. Different levels of cultural affinity are of interest to the Hopi. At a general level, Hopi are concerned about all *Hisatsinom* human remains, which can often, but not always, be identified contextually by association with pueblo architecture or pottery types. No osteological analysis is required for this type of identification. More specifically, some Hopi are also interested in the genetic affinity among different southwestern tribes and what this means for prehistoric migrations. In addition, the age, sex, and pathologies of disinterred human remains are important, as well as associated funerary objects indicative of social status that would warrant a specific treatment. Nondestructive osteological analyses and study of artifacts are thus seen as appropriate.

Members of the advisory team want to make informed decisions on the appropriate techniques for studying human remains. In consultation on the Fence Lake Mine Project, SRP facilitated a meeting where a physical anthropologist, Charles Merbs (Arizona State University) reviewed the state of the art of osteological analyses and what can be learned using the various methods and techniques. This allowed the Hopi to develop recommendations for the appropriate osteological analysis, fully understanding research procedures and potentials for interpretation. For instance, some Hopi think tribal affinity and clan migration might be understood through genetic studies that entail destructive analysis of human remains, and they are willing to consider this as an analytical option. Others with a more conservative view think that such analyses, while interesting, would be culturally inappropriate. The important point here is that the Hopi cultural advisors are willing to consider professional research designs that address specific problems for specific sets of data, with mutual benefits to anthropologists and the Hopi, and then base their recommendations on presented information, as tempered by cultural values.

The Hopi realize they share a cultural affinity to many *Hisatsinom* archaeological sites with other pueblos and non-pueblo tribes, creating a need to consult with other tribes, especially with regard to the proper treatment of human remains and funerary objects. On the Fence Lake Mine Project, the SRP sponsored a series of meetings between the Acoma, Hopi, and Zuni tribes, allowing discussion among tribal elders, and resulting in a uniform set of recommendations for the proper disposition of human remains and grave goods under the provisions of NAGPRA.

Knowledge that the Hopi tribe burial treatment recommendations to SRP did not conflict with other pueblos' recommendations allayed many anxieties. The intertribal pueblo meetings were in everyone's best interest.

Archaeologists conceptually can reduce human remains simply to classification as "artifacts," and make sampling decisions for a project area, allowing sites containing human graves to be destroyed without data recovery. Hopi, however, apply more humanistic criteria when consulted, and have recommended that every ancestral grave in the direct impact zone be relocated, reburied as closely as possible to its original location. For the Hopi, reinterment is the only acceptable mitigation for grave disturbance because of their concept of death. Death initiates two distinct but inseparable journeys: the physical journey of the body as it returns to a oneness with the earth, and the spiritual journey of the soul to a place where it finally resides. Disruption of the physical journey obstructs the spiritual journey, creating an imbalance within the spiritual world and, hence, the natural world.

The Hopi conduct a reburial ceremony when ancestral remains are reburied. Elders from the advisory team have traveled extensively to conduct the appropriate rituals.

Role of Ethnohistory

The CPO uses ethnohistory in conjunction with archaeology for consultation. This research entails the collection and analysis of information from archival sources, published literature, and oral history interviews. Published Hopi literature is extensive, but the information itself is not always accurate from the Hopi perspective. Formal interviews with Hopi elders are useful to verify published information. The CPO prefers to tape record and transcribe interviews, building a body of archival documentation, and thus allowing the interviews to be referenced and cited in the same scholarly fashion as other written sources.

The interviews and ethnographic research are conducted on a "need to know" basis, where only that information needed for management purposes is made available. Basic questions pertaining to historic preservation include the antiquity of a traditional cultural property, the way in which it functions to retain or transmit cultural identity, and whether its integrity has been compromised through alteration of location, setting, design, or materials. Research generally does not require esoteric aspects of rituals to be divulged. A filtering process keeps esoteric information from being needlessly divulged to non-Indians, and also to safeguard it from other Hopi clans or villages. Many interviews are conducted entirely in Hopi, and only portions are transcribed or summarized in English.

This ethnohistorical research uses documentary sources to fill in gaps. During the SRP Fence Lake Mine Project, none of the Hopi elders knew the entire pilgrimage route from the Hopi Mesas to the Zuni Salt Lake in New Mexico. Even though the old trails are not precisely known, the shrines and offering places along some of the trails are still used in prayers and, conceptually, the trails have not lost their significance. For this reason, the advisory team thought it was important to locate the old trails and identify how the SRP project impacted them. Ethnohistorical research used oral history interviews, review of published literature, analysis of aerial photographs and remote sensing, and extensive fieldwork to locate them. This methodology successfully located one pilgrimage trail, and determined general locations of two others.

Documentation of contemporary Hopi values and beliefs about sites is another important component of ethnohistorical research. This information provides the CPO with the documentation it needs to consult with regulatory agencies and help evaluate historic properties in terms of eligibility for the National Register of Historic Places.

Cultural Preservation vs. Historic Preservation

The Hopi tribe approaches consultation from a cultural preservation perspective, yet the framework with which this research is conducted is one of historic preservation. While these two pursuits overlap substantially, there are also important differences that need to be considered for the design of appropriate research and the dissemination of results. For instance, while preservation of Hopi culture requires that esoteric religious information remain secret, the historic preservation compliance process requires documentation of Hopi values and beliefs in order to assess the historical character of properties—a potential source of conflict. This conflict was resolved effectively during the SRP project and the Glen Canyon Environmental Studies by allowing the tribe to collect the necessary data and decide what information could be released. By guaranteeing information confidentiality and by directly participating in the research, the CPO is able to successfully balance cultural preservation with historic preservation and help agencies satisfy their federal mandates.

Implementation of an intense CPO review process ensures confidentiality of esoteric information. Draft reports are read by the director and staff, and then submitted for review by the advisory team. This is a time-consuming process, and the internal review schedules do not always coincide with project schedules. The final review for the Fence Lake Mine Project, for instance, was initiated six months after the draft report was completed, at the same time the report was released for review by state and federal regulators.

The advisory team review entailed reading the entire report aloud in both English and Hopi. English words and cultural resources management concepts were defined and discussed when these were not readily understood, and there was detailed discussion of all information, recommendations, and conclusions. The primary concern was that the report be accurate, using the advisors' knowledge to verify anthropological data. Another concern was whether use of the information should be restricted to the sponsor and regulators, or released to the public. Review took six full days, involving working groups from 12 to 22 people. Those who are quoted or cited in the report gave explicit permission to be identified. Similar permission from those unable to attend the meeting was obtained by reviewing the report with them privately. The intense scrutiny the SRP report was subjected to guarantees both that the advisory team fully understands the information contained in the report and that it contains no erroneous information.

Accommodation of Academic and Hopi Values in Dissemination of Knowledge

After review of the SRP Fence Lake Project ethnohistory report, the advisory team recommended that the CPO only release this information to the project sponsor and the regulatory agencies. It did not feel comfortable with a public release which would make it available for scholarly research outside the auspices of the Hopi Tribe. The CPO released only a limited distribution of the final report with the caveat that it cannot be copied or used for scholarly purposes unrelated to project management without written tribal permission

There is some irony in the restriction of ethnohistorical reports prepared by the CPO, given the fact that these reports draw upon past anthropological work that would not be available if it had been similarly restricted. Report restriction may result in the unavailability of that data for future use. Quite honestly, report restriction creates a tension between the professional ethics of the CPO anthropologists who are expected to disseminate the results of their work to other scholars, and the cultural ethics of Hopi tribal members to not divulge information. This tension is diffused by open discussion of the issue between the Hopi and their non-Indian employees and consultants, and by an ongoing evaluation of the respective cultural preservation and scholarly research goals. It is also mitigated by the approval of dissemination of some publications [see "Ethics of Field Research for the Hopi Tribe," *Anthropology Newsletter* (January 1994:56)].

Hopi people use archaeology and ethnohistory to verify their own beliefs and enrich their personal understanding of their place in the universe. Archaeologists have a less personal and more abstract interest in adding to the general store of knowledge and reaching scientific or historical conclusions. These two objectives are not mutually exclusive, but their joint accommodation is still being developed, which is not surprising given that the CPO is still a relatively new organization working in uncharted territory. Perhaps in time the Hopi will decide that cultural resource management projects provide an appropriate means for the Hopi Tribe to advance scholarly knowledge, as well as their self-defined preservation goals.

Prospects for the Future

Archaeological research is of concern to the Hopi, particularly when their ancestors are the subject of research and their self-perception is affected. The destruction of archaeological sites, be it by construction projects, land development, or scientific excavation, is of great concern, because their ancestral record is obliterated. Hopi participation in research and consultation will ensure that Hopi perspectives and concepts are incorporated into the written record that will remain after archaeological sites are destroyed.

Beyond consultation, the Hopi want to be treated as peers in archaeological research so that their knowledge, values, and beliefs are respected in the same way that archaeologists respect one another when they differ in research methods or interpretations. The Hopi do not want to indiscriminately impose their sacred knowledge on the archaeological record, or unfairly constrain archaeological interpretation. They do not want to censor ideas, nor do they wish to impose research designs on archaeologists.

However, not all information should be divulged and not all archaeological research is suitable for direct tribal involvement. No guidelines define what is appropriate research or what research is appropriate for Hopi to participate in. Hopi standards for appropriate research and how research should be conducted will certainly evolve in the future as

Hopi Cultural Advisory Task Team members Harlan Williams, Frank Mofsie, Merwin Kooyahoema, and Daldon Taylor review ethnohistory report with T. J. Ferguson, Hopi Cultural Preservation Office, February 22, 1992.
Photo by and courtesy of HCPO.

archaeological method, theory, and techniques also develop, and as tribal members see a need to obtain new information about their past. Future cooperative research ventures between the Hopi Tribe and anthropologists may serve to identify and advance mutually beneficial research interests. Archaeologists should not be discouraged if the Hopi Tribe does not presently choose to support proposed research. With continued communication and increased understanding of the research process, the tribe may support research in the future that is not considered appropriate today.

Conclusion

Cultural preservation is important to the Hopi Tribe. As Vernon Masayesva, tribal chairman, remarked at the 1991 Hopi Cultural Preservation Day:

> it is true that . . . early in life . . . when we are taught to plant, the elders would tell you that if you want to plant a straight row of corn, you have to first pick where you are going to be going, where you wish to end up at. And then you start planting, but every so often you have to look back. Because it is what happened that tells you where you are at, and where you are going. So, when we talk about cultural preservation, its not just because we want to save something, I think it's because we don't want to forget who we are as Hopis. That we don't want to ever forget our responsibilities, and our traditions and values—all those things that make us different in many ways from other cultures. And this is why cultural preservation . . . is very important. Because you will never know who you are unless you know where you came from. You never know where you are going unless you understand where you have been.

The Hopi CPO thinks that archaeology, ethnography, and ethnohistory play important roles in cultural preservation, and that the research conducted for consultation with state and federal regulatory agencies will result in lasting benefits for the Hopi people.

SAA Bulletin, March 1995

Postscript

Following the publication of this article, several comments were received about the Hopi Tribe's perception of ancestral puebloan habitation sites as traditional cultural properties. The point that raised the most debate was the Hopi Tribe's conclusion that these archaeological sites should be considered eligible for the National Register under other criteria than criterion *(d)* (Anyon 1995; Dongoske et al. 1995; King 1996; Phillips 1996; and Sebastian 1995a, 1995b). The difference between these opinions and those represented in our article was in how traditional cultural properties are perceived by the Hopi vs. federal agencies and SHPOs charged with evaluating and managing these properties. These diverse views, while not entirely in opposition, reflect the dichotomy created by identifying and evaluating important historic resources under the broader values of the National Historic Preservation Act (NHPA), and then forcing them into the development-oriented process defined within Section 106. Since the publication of this article, the regulations (36CFR 800) governing the implementation of Section 106 have been revised as a result of the 1992 amendments to the NHPA. The new regulations have made some of the procedurally-based disagreements moot. For example, in the past there often was debate among the Hopi Tribe, various federal agencies, and the Arizona and New Mexico SHPOs regarding the eligibility of archaeological sites (ancestral puebloan habitation sites) for the National Register of Historic Places under criteria other than criterion *(d)*. The Hopi Tribe also considers these sites to be eligible under criterion *(a)* because of the important relationship of these sites to significant events (i.e., clan migrations) in Hopi history. Recognition of these sites as eligible under criterion *(a)* would not afford greater protection for them, but it may have led to some project delays because of the time involved in additional review and consideration of those values which would make the property eligible under criterion *(a)*. In the new regulations, sites evaluated as eligible for the National Register under any criteria are treated the same; the "research exception" for properties (principally archaeological sites) eligible only for their research value [criterion *(d)*] is no longer a part of the regulations.

Other more fundamental issues, however, remain unresolved and will need to be addressed within the broader philosophy guiding the federal historic preservation program. One issue is the evaluation of traditional cultural properties. Often, traditional cultural properties are viewed as a separate category of historic property that only marginally fits into the federal historic preservation arena. For some traditional cultural properties, this will likely always remain the case, because their value truly is in their continued religious use. For the majority of traditional cultural properties, however, simple recognition by federal agencies and SHPOs of the traditional value and historic importance as viewed by the culture to which it relates is all that is necessary to adequately incorporate it into the existing concept of historic property. Another issue deals with mitigating project impacts to historic properties—one likely to remain contentious. As Native American traditional cultural values of historic properties (particularly archaeological sites) become increasingly recognized, the simplicity of diminishing project impacts through conventional archaeological data recovery will no longer be sufficient. The development of appropriate strategies will thus become increasingly complicated. We believe that the potential for developing and conducting innovative and intellectually stimulating archaeological research through the incorporation of Native American values and traditional knowledge should offset the added complexity of bringing anthropology back into archaeology.

Native American Oral Traditions and Archaeology

Roger Anyon, T. J. Ferguson, Loretta Jackson, and Lillie Lane

The purpose of this position paper is to present ideas to the Arizona Archaeological Council membership on the appropriate use of oral traditions in archaeological research. It provides a basis for continuing a dialogue between Native Americans and archaeologists about how and why archaeology is conducted in Arizona.

Historical Perspective on the Use of Oral Traditions in Archaeology

The first archaeologists to work in the Southwest had a keen interest in the relationship between Native American oral traditions and the archaeological record. Archaeologists such as Frank Hamilton Cushing, Jesse Walter Fewkes, Cosmos Mindeleff, and Victor Mindeleff routinely collected information about Native American oral traditions and used it in their research to help interpret the chronology, function, and cultural affiliation of the archaeological sites they investigated. During this period, Fewkes (1900:579) astutely observed that "This work . . . can best be done under guidance of the Indians by an ethnoarchaeologist, who can bring as a preparation for his work an intimate knowledge of the present life of the Hopi villagers."

In the early twentieth century, however, many cultural anthropologists began to discount the historical value of Native American oral traditions. Writing about the Zuni, for instance, A. L. Kroeber (1917) noted, "The habitual attitude of the Zuñi, then, is unhistorical . . . That now and then he may preserve fragments of a knowledge of the past that approximate what we consider history, is not to be doubted. But it is equally certain that such recollection is casual and contrary to the usual temper of his mind." Similarly, Robert H. Lowie said, "I cannot attach to oral traditions any historical value under any conditions whatsoever" (quoted in Eggan 1967). Archaeologists were influenced by the attitudes of cultural anthropologists, and for many decades, oral traditions were generally ignored in archaeological research.

Recently, there has been a renewal of interest in the historicity of Native American oral traditions (e.g., Bahr et al. 1994; Teague 1993; Wiget 1982). Indicative of this work is Teague's analysis of the oral traditions of the O'Odham and Hopi, oriented toward increasing our understanding of the cultural events and processes of the period before documentary history in southern Arizona. Teague (1993:436) concluded that, "oral histories can be shown to conform to . . . archaeological evidence to an extent not easily attributed to the construction of an after-the-fact explanation for the presence of numerous ruins throughout the region. These histories reflect direct knowledge of events in prehistoric Arizona." Her article represents the renewed respect archaeologists are beginning to afford native accounts of traditional history.

The Nature of Knowledge in Oral Traditions and Archaeology

As archaeologists begin once again to incorporate Native American oral traditions into archaeological research, it is important to recognize that oral traditions and archaeology represent two separate, but overlapping, ways of knowing the past. Because they are qualitatively distinct, different standards apply in the way that information is collected, evaluated, and used to understand the past. These sources of knowledge converge in a broad sense on certain issues and themes, however, such as migrations, warfare, residential mobility, land use, and ethnic coresidence. Both sources can therefore be used productively to investigate these issues, among others.

There is no doubt that a real history is embedded in Native American oral traditions, and that this is the same history that archaeologists study. Oral traditions contain cultural information about the past carefully preserved and handed down from generation to generation within a tribe. The archaeological record contains material remains of past human behavior that provide physical evidence for many of the same events and processes referred to in oral traditions. Since oral traditions and archaeology have inherent limitations, combining them in research can create knowledge that goes beyond what is possible using either source by itself.

Tessie Naranjo (1995) recently pointed out that Native American oral traditions are often axiomatic rather than hypothetical. Whereas scientists search for exclusive and universal truth, Native Americans use their oral traditions to attain a multiversal understanding of the past that simultaneously operates on many different levels of meaning.

In this regard, it needs to be understood that oral traditions and archaeology are both palimpsests of history. Oral traditions incorporate the cultural knowledge of many ancestors at multiple levels of signification. Similarly, archaeological sites incorporate a complex record of past human behavior embedded in artifacts and archaeological deposits. Both oral traditions and archaeology thus constitute sources of knowledge that have intricate structures that must be systematically and carefully analyzed in terms of their own internal logic to use them in scholarly research.

Methodologies for Using Oral Traditions in Scholarly Research

Studies by David Pendergast and Clement Meighan (1959), Eggan (1967), and Wiget (1982) have unequivocally demonstrated that a real history is embedded in Native American oral traditions. As Eggan (1967) pointed out, anthropologists now have more data and better historical controls than earlier generations of anthropologists, and consequently, we should be able to analyze social and cultural data in a more sophisticated manner so as to develop the means to segregate history from other aspects of oral traditions. Jan Vansina (1985) presents a rigorous methodology for incorporating oral traditions in historical research. These methodologies need to be incorporated into archaeological method and theory to establish the scholarly basis for using oral traditions in historical research.

Good scientific research uses a methodology based on the falsification of hypotheses. In essence, archaeologists disprove what they can, and then create theories to explain the residual hypotheses. This scientific methodology may not always be appropriate for the research of oral traditions, where a more humanistic and qualitative approach is sometimes warranted. Applying a humanistic rather than a scientific methodology in the use of oral traditions should be done in a manner that meets high scholarly standards.

Uses of Oral Tradition and Archaeological Research

Archaeologists are interested in learning about the past. Native Americans are interested in maintaining the cultural traditions they inherited from their ancestors who lived in the past. For Native American tribes with strong oral traditions, the primary sense of history comes from the narratives, stories, and accounts told by tribal elders. In this context, archaeology constitutes a secondary source of supplemental information about tribal heritage. Some, but not all, tribal members may find this supplemental information useful in the transmission of family values.

Archaeology can also be used by tribes to achieve their own political and legal goals in relation to the larger society. Archaeological data can be used to help document land claims and water rights, and manage tribal cultural resources on lands managed by state and federal agencies. A small but increasing number of Native Americans are realizing that archaeology can be used constructively to validate tribal history.

In recent years, archaeologists have been called upon to expand their professional activities with respect to historic preservation by collecting information about traditional cultural properties and sacred places, as well as historic archaeological sites of interest to particular tribes. Native American oral traditions contain essential information about cultural values and beliefs pertaining to traditional cultural places, natural features, specific sites, and landscapes that are important cultural resources for Native Americans (e.g., Kelley and Francis 1994). To successfully meet the mandate for historic preservation, contemporary archaeologists must either work with oral traditions or coordinate their work with other researchers who are working with this source of information. This creates an ethical and methodological imperative for archaeologists to work closely with Native Americans so that the information needed to properly manage tribal cultural resources can be collected and reported in an appropriate manner.

The Need for Respect in the Research of Oral Traditions

Indiscriminate references to oral traditions as "myths and legends" is demeaning to Native Americans. It perpetuates a false dichotomy that implies that oral traditions are less valid than scientifically based knowledge. Oral traditions and scientific knowledge both have validity in their own cultural context. Scientific knowledge does not constitute a privileged view of the past that in and of itself makes it better than oral traditions. It is simply another way of knowing the past.

Archaeologists need to have respect for sources of knowledge about the past that are unique to Native Americans. Even in situations where oral traditions are not used in archaeological research, archaeologists should be sensitive to both the inherent limitations of scientific knowledge and to the ways that oral traditions can transcend scientific knowledge with respect to cultural heritage.

Sometimes archaeologists publish findings that contradict Native American oral traditions. This need not be done in a belligerent manner that directly challenges these traditions, and archaeologists should strive to place their conclusions in a cultural and intellectual context to help Native Americans understand the nature of scientific knowledge and other archaeologists understand the nature of oral traditions. By respecting the values of Native American oral traditions, archaeologists will lay a foundation for Native Americans to respect the values of scientific knowledge, and for scientists to respect the values of oral traditions.

Sensitive Issues in the Use of Oral Traditions

Oral traditions are intimately connected with Native American religious beliefs and knowledge, much of which is esoteric in nature. For this reason, it is essential for archaeologists to collaborate with tribal cultural advisors regarding the use of oral traditions in archaeological research. These advisors are needed to determine what aspects of oral traditions are appropriate for use in scholarly research, to help interpret the results of research, and to guide decisions about publication.

Reducing oral traditions to a written form has a cultural impact that needs to be considered in research. As Whiteley (1988:xvi) has observed, written texts turn oral traditions into fixed literary images widely disseminated in the larger American society in a manner that Native Americans cannot control. This is a critical concern when sacred knowledge is misappropriated for scholarly research, and a dynamic oral tradition is reduced to a static point of reference.

The preferences of each tribe regarding the use of oral traditions in archaeological research should be respected. Some tribes—such as the Hopi—encourage the use of oral traditions in archaeological research, especially when this research is done by researchers working in collaboration with Hopi cultural advisors (Dongoske, Ferguson, and Jenkins 1993). These advisors are the best judges of what aspects of oral traditions constitute historical information and what aspects constitute esoteric religious knowledge that should remain confidential.

The Navajo people have an abundance of oral traditions that coincide with and complement contemporary archaeological research. The store of Navajo traditional knowledge can enhance archaeology and the Navajo Nation by furthering our understanding of the past. Many Navajo people are fascinated by the oral traditions that ground historical stories in the context of places that can still be seen in contemporary landscapes. An important part of the physical counterpart of stories are the ruins studied by archaeologists. The Navajo Nation therefore recommends that archaeologists augment their scientific conclusions with Navajo oral traditions. To facilitate this approach, the Navajo Nation Historic Preservation Department is developing ways for the Navajo people to interact with the science of archaeology.

The Hualapai Tribe places a great value on the oral traditions of its elders, and these traditions are an important part of the cultural heritage of the Hualapai people. When Hualapai culture is the subject of research, it is the Hualapai people who are the cultural experts. Consequently, the Hualapai Tribe prefers that research using oral traditions be conducted by tribal members so that sensitive information can be controlled and the tribe can be sure it is used for appropriate purposes.

Some tribes, like the Pueblo of Zuni, are reticent about the use of oral traditions in scholarly research. At present, the Pueblo of Zuni does not encourage the use of oral traditions in scholarly research, except in a very limited fashion by researchers employed directly by the tribe. This makes it imperative for scholars researching Zuni oral traditions to consult with the tribe.

Some Native Americans think that in the past archaeologists have "mined" archaeological sites to collect the artifacts that form the basis of archaeological research. There is an increasing concern that archaeologists now want to "mine" oral traditions to interpret the archaeological record. There is a growing anxiety that unless tribal members fully collaborate in the research process, this approach will result in the continuation of cultural exploitation.

Recommendations for Use of Oral Traditions

- By asking tribal officials, determine whether or not a tribe wants its oral traditions used in archaeological research.

- If tribes want oral traditions to be used in archaeological research, then establish at the outset the parameters of that use with Native American cultural advisors and tribal officials.

- Compensate subject specialists such as tribal cultural advisors for their time (like other professional researchers) on funded cultural resources projects.

- If tribes do not want oral traditions used in archaeological research, then state this in reports. These reports should acknowledge that the review of culture history and the scientific findings do not include oral traditions at the request of the tribe.

- Encourage tribal review of archaeological research, especially if it uses oral traditions.

SAA Bulletin, March 1996

The White Mountain Apache Tribe Heritage Program: Origins, Operations, and Challenges

John R. Welch

Editors' Note: The author has chosen to rewrite his original article, rather than provide a postscript.

Perhaps because most archaeologists spend so much time looking for patterns in the past, few are prepared for the dynamic, contemporary settings in which Native Americans are asserting interests in their heritage. Empowered by favorable shifts in laws, public opinion, and self-governance, many tribes are establishing sophisticated programs dedicated to regaining control over and resuming responsibility for the places, objects, and intangibles that connect American Indian history, culture, and group identity. As a process with profound implications for the future of both archaeology and tribal sovereignty, and as a means for discovering alternative views of the past and values of the archaeological record, tribal program development merits close and thoughtful attention.

This essay describes how the White Mountain Apache Tribe of the eastern Arizona uplands has established an ambitious program to tackle the often unwieldy and emotionally charged issues involving archaeology, repatriation, museum development, historic preservation, community representation, and cultural perpetuation—all wrapped up in the context of tribal interpretation of Fort Apache, an outpost the United States once dedicated to White Mountain Apache subjugation and acculturation. I will describe the tribe's conceptual approach and concrete program initiatives through 1999 and discuss how these relate to policy and ethical issues being confronted by archaeologists.

The scope of White Mountain Apache interests and concerns regarding their history, culture, and geography is encompassed by the term "heritage resources," defined as cultural, historical, archaeological, and paleontological sites and objects, as well as the intangible cultural and oral traditions that derive from these resources and endow them with significance. Like many Native Americans, Apaches often experience a connectedness to heritage resources that is foreign to researchers and agency staff who are generally trained to be analytical and dispassionate. Many White Mountain Apaches cultivate ties between tangible (i.e., places, objects, practices) and intangible (i.e., beliefs, traditions, values) aspects of culture and history, while researchers and government agency personnel are more apt to value divisions (e.g., natural vs. cultural; archaeology vs.

ethnography; archaeological vs. historical vs. cultural sites; history vs. prehistory). Apaches' culturally derived respect for heritage resources and their preference for in situ preservation through complete avoidance often contrasts sharply with researchers' approaches (who focus on informational values) and government agencies (where legal and policy frameworks drive most decisions and cultural resources vie with many others for management priority). A final contrast often creates or revivifies conflicts between archaeologists and Apaches: Unlike most non-Indians, and regardless of current land ownership, White Mountain Apaches have enduring spiritual and affective links to expansive landscapes and difficult-to-pinpoint localities important to their past and their identity.

Although differences between non-Indian and Indian views have always existed, recent statutory changes and related program developments have obliged archaeologists and related professionals to more fully consider Native American perspectives. The academic, management, and economic goals embraced by archaeologists and agencies are now balanced against spiritual, political, community health, and cultural perpetuation objectives embraced by Native Americans. The process of assessing the diverse values of heritage resources and prioritizing the often conflicting objectives of those interested in such resources is drawing history and culture into the present. From my vantage, I see many archaeologists still looking backward—to the puzzles of the past they seek to solve and to a simpler time, when academic principles ruled—while tribes look forward to having Native American voices given full hearing in all matters pertaining to their culture and history.

The good news is that divergent views on heritage resources and their contemporary roles give rise to opportunities for learning from and working with one another to protect and conserve places, objects, and cultural intangibles.

I will first sketch the history of White Mountain Apache involvement in heritage resource conservation and the tribe's strategy for integrating heritage conservation into economic and community development initiatives. I will then review Heritage Program operations and challenges as of 1999 and note my sometimes conflicting responsibilities to tribal leaders, the broader Fort Apache Indian Reservation community, federal agencies, professional ethics and colleagues, and the heritage resources that the White Mountain Apache have asked me to help them protect and conserve. The reservation has been my backyard since 1984 and my home since 1992. I am honored that the tribe and its members have shared their lands, convictions, and hopes with me.

Heritage Program Predecessors

With a rapidly growing membership of about 12,500 members, the White Mountain Apache Tribe occupies the 6,734 km^2 (1.7 million acres)

Fort Apache Indian Reservation. Ranging in elevation from less than 2,500 ft to more than 11,400 ft, the reservation encompasses a dazzling array of landforms, biota, and heritage resources. More than 2,100 heritage sites—many of which derive from ancestral Pueblo occupation—have been documented. The reservation likely contains some 8,000 more undocumented historical, archaeological, and paleontological sites. If place-naming is used as an index of cultural significance (for the White Mountain Apaches, it is), then the number of localities requiring respectful consideration is virtually infinite (Figure 1).

Long a destination for hunting and fishing enthusiasts, as well as looters, the Fort Apache reservation is today becoming a mecca for gentler adventurers drawn by Apache culture, observable wildlife, remote canyons, and little-visited pueblos and cliff dwellings. The shifting interests of refugees from the Phoenix and Tucson summers, together with depressed livestock and forest products markets, have spurred the tribe's interests in expanding tourism on the reservation. In 1993, the tribe opened a modestly successful casino and launched an effort to incorporate its vast heritage resources into innovative community and economic development initiatives. These initiatives are breathing new life into Apache interest in its history, spurring a renewed search for innovative and adaptive uses for heritage resources.

Figure 1—The collapsed remains of a *gowa* (wickiup), a White Mountain Apache heritage site (21036 [FAIR]).

Because funding for proactive initiatives is scarce and Apaches often view the past with ambivalence, partnerships among heritage resource conservation and economic and community development organizations are crucial. On one hand, all ancient places, objects, and intangibles are said to deserve respect and, if possible, avoidance. On the other hand, the past often is treated as a closed subject, and those interested in the dead and their possessions are sometimes viewed with suspicion or scorn. In *Apaches and Longhorns*, Will Barnes (1941) recounts the threatening 1883 appearance of Apache men at Fort Apache to demand the return of heritage objects looted from a nearby cave by unthinking cavalrymen. A century later, while attending a ceremonial dance during a break from my work on the reservation with the University of Arizona field school at Grasshopper, an elderly tribal member approached me, held my attention with a fierce gaze, gritted his teeth, and hissed, "bonedigger." The remark surely signaled his disapproval of excavations (although the Grasshopper project ceased removing burials after 1977), but also may have reflected a concern that my contact with the long-dead could corrupt the unfolding ritual.

White Mountain Apache involvement in heritage management was initially confined to Tribal Council reviews of excavation proposals (e.g., Grasshopper, Canyon Creek Ruin, Kinishba, Forestdale Valley) and short-term tribal member employment as project field workers. In 1969, however, the tribe acknowledged the need to record disappearing cultural and oral traditions by opening a Culture Center in the only log cabin remaining at Fort Apache, appointing Edgar Perry as its director. Working with his wife Corrine, John Quintero, and Anne Skidmore, Perry made some 600 recordings of White Mountain Apache stories and songs and produced the first Apache-English dictionary. The Culture Center was relocated in 1976 to the only surviving barracks at the fort and, in this larger space, thrived as a gathering place for Apache elders and cultural specialists, an Apache crafts outlet, and a favorite destination for visitors from many countries. The 1985 fire that destroyed the barracks building and most of the tribe's collections dampened, but did not eliminate, enthusiasm for further development of the Culture Center.

By the mid 1980s, tribal and SHPO concerns led Raymond Palmer, a tribal member and forester with the Fort Apache Agency, Bureau of Indian Affairs (BIA), to lay the basis for BIA involvement in heritage management by assuming responsibility for the protection of heritage sites from BIA projects. Palmer succeeded in identifying and gaining protection for endangered sacred sites as well as archaeological resources, and Palmer's non-forestry duties quickly became overtaxing. Responding to still-escalating tribal needs and agency legal obligations, the local BIA superintendent, Ben Nuvamsa, developed an agreement that provided for the occasional assistance of Bruce Donaldson, the archaeologist on the neighboring Apache-Sitgreaves National Forests. Through field trips and training sessions, Palmer and Donaldson enlisted land managers, field technicians, and archaeologists with regional interests to assist in the identification, interpretation, and protection of the reservation's heritage sites. Their emphasis on Apache culture, history, and archaeology was among the groundbreaking approaches Palmer and Donaldson took in training tribal member para-archaeologists . These subjects had been neglected in most previous archaeological studies on the Fort Apache Reservation, which had focused on the occupation by ancestral pueblo groups of areas below the Mogollon Rim. From 1987 through 1992, I served as an occasional consultant for these training sessions, conducting field inventories done as part of the BIA's timber sale planning process and establishing protocols for protecting heritage sites from project impacts and wildfire suppression activities (Figure 2).

Figure 2—Archaeologists and tribal member para-archaeologists, partners in protecting Apache heritage sites from forest fire suppression activities (left to right: I. Lupe, M. Altaha, D. Gregory, P. Alsenay, O. Cassadore, L. Benally, D. Goseyun, author).

Heritage Program Establishment

Despite early involvement in heritage management and the exemplary cooperation between the BIA and their client tribe, the White Mountain Apache have only recently pursued substantial and sustained participation in the academic, governmental, and resource management programs and activities affecting their heritage. The tribe's escalating participation derives from long-stifled desires to reassert control over aspects of their culture and history, and from the partial recognition of these interests through the Native American Graves Protection and Repatriation Act of 1990 (NAGPRA) and the 1992 amendments to the National Historic Preservation Act (NHPA). The White Mountain Apache Tribe's prevailing interest in NAGPRA involves the return of cultural items (i.e., human remains, funerary objects, sacred objects, and objects of cultural patrimony) to Native American control. The NHPA amendments take affirmative steps towards making tribes full partners in the national historic preservation program by (1) requiring more and better tribal consultation by federal agencies, (2) recognizing Native American cultural and religious sites as potential historic properties, and (3) establishing the basis for tribal assumption of SHPO functions on tribal lands. This new legal framework is assisting the tribe by defining opportunities that may be exploited when and where appropriate.

Encouraged by the statutory changes, White Mountain Apache Tribal Council Chairmen Ronnie Lupe and Dallas Massey positioned the tribe to maximize new opportunities in heritage resource management through a series of far-reaching initiatives. In 1992, the tribe supported a BIA agency plan to hire an archaeologist, allowing me to address problems I had identified during earlier consultant work. My job initially centered on improving the Fort Apache Agency's NHPA compliance and on protecting archaeological sites from land modification activities and looters. As discussed below, my responsibilities evolved to focus on providing technical assistance to the tribe in archaeology and historic preservation, as well as in museum and economic development.

In 1993, the tribe published the *Master Plan for the Fort Apache Historic Park* to rehabilitate the rapidly deteriorating Fort Apache Historic District. Supported by the Arizona State Parks Heritage Fund and the Fort Apache BIA Agency, the *Master Plan* involved an advisory team whose members have remained closely involved in program development. The move to integrate cultural education, historic preservation, community health, and tourism initiatives in the development of a historic park set the stage for Heritage Program evolution and signaled the tribe's interest in balancing Euroamerican-authored accounts of local history and culture with perspectives derived from Apache oral traditions and historical experience. The *Plan's* strategy for boosting Apache pride and tribal revenues asserted control over Fort Apache and put the place to work for the reservation community.

The final catalyst in the creation of the Heritage Program came with the tribe's recognition of the need for prominent representation of Apache elders and cultural specialists. In 1994, the tribe appointed Ramon Riley as the cultural resources director, to manage repatriation and cultural revitalization programs. Riley faced many sensitive issues, including the disposition of ancestral Pueblo burial assemblages removed from the reservation through archaeological research. The tribe had asserted ownership of all materials collected from their reservation; however, instead of requesting the return of tribal property from the Arizona State Museum (the repository for most collections from the Fort Apache Reservation) or seeking expeditious repatriation of the burial assemblages pursuant to NAGPRA, the tribe joined forces with the Hopi Tribe and Zuni Pueblo. This intertribal consortium leap-frogged many potentially divisive questions concerning cultural affiliation and other legalities by focusing on assemblage disposition, especially on requirements for documentation, ceremonial treatment, avoidance of damage to undisturbed heritage site areas, and long-term security for repatriated cultural items. The White Mountain Apache Tribe's overriding interests in respectful interaction with other tribes and the appropriate disposition of cultural items—interests widely shared with other tribes—has allowed for the thorough, and still ongoing, deliberation of potentially sticky issues involving ownership and cultural affiliation.

In part because of the positive impression made by the expert advisory teams from Zuni and Hopi, the tribe established a Cultural Advisory Board (CAB) of elders and cultural specialists to oversee the protection, repatriation, and appropriate use of the tribe's heritage resources. The CAB meets periodically to clarify Apache cultural principles and their application to heritage management issues, plan repatriation efforts, review proposals for research or other use of White Mountain Apache heritage resources, and address implications of Apache cultural and religious sites threatened by projects. The CAB meetings reaffirm the deep concerns of many White Mountain Apaches with the protection of their heritage, the health and vitality of Apache communities, and the need to reach into Apache history and culture for guidance and principles useful in addressing contemporary problems (Figure 3).

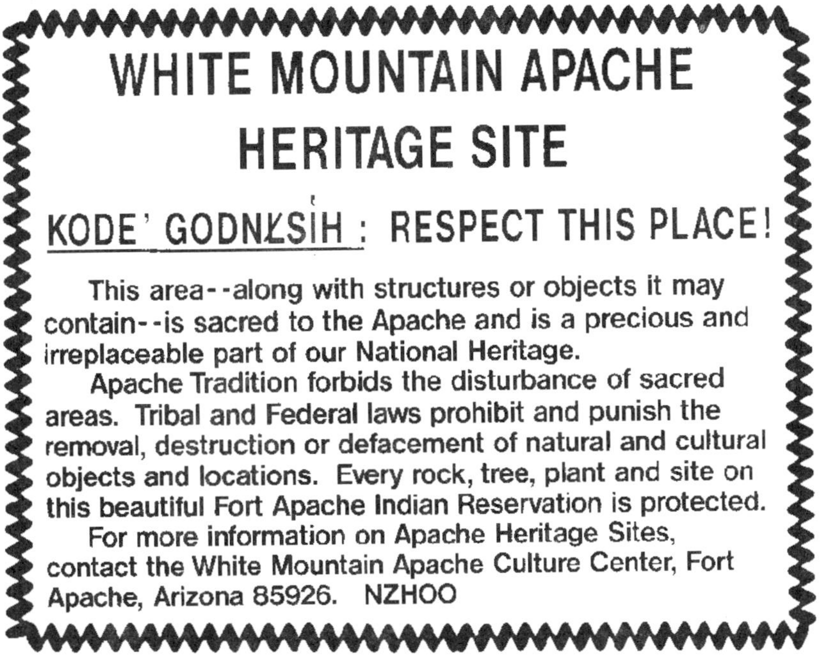

WHITE MOUNTAIN APACHE HERITAGE SITE

KODE' GODNŁSIH : RESPECT THIS PLACE!

This area--along with structures or objects it may contain--is sacred to the Apache and is a precious and irreplaceable part of our National Heritage.

Apache Tradition forbids the disturbance of sacred areas. Tribal and Federal laws prohibit and punish the removal, destruction or defacement of natural and cultural objects and locations. Every rock, tree, plant and site on this beautiful Fort Apache Indian Reservation is protected.

For more information on Apache Heritage Sites, contact the White Mountain Apache Culture Center, Fort Apache, Arizona 85926. NZHOO

Figure 3—Heritage site sign that integrates educational and warning messages.

Heritage Program Missions and Initiatives

With the vision and personnel in place, the White Mountain Apache Tribe's Heritage Program became a reality in 1996. The program is charged with the protection, management, and culturally appropriate use of all places, things, and traditions deriving their significance from White Mountain Apache culture and history. Perhaps the most distinctive characteristic of the Heritage Program is the emphasis placed on the *conservative use* of heritage resources to create a healthier Apache community, attract visitors and represent the community to them, and foster employment. The tribe views carefully managed heritage tourism as an important alternative to resource extraction industries and project a more accurate and dynamic Apache identity as an alternative to Apache stereotypes propagated in popular media.

By uniting community and economic development with cultural, linguistic, and historic preservation, the White Mountain Apache Tribe seeks to harness its sometimes unfortunate, often misunderstood, and always fascinating past in pursuit of an exciting future. The Heritage Program today, although still a work in progress, embraces three overlapping domains: (1) repatriation and cultural documentation, (2) museum and collections management, and (3) historic preservation and the Fort Apache Historic Park. Activities in each of these program areas involve important partnerships and collaborations with various White Mountain Apache Tribal offices, other tribes, state and federal agencies, universities, and a growing number of private benefactors.

Repatriation and Cultural Documentation

The CAB provides Heritage Program oversight and contributes, as needed, the often sensitive information required to identify, assess the significance of, and protect Apache heritage resources. Ramon Riley coordinates CAB activities, serves as a member of the tribe's Project and Plan Environmental Review Board, and manages repatriation, ethnohistorical research, and traditional lifeways documentation initiatives. CAB members are encouraged to act as liaisons between the Heritage Program and cultural practitioners present on and off White Mountain Apache lands. Mutually beneficial relations between program staff and heritage resource stakeholders (e.g., cultural practitioners, educators, elders, youth, community health advocates) are seen as critical to long-term program success (Figure 4).

Repatriation is the Advisory Board's first priority. The CAB holds, consistent with NAGPRA, that most White Mountain Apache *cultural items* (i.e., human remains, funerary objects, sacred objects, cultural patrimony) stored in off-reservation repositories should be expeditiously returned to the control, if not the possession of the most appropriate tribal steward. In general, this means the return of cultural items to their original resting

Figure 4—Bert Hinton, Ramon Riley, and Levi Dehose, members of the White Mountain Apache Cultural Advisory Group, conduct a field review of the Silver Creek Archaeological Research Project.

places or another safe place under tribal protection or jurisdiction. These guiding principles, together with the cooperative spirit essential for an Apache nation divided into many tribes, were established through the *Inter-Apache Agreement on Repatriation and the Protection of Apache Cultures*, which was signed by nine Apache tribes in 1995.

Also in 1995, the five Arizona tribes with Apache affiliations (Camp Verde, Payson Tonto, White Mountain, San Carlos, and Fort McDowell) began work under the terms of a National Park Service (NPS) NAGPRA grant. A working group of elders and cultural experts has been assembled and dispatched to more than 20 museums to participate in consultations and initiate repatriation claims. Several of these claims have been filed jointly by multiple Apache tribes. The attitudes adopted by museum personnel regarding the Apache delegations have varied significantly. Most museum professionals approach NAGPRA as an opportunity and have welcomed tribal members as colleagues bringing unique knowledge about collections under their care. Other institutions, seemingly threatened by NAGPRA's recognition of tribal rights, elect to limit interaction with tribal representatives to that mandated by the statute.

White Mountain Apache research and documentation interests center on ethnography and ethnohistory, with archaeological collections and excavations discouraged except in the case of essential land modifications. Ethnographic research expertise is being refined through programs to document traditional cultural properties, land use, and oral traditions. Because critical data and irreplaceable wisdom are lost with the passing of tribal elders, current work is emphasizing stories, place names, and native historical viewpoints. With support from the Lila Wallace-*Readers Digest* Fund, the Heritage Program has expanded and duplicated a unique library of audio and video tapes of Apache craft, lifeway, and oral traditions. Beverly Malone, the Heritage Program language specialist, and Anna Goseyun have used expertise and equipment acquired through the grant-funded work to assist with ethnohistorical studies of portions of White Mountain Apache aboriginal territory endangered by proposed copper mines and other federally permitted projects. Proactively mandated by the Tonto and Coronado National Forests and coordinated by Payson Tonto Tribal Historian Vincent Randall (now chairman of the Camp Verde Yavapai-Apache Nation Tribal Council), these surveys are employing Apache experts to identify places and values significant to Apaches threatened by federal actions. For the first time, the people entrusted by their communities with knowledge and wisdom of the Apache past are being given a meaningful opportunity to share their knowledge to preserve aspects of their heritage. For Apaches, whose ancient material remains are scarce and elusive, this oral history-based approach is a welcome complement to the archaeologically focused process that prevails in most NHPA compliance efforts.

Also in progress, thanks to a grant from the NPS Historic Preservation Fund grants to Indian tribes program, is intertribal collaboration to systematically collect the Apache names for landscape features and sites within and adjacent to western Apache aboriginal territory. The project has already collected names and oral traditions for dozens of places and may result in an atlas or other teaching tool, a basis for consultations with federal and state agencies and repositories, or both.

Nohwiké Bagowá:
The White Mountain Apache Culture Center and Museum

The reservation community's rapidly growing interest and involvement in heritage resource issues provided the justification for a proposal to rehabilitate a vacant architectural shell located within the Fort Apache Historic District for use as a significantly upgraded Cultural Education and Museum Facility. With grant support from the U.S. Department of Housing and Urban Development, the new facility opened in 1997. In addition to classroom, crafts production, and exhibit space, the new facility provides secure storage for the tribe's growing collections. Nancy Mahaney, the tribe's museum director, is responsible for the maintenance of all collections, exhibit development, and initiating long-range planning for public interpretation of the facility in the broader context of the Fort Apache Historic Park.

The White Mountain Apache Tribe seeks to acquire, preserve, and make appropriate use of non-sensitive objects, photographs, and documents relating to Apache history and culture. The new Cultural Education

Facility houses the tribe's Archives and Research Library. This segment of the tribe's collections was developed with a grant from the U.S. Department of Education. The photographs and documents now housed in the library have already been used in genealogy projects, the Fort Apache restoration and revitalization effort, and identification and documentation of heritage sites threatened by logging, road construction, and other activities. Programmatic funding is being sought to expand the Archives' mission to include long-term management of the tribe's administrative records.

Historic Preservation and the Fort Apache Heritage Foundation

In accord with the *Master Plan* for the Fort Apache Historic Park, the Heritage Program seeks to exploit the fort's name recognition and national significance to draw attention to Apache perspectives on Apache history and celebrate local traditions. The Fort Apache Historic Park includes the former military cemetery, a badly disturbed ceremonial cave ("Geronimo's Cave"), a historic adobe church located in Cibecue, and Kinishba Ruins National Historic Landmark, a partially reconstructed fourteenth-century pueblo that is deteriorating for the second time. Restored in 1998, the mission church serves as a satellite learning center for the Cibecue Community School. Kinishba and other sites offer unique opportunities for visitors to experience heritage destinations under the tutelage of tribal members (Figure 5).

During the five years (1994–1999) following the publication of the *Master Plan*, 10 of the fort's 27 historic buildings received restoration and

Figure 5—Kinishba, a partially restored (and re-collapsing) ancestral pueblo village under the protection of the White Mountain Apache Heritage Program.

rehabilitation treatments. Comprehensive documentation and preservation planning documents also have been completed. With the greatest threats to individual structures now mitigated, the tribe has initiated a series of interpretive and site development projects intended to restore Fort Apache to active duty—this time in support of rather than against the Apache community. To develop Fort Apache as a source of Apache pride and employment, the tribe has obtained grant support for diverse projects (Table 1), chartered a 501(c)(3) corporation (the Fort Apache Heritage Foundation), and forged or expanded partnerships with the World Monuments Fund, NPS, and Arizona State Parks. The Heritage Foundation Board of Directors includes a roster of distinguished tribal members (Tribal Council Chairman Dallas Massey, Ramon Riley, Paul Ethelbah), notable Arizonans (Honorable Rose Mofford, Eddie Basha, Jeanne Westphal, Larry Vicario), national service leaders (Kareem Abdul-Jabbar, Neil Mangum, Charles Vehlow), and me.

The 1997 World Monuments Watch Program of the World Monuments Fund designation of the Fort Apache Historic District to the world's *100 Most Endangered* heritage sites served to focus local, historic preservation, and economic development interests on Fort Apache and on plans to realize the site's potential to offer visitors the uniquely Apache perspective on Apache culture and frontier history. This designation facilitated the ongoing preservation effort, but more importantly, fostered new initiatives involving site interpretation, visitor planning, and the development of enterprises and services intended to enhance visitor experiences and create revenues and tribal member jobs. To these ends, the Rivers and Trails Conservation Assistance Division of NPS has provided technical support for the establishment of the Fort Apache working group. Intended as a grassroots complement to the Heritage Foundation, the Working Group is comprised of community service and educational representatives dedicated to the vision of a Fort Apache Historic Park that fully represents the best interests of the Apache community. Issues raised at foundation and working group meetings run the gamut from the appropriateness of specific structural preservation treatments and research proposals, to policies for cavalry reenactments and the stories to be narrated to visitors. The representation of Fort Apache as a place with multiple, distinctive histories is the central theme to be explored in the interpretive planning process. Funded by a grant from the National Endowment for the Humanities, this process is expected to provide plans for relating seldom-available White Mountain Apache perspectives on regional culture and history.

Underlying the diverse preservation initiatives at Fort Apache and Kinishba is the tribe's willingness to take the lead in preserving and allowing for the respectful use of non-Apache heritage sites, provided that other partners and local economic development opportunities are involved. Unfortunately due to the neglect and mismanagement of Fort Apache by the BIA, the tribe has been obliged to file a claim against the federal government for the nearly $14 million required to repair damages to the Historic District and bring the facility up to code without sacrificing its historic character or integrity.

As the White Mountain Apache Historic Preservation Officer (WMAHPO), I have primary responsibility for four Heritage Program elements: tribal assumption of SHPO functions, heritage site inventory and protection, non-NAGPRA consultations concerning projects proposed within White Mountain Apache Aboriginal Territory, and coordination of the Fort Apache restoration and revitalization effort. For the White Mountain Apache Tribe, the assumption of SHPO responsibilities is a means for advancing sovereignty and rights of self-governance and self-determination while enhancing control over Apache heritage resources and processes for planning and implementing land modification projects on the Fort Apache Indian Reservation. The 1992 NHPA amendments that gave tribes the authority to assume SHPO responsibilities and encouraged tribal HPOs to embrace professional standards and guidelines also ensure that tribal values are considered to the extent feasible. The White Mountain Apache Tribe has assumed responsibility for heritage site inventory, education, and planning for the Fort Apache Indian Reservation and is working to assume from the Arizona SHPO all Section 106 consultation duties and the submission of National Register nominations to the keeper of the Register.

The most important impediments to WMAHPO progress are financial and institutional. Tribal HPOs have yet to achieve parity with State HPOs in terms of annual allocations from the Historic Preservation Fund. The National Association of Tribal Historic Preservation Officers (NATHPO) has joined other preservation partners in encouraging Congress to dedicate the support necessary to make tribes full partners in the national historic preservation program. The Historic Preservation Fund, fueled by proceeds from offshore mineral leases, has never been adequately tapped by Congress to support the historic preservation and environmental conservation purposes for which it was created. The long-range objective is to develop, as a part of the Heritage Program, a HPO that draws much of its funding from nontribal sources while maintaining commitments both to White Mountain Apache heritage conservation and to the operational and ethical principles that guide professional archaeology and historic preservation.

Support for the tribe's effort to reach this goal has come from many sources, but archaeologists have been slow to provide assistance. The tribe's effort to establish and administer its heritage site inventory system (FAIRsite) illustrates some of the challenges posed by the archaeological community's apparent lack of enthusiasm for tribal program development. FAIRsite exists in both digital and hardcopy formats. USGS quadrangle maps showing cultural, historical, archaeological, and paleontological sites and inventoried areas are supported by paper files for each locality and heritage site survey project, all maintained in a high-security, fire-resistant environment. The digital format consists of an ArcInfo-based GIS and database that contains about half of the more than 2,000 documented heritage sites. FAIRsite incorporates more, higher quality information pertaining to the reservation than that contained in all off-reservation site files combined.

Prior to FAIRsite creation, a consortium of Arizona institutions joined forces in response to the perceived need for a single, statewide site file and database. The Azsite Consortium (Arizona State University, Arizona State Museum, Arizona SHPO, and the Museum of Northern Arizona) works to enhance the state's resource management capacity and streamline the NHPA compliance process.

This effort has included the entry of tribal lands site inventory data into Azsite against the expressed wishes of the tribe and over the many warnings about making site locational data available on the Internet. A conflict between the tribe and the consortium exists over the incorporation of tribal lands data into the statewide database. Tribal concerns with sovereignty and long-term security are foremost. The White Mountain Apache Tribe asserts an ancient, undiminished, and exclusive authority to manage resources located on tribal lands and information pertaining thereto. The tribe objects to the incorporation of data from its lands into a massive, Internet-accessible database without consent. Dismayed by the rampant looting and unauthorized visitation that have followed the documentation of archaeological sites on the reservation, the tribe has yet to experience the far-reaching benefits that can derive from archaeological research and data sharing. Consequently, the tribe does not release FAIRsite data except to assist with tribally endorsed plans entailing land modifications or when there are other, specific benefits for the tribe or its members. Visitation to heritage sites outside of the Fort Apache Historical Park requires a special permit issued by the Heritage Program director.

The conflict over Azsite boils down to divergent views on the values and interests which should govern the use and circulation of site survey data. Tribal interests in this case are somewhat at odds with my professional inclination to share data with colleagues, but at least three factors outweigh this inclination: (1) tribal willingness to ensure FAIRsite data compatibility with Azsite and to allow use, with tribal permission, of reservation data bearing on interregional planning and research initiatives; (2) official tribal assumption of SHPO inventory responsibilities for the reservation; (3) FAIRsite availability as the most automated and comprehensive means for storing and retrieving information concerning archaeological surveys and heritage sites on the reservation, including hundreds of sites missing from Azsite. In sum, Congress has invited the tribe to manage its heritage sites as it sees fit. The tribe has accepted this invitation, and archaeologists and others must now recognize the tribe's sovereign right and responsibility to control access on the basis of White Mountain Apache, rather than academic-, national-, or State of Arizona-derived values. The Azsite Consortium has not accepted the tribe's standing offer to include Fort Apache Reservation data so long as tribal officials are authorized to act as gatekeepers. Tribal leaders remain open to suggestions and proposals from prospective partners, but until tribal decisionmakers are convinced that research on their heritage resources will contribute to social, educational, management, and economic objectives for White Mountain Apache people and land, data access will be tightly controlled.

For projects with federal involvement, which require Section 106 compliance, the White Mountain Apache and other tribes with heritage management programs have the opportunity to define *historic property* and *significance* according to their values and interests. For federal projects or activities beyond reservation boundaries, but within the enormous Aboriginal Territory in which White Mountain Apache ancestors lived, migrated, farmed, hunted, collected plants and minerals, prayed, and were interred, heritage resource management issues are more ponderous. In response to announcements of projects that threaten Apache landscapes or heritage sites, the tribe's cultural resources director, environmental planner, attorney, and I work together with project proponents to seek resource protection and appropriate treatment. For larger and more destructive projects, the tribe generally holds that the NHPA compliance process should employ tribal members who are uniquely qualified to assist the agency with historic property identification, National Register eligibility determination, and significance assessment. Federal agencies, project proponents, and their contractors are gradually recognizing the legal, informational, and political advantages of this approach. Even as mutualistic collaboration in the Section 106 process continues, however, the situation will still resemble the chaos that followed initial NHPA enactment. We have far to go in agreeing upon the meanings for "consultation," "cultural and religious importance," and "scale of federal involvement."

The Future of the White Mountain Apache Heritage

Apaches are rejecting the powerful dichotomy between the highly marketable and wildly exaggerated caricature of their forebears as the fierce military masters of the frontier Southwest, as opposed to their historical identity as a diverse group of foraging-farming peoples that briefly impeded Manifest Destiny. The Apache knack for creating opportunity in diverse and challenging circumstances has prevailed in Heritage Program evolution. Instead of choosing between the former stereotype as a means for drawing tourists and creating jobs, or the latter to lay the foundations for cultural education, historical rectification, and community development, the White Mountain Apache Tribe has embraced both. Apaches have decided to bring their past with them into the future. This is good news for all parties, the possible exception being non-Apaches who presume that their notions about Apache history and culture, or the management thereof, take precedence.

Indian land is where conflicting tribal and nontribal perspectives on heritage resource management are coming most poignantly into contact with a still-unfolding legal framework for archaeology in the post-NAGPRA era. Archaeology, historic preservation, and public museums will continue to adjust as tribes assert their values, beliefs, and rights. Tribes' holistic views concerning the tangibles and intangibles that non-Indians often distinguish as archaeological sites, historic properties, cultural resources, traditional cultural properties, and intellectual property may be seen as a major source of far-reaching change in archaeology and cultural resources management in the United States. Tribes are likely to continue to press the view that American Indian heritage resources, regardless of current ownership or control, should be protected and managed in accord with American Indian values, beliefs, and interests.

By expanding their participation in government, museum, and research projects and policies, the White Mountain Apache and other tribes are obliging important reexaminations of roles, values, and assumptions involving the past. Indian tribes may be the last of the four principal partners to join the national historic preservation program but their participation is likely to have the greatest cumulative impact since the program's 1966 inception. The realization that Native Americans—as intellectually potent, politically astute, and increasingly organized groups endowed with substantial rights and privileges in the United States—have significantly divergent, though equally valid views concerning the goals and processes of the national program, is inexorably infiltrating even the most remote and intransigent corners of academia and agency bureaucracy. The White Mountain Apache Tribe is likely to continue its vigorous efforts to create and exploit opportunities for the management of Apache heritage resources in accord with Apache cultural principles and contemporary interests.

Archaeologists need not abandon their discipline, much less their worldview to learn from or establish mutual respect, trust, and partnerships with American Indian people and tribes. What archaeologists should relinquish, however, is the outmoded and paternalistic view that they know how best to treat heritage resources and that research—especially excavation and other forms of destructive analysis—are the highest and best uses of the material legacy of the past. The dozen or so Native American tribes I have worked with during the last decade share a deep concern with educating their youth, treating their elders with respect, and honoring and reaching into their rich past and its legacies to help them chart a better future. These positions provide ample common ground for building enduring and mutually beneficial relationships between archaeologists and American Indians. The key to this relationship lies with archaeologists and others who have had the privilege of working on Indian history and Indian lands. Because Indian tribes are frequently consumed with challenges only tangentially related to history and culture, it is up to archaeologists, both Indian and non-Indian, to seek ways to make their information and methods relevant and useful to the people to whom they owe a debt of gratitude for their careers.

SAA Bulletin, November 1997 and August 1999

NAGPRA, the Conflict between Science and Religion, and the Political Consequences

G. A. Clark

I am a paleoanthropologist interested in epistemology—how we know what we think we know about the remote human past (Clark 1992, 1993). More precisely, I am interested in the logic of inference in "deep time"—the Plio-Pleistocene archaeopaleontological records of Africa and western Eurasia (Clark 1997a). So I am a different "kind" of archaeologist from those who deal with NAGPRA issues on a daily basis. I mention this because I think the kind of archaeology one practices has implications for how NAGPRA is regarded, and whether or not one is disposed to be sympathetic to it as a mechanism to redress historical wrongs. In terms of my biases, I am a committed evolutionist and, like most evolutionists, a materialist to the core. These philosophical considerations in turn affect how I view archaeology, and my construal of the place of archaeology within the broader context of western science (Clark and Barton 1997).

While I readily acknowledge its defects, I am a staunch and unapologetic admirer of western science. Like it or not, the modern world is almost entirely a product of western science. Despite unparalleled success, however, western science is currently under assault by various pseudo- and anti-science constituencies which attack the materialism that is the central ontological bias of the scientific world view. Usually considered a "science-like" endeavor, archaeology is caught up in this controversy. Laws like NAGPRA strike at the heart of a scientific archaeology because they elevate the cultural traditions and religious beliefs of Indians to the level of science as a paradigm for describing or explaining the experiential world. Political considerations thus take precedence over disinterested evaluation of knowledge claims, with tragic and irreversible results (Clark 1996).

Because of my preconceptions about the place of humans in the natural world, I subscribe to what might be called "the materialist view" on NAGPRA. I think archaeology is, or should be, a "science-like" endeavor—as opposed to a political enterprise, an industry, a platform for promoting a social agenda, or an exercise in public relations. Archaeologists, whether or not they acknowledge it publicly, subscribe to the same kinds of materialist biases and assumptions about the nature of the world, and the place of humans in it, that underlie all of western science. The problem is that they are forced to compromise their beliefs, or keep silent about them, for the sake of political expediency.

A Few Definitions

Science can be defined as a collection of methods for evaluating the credibility of knowledge claims about the experiential world. Science does not pretend to certainty; it only seeks better and better approximations of it. Scientific conclusions are continuously subjected to critical scrutiny. Science is, therefore, self-correcting. No topic or question is "off-limits" to science. The only thing that is antithetical to the scientific worldview is dogma. Dogma is the stuff of religious belief. From the standpoint of science, the illusion of absolute, unchanging truth is the most pernicious of vanities.

There are, of course, many views of humans and the place of humans in the natural world. I would argue, however, that there is only one scientific view—that of neo-Darwinian evolutionary theory. As the most powerful explanatory framework that humans have ever devised to account for the origins and diversity of life on earth, evolution is central to western science, extends far beyond the life sciences in which it first arose, and subscribes to the same materialist biases and assumptions that underlie all science.

Materialism is the idea that only matter and energy exist, and that what we regard as "mind" or "spirit" consists exclusively of matter and energy arranged in complex ways. More precisely, "mind" is a consequence of brain evolution and, since our brains have evolved over the 5 million years for which we can document the existence of the Hominidae, what constitutes "mind" also has evolved. From this perspective, humans are only animals (albeit highly intelligent, technologically sophisticated, socially complex ones). Religious views of humans and their place in nature, dependent as they are on concepts that have no reality outside the mind, are epiphenomena (and—for a materialist—absurd). In other words, one cannot simultaneously understand and accept evolution and sustain a belief in the nonmaterial. From the standpoint of science, religious beliefs are curious survivals of earlier cognitive evolution. What probably happened is that, as our cognitive capacities expanded slowly over the long millennia of the Pleistocene, we came to imagine more and more complex realities, and populated them with the gods, demons, and spirits that are the stuff of religious belief. The question science would put to religion is: Why do humans have religious beliefs at all, since there is absolutely no empirical support for them?

My view, then, is that (1) philosophical and methodological materialism underlie the scientific worldview, (2) the scientific worldview in respect of humans is grounded in Darwinian evolution, (3) archaeology is "science-like" in terms of the preconceptions that underlie its logic of inference and its knowledge claims, and (4) this worldview puts those archaeologists who worry about such things at odds with the anti-materialist belief systems of Indians (and those of Americans in general). NAGPRA is, therefore, only a very small part of a much larger controversy that extends to many aspects of modern American life. That controversy turns on the conflict between the worldviews of religion and science. The late Carl Sagan summarized the issues underlying this debate in *The Demon-Haunted World*—recommended reading for archaeologists of all persuasions, regardless of their views on NAGPRA (1996; see also Sagan and Druyan 1992).

Science and NAGPRA

NAGPRA is basically about the repatriation to Native American claimants of human remains and funerary objects from museum or federal agency collections, and/or those recovered from Indian lands (Ferguson 1996). These remains, and their counterparts elsewhere, are perceived by western science to pertain to a generalized human past, to be part of a universal heritage not circumscribed by ethnic or cultural boundaries. However, legislation enacted in recent years has given the cultural traditions and religious beliefs of Indians greater weight under the law than those of other Americans, and weights those traditions and beliefs more heavily than the universalist perspective that underlies scientific inquiry. Motivated by political expediency, and the kind of anti-science sentiment to which I have just alluded, NAGPRA requires the consultation in archaeological excavation of very broadly defined Native American constituencies, and mandates the repatriation and reburial (if so desired by native claimants), of human remains and funerary objects, sometimes including those not affiliated with any known or recognized Native American group.

NAGPRA creates both short-term opportunities and long-term problems for archaeologists, bioarchaeologists, and physical anthropologists concerned with the study of human skeletal remains. It creates opportunities because the NAGPRA-mandated inventories (1) employ many archaeologists and physical anthropologists (albeit temporarily); (2) because it forces the profession to "clean up its act" in regard to curation and record keeping, and (3) it applies minimum descriptive standards to the human skeletal collections (Rose et al. 1996). It creates problems because NAGPRA puts ethnicity and religious belief on an equal footing with science, and thus provides a mandate for claims of affiliation by virtually any interested party. As is true of any ethnic or racial category, however, "Native Americanness" has only a political definition. Anthropologists acknowledge the statistical, clinal character of race and ethnicity; the government does not. Federal agencies and state legislatures, which have often gone far beyond NAGPRA in their zeal to be politically correct, don't want to be bothered with such subtleties (after all, anthropologists are an even weaker political constituency than Indians), with the result that claims for the repatriation of human remains and "objects of cultural patrimony" can be extended to include just about anything identified as "affiliated" by a claimant. The process thus becomes entirely political, with western science, represented by archaeology, the inevitable loser.

Archaeology is admittedly a "small science," with a weakly developed conceptual framework that lacks the powerful law-like generalizations that underlie the spectacular progress of experimental "big science" disciplines like physics. Despite its many shortcomings, however, archaeology in the United States has always been a "science-like" endeavor in the sense that it subscribes to the same collection of materialist biases and assumptions that underlie all of western science. Moreover, its achievements have been substantial. It is simply a fact that most of the precontact aboriginal societies of the New World would have vanished without a trace were it not for archaeology (and the occasional presence of a western observer to record information about them). We all lose if, for reasons of political expediency, Indians rebury their past. One of the many ironies in the situation provoked by NAGPRA is that many Native American groups who favor the preservation of archaeological and skeletal collections are being co-opted by the actions of small, but vocal, activist minorities in cahoots with ignorant legislators willing to sell the profession down the pike for the sake of short-term political gains.

The problems with putting NAGPRA into operation are thrown into sharp relief by the ridiculous situation surrounding Kennewick man. NAGPRA is predicated on the assumption that archaeologists can, in fact, identify prehistoric antecedents to extant identity-conscious social groups. However, I don't believe they can do that reliably, consistently, or—usually—at all. Race and ethnicity are fleeting, transient things—written on the wind. They do not partake of the timeless "essences" the public, in its ignorance of biology, would impart to them (Clark 1997b, 1997c, 1998, 1999a). Race and ethnicity are in a constant state of flux. There is no scientific basis for thinking that present-day ethnic groups even existed as recently as 400 or 500 years ago, much less in more remote time ranges. The notion of fixed, enduring, bounded ethnicity is positively quaint from the perspective of modern population biology (e.g., Molnar 1998). Nevertheless, it is endorsed and reified by the simple-minded, essentialist, typological thinking institutionalized in public policy by our own government. For example, take a look sometime at the absurd racial and ethnic categories concocted by the U.S. census and replicated, in the name of affirmative action, on application forms throughout the land (Clark 1997c, 1998). The point is simply that popular conceptions of race and ethnicity, as discrete or bounded entities, have no basis in modern science. Consequently, efforts by archaeologists to trace them back very far into the past are likely to be doomed to failure.

Wreaking Vengeance on History

In closing, I question the advisability of wreaking vengeance on history—for that is exactly what NAGPRA tries to do. Not a good idea. No one disputes that Indians have suffered mightily at the hands of the European colonists who have come to dominate U.S. society. No one is claiming that scientists have always acted responsibly with respect to human skeletal material under their curation. No one is suggesting that if we can just "decode" nature correctly, moral truth will be revealed. I am saying, however, that the loss of prehistoric skeletal material to science is incalculable, and that that consideration takes precedence, or should take precedence, over the religious concerns of Native Americans. The worldviews of science and religion are fundamentally incommensurate. They cannot be reconciled. Science is not "about" religion, however. It is not about moral truth, although it can sometimes help us in our struggle to reach moral decisions. Clearly, humans did not evolve in this hemisphere. Indians haven't always been here, haven't always been where they're found today, regardless of what their origin myths might say. I am curious as to how they came to be here, and what happened to them subsequent to their arrival. The only way to answer these questions is through the analysis of prehistoric human skeletal material. The idea that we should spend a bundle now to study it "completely," before we give it back, is ridiculous, since it presupposes that science will not advance, and that new avenues of inquiry will not be opened to us later. It also assumes that data exist independent of the conceptual frameworks that define and contextualize them, which, from an epistemological standpoint, is terminally naïve (e.g., Clark 1991, 1999b). A direct consequence of the national paroxysm of guilt surrounding the quincentenary, NAGPRA is bad law. It is in the interests of Indians and anglos alike that it be repealed.

NAGPRA clearly has implications for the future of archaeology as a "science-like" endeavor. It also speaks volumes about the status of western science in general, and the role that reasoned inquiry plays in U.S. society. The worldview of western science is under serious and sustained assault, and there is a danger that "science-like" views of reality will perish in the face of a multipronged attack in which mysticism, religious fundamentalism, creationism, and the believers in the paranormal align themselves with postmodernist academics to attack the critical realism and mitigated objectivity which are the central epistemological biases of the scientific worldview. The political climate has also become increasingly problematic in recent years as politicians, who generally misunderstand what science "is" or "does," have pandered to the often-vocal concerns of the various anti-science constituencies. The result is a loss of public confidence in the ability of science to resolve significant problems, an increase in the popularity of the various pseudo- or anti-scientific worldviews, and a decline in the perceived credibility of rational thought as a method of inquiry about the nature of the world and the place of humans in it. These threats to rational behavior even have the potential to undermine the democratic process itself, since it depends upon the capacity of an educated citizenry to make reasonable decisions in the face of uncertainty.

SAA Bulletin, November 1998

Native Americans, Western Science, and NAGPRA

Joe Watkins

Geoffrey Clark presents a well-reasoned presentation of the view of a "paleoanthropologist" (a snazzier term than "archaeologist") regarding the place of science in Western culture and the way that the scientific study of humanity has and will "suffer" under NAGPRA. In fact, he has received a wide audience for his views: his paper in this exchange has been presented at the Annual Meeting of the American Anthropological Association (in the public policy forum, "NAGPRA Revisited: Where Do We Go From Here?") and the SAA Annual Meeting (in the symposium, "The Impacts of Repatriation: International Perspectives"), as well as published in the April 1998 *Anthropology Newsletter* (pp. 24–25).

Clark's perception of the conflict between science and the Native American is well presented. But the keyword here is "perception." As with most scientific writings aimed at the rather specialized population of scientists studying Native American human remains, one of the paper's fundamental flaws is its failure to deal with the differing perceptions of the scientific and Native American communities. While it is extremely difficult to offer a single "Native American perspective" on anything, I will proceed to offer a generalization as if it were possible to do so.

Passion vs. Dispassion

Logically, Clark's arguments make sense: NAGPRA should not hinder science's quest for answers which explain the natural world and humanity's place within it. But, unfortunately (or perhaps, happily?), we humans are not logical creatures. We are emotional beings, given to outbreaks of whimsy and passion. Maybe American Indians and scientists are doomed to operate on opposite ends of the emotional spectrum—passion versus dispassion. Where scientists feel drawn to cold facts, American Indians feel drawn to those things outside of the demonstrable world (Clark's "epiphenomena"). Perhaps scientists should stop being so dispassionate, stop trying to step outside humanity, and join the rest of the world. I don't trust a person who has no passion!

Clark's comment that ". . . one cannot simultaneously understand and accept evolution and sustain a belief in the nonmaterial" reminds me of a joke: "What do you get if you cross a scientist with the Ku Klux Klan? Someone who burns question marks on the lawn." I believe science and religion are remarkably intertwined, a double helix spiraling across time and space. Neither should exist without the other, for each one gives us different information and different perceptions on the human condition. I argue, unlike my materialist colleague, that it is the very fact that we are aware of such things (rather than blindly accepting of them) that places us at the top of the intellectual pyramid. The very fact that we recognize the difference between life and death, that we cannot quantify "life" as it exits the corporeal materialist mass but only the resultant "death," sets us apart from those lesser animals that recognize only an inanimate form in their midst, perhaps only as a source of food.

Perhaps some American Indians place an apparent undue emphasis on human remains—the last material reminder of a person's life—but the uncertainty with which we all face the afterworld imbues in us an obligation to see that those remains are protected from unnecessary and unwanted disturbance. If the disturbance and study of human remains is deemed unnecessary by American Indians, then the entire process is seen as an affront to American Indian cultural beliefs. Anthropologists should be among the first to realize that messing around with a culture's belief system is asking for trouble. But if a disturbance is seen as accidental or unavoidable, then the chance of compromise is greater. The second word, "unwanted," is perhaps more loaded than "unnecessary," because it implies a lack of power, a helplessness of American Indians, to control—or at least participate—in determining their own destiny. Many projects dealing with human remains are unwanted by American Indians. This is plain truth. But there are some American Indian groups who can be persuaded to allow studies when they see the utility for them. The utility must be real to them, not just to the researcher.

NAGPRA: Equal Protection

Perhaps certain portions of NAGPRA are aimed at "redressing historic wrongs," as Clark comments, but NAGPRA itself is, more importantly, a piece of human rights legislation designed to provide Native American human remains equal protection under the law. Timothy McKeown, program leader for the National Park Service, says that NAGPRA ". . . formally reaffirms the rights of lineal descendants, Indian tribes, and Native Hawaiian organizations to have custody of Native American human remains, funerary objects, and objects of cultural patrimony" (McKeown 1995:15). J. Trope and W. Echo-Hawk present five sources of existent law (other than NAGPRA) that ". . . can provide the underpinning for tribal grave protection efforts and repatriation claims" (1992:47). R. Tsosie (1997:71) notes that NAGPRA does not go far enough toward protecting all Native American remains, since it covers only those items found on federal or tribal property or which reside in federally funded institutions. If NAGPRA is human rights legislation, as these authors assert, it does not matter whether there is a Native American political agenda at work here. Anthropologists must stop taking NAGPRA personally! The law was not created to make their lives miserable, but to take another's belief system into consideration and to provide equal treatment for all human remains. Anthropologists also have forgotten that, although NAGPRA is a national law, it is not applied nationally. Each American Indian tribe or nation can choose to apply the law as it sees fit. Consultation is a face-to-face and person-to-person business.

Contrary to what Clark feels, I do not think that, under NAGPRA, "[p]olitical considerations thus take precedence over disinterested evaluation of knowledge claims." While Clark thinks archaeology should be "... a 'science-like' endeavor—as opposed to a political enterprise, an industry, a platform for promoting a social agenda or a public relations exercise", I find it difficult to believe that science has ever presented a "disinterested evaluation of knowledge claims . . .," or that science is not "... a platform for promoting a social agenda or a public relations exercise." Science is never above nor outside of the society or political system in which it exists. Society not only influences science, it actively molds it—from the topics scientists study and the levels of freedom they have to study touchy topics, to the ways in which the society punishes those who do not work within its system. As an example of perhaps science at its worst, Nazis did "science." It is not the results of Nazi science which the world finds unacceptable but rather the political enterprise behind it, the "industry" it created, its platform for promoting a social agenda, and its exercise in public relations. Science in the modern world also has political and social agendas that often go unrecognized.

Clark also congratulates archaeology for its achievements by stating: "It is a fact that most of the precontact aboriginal cultures of the New World would have vanished without a trace were it not for archaeology (and the occasional presence of a western observer to record information about them)." Like the philosophical tree in the forest, if "a precontact aboriginal culture of the New World vanishes without a trace," and there is no "Western observer there to record information about them," do they make a sound? Moreover, I suppose we "precontact aboriginal cultures in the New World" should be happy that we weren't in the presence of Western observers like those who helped record information about the Tasmanians!

An Anthropology of All Americans

I agree with Clark, however, when he states "NAGPRA creates both short-term opportunities and long-term problems for archaeologists, bioarchaeologists and/or physical anthropologists who study human skeletal remains." It is indeed a fact that some anthropologists will lose their primary research focus, but there are too many options available to begin making arrangements for the discipline's funeral. We may be too short-sighted to comprehend the opportunities we may have been given, but we can make American anthropology an anthropology of all Americans, not just white Americans. By working with American Indians instead of in spite of them, we might actually develop programs that have meaning outside of the ivory tower of academe, programs that impact the human condition and provide useable information beyond The Learning Channel or PBS, programs that will provide answers to everyone about what happens when humans enter an unknown world without an idea of food or raw material sources, or even whether the sun will rise the next morning. We must earn the right to wear the mantle bestowed on us as chroniclers of the vast store of knowledge about what it is to be human.

We, as anthropologists, are standing on the edge of a forest with an almost impenetrable growth in front of us. We can try to bulldoze our way through it, but we will destroy all that might be ahead of us; we can try to circumvent the forest, and run the risk of losing our collective lives in the resultant uncharted wilderness; or we can look for the path between the trees, moving carefully, taking the journey one step (and roadblock) at a time. An army does not pass through a forest as a single body, but rather as an allied group of individuals. We must be an army on a common campaign—an army of individuals working to reach a common goal.

SAA Bulletin, November 1998

Postscript

Has archaeology changed in its attitude toward Native Americans and other nonscientific stakeholders? Yes, I believe so. While a select number of archaeologists in the past have tried to integrate Native American and archaeological viewpoints [see Ferguson (1996) for a more recent discussion of perspectives of Native Americans and the practice of archaeology], recent articles in *American Antiquity* by Dongoske et al. (1997: 600–608), and Shaul and Hill (1998), as well as a poster session at the 1998 SAA Annual Meeting seem to indicate that archaeologists have become more concerned with reaching and involving others outside of the discipline. And well we should, since Principle 2 of the SAA Principles of Archaeological Ethics (Lynott and Wylie 1995:23; Lynott 1997:592) and Part III(A)(1) of the newly revised *AAA Code of Ethics* (*AAA* 1998:19) urge practitioners to ". . . consult actively with the affected individuals or group(s), with the goal of establishing a working relationship that can be beneficial to all parties involved."

Has archaeology benefited from this change in attitudes? Again, I think it has, and, to some extent, NAGPRA is responsible for that. NAGPRA continues with us as perhaps an artificial conscience which goads archaeologists, anthropologists, and other scientific practitioners to question the nature of our practices, as well as to interact with others around us who, perhaps, question the value or even existence of our discipline. While science has not slowed down in its struggle to explain better the natural world of which we are a part, individual scientists have at least slowed down and examined the ways by which we develop those explanations. While we still go about our business of interpreting that which we encounter in the ground known as the cultural record, as archaeologists we are now more than ever aware that those human and cultural remains have someone who wish to speak for their protection. Public education is more strongly encouraged as a means of reaching those populations which in the past have been involved only marginally with archaeology's business.

Is there a risk to archaeology from NAGPRA? That is, will NAGPRA mean the end of archaeology? Not unless archaeologists become numb from the neck up. We all must continue to work with not only Native Americans, but all groups who indicate a concern with the way we conduct our business—including legislators, developers, and any other group of individuals. If we can. we'll be able to demonstrate the utility of the archaeological method for obtaining information about the past. It soon might become more common for archaeology to reestablish connections between current cultures and those represented within the archaeological record, connections which will help us better understand how humans in the past have adapted to their environments, and provide a firmer foundation to the written and unwritten histories of existing cultures.

Native Americans and Archaeology: A Vital Partnership

Robert Kelly

A couple of years ago, while speakers at a conference wrestled with defining archaeology's purpose, my mind wandered to that day's Ku Klux Klan rally on the courthouse lawn in my small Kentucky town. That, for me, solved the speakers' conundrum. It seems too simplistic, but archaeology's purpose today is to play a role in ending racism. Everything follows from this fact.

In the postmodern world, truth seems to be elusive. As in Akira Kurosawa's film, *Rashomon,* in which an event is retold through the eyes of four characters, truth arises from multiple perspectives. But it is the audience, not the participants, who are the beneficiaries of any insights. Extending the analogy, it is those who watch archaeologists, our students, and the public, who benefit from multivocality. Archaeology achieves its goal through education.

Archaeologists in the academy have changed over the years. I suspect that the first generation of academic archaeologists—Alfred Kidder, Nels Nelson, and their contemporaries—knew Native Americans as people, not just as objects of study. Reasons for this include a humanistic bent in the field, the presence of Native Americans as laborers on large projects, and the four-fields approach with its emphasis on ethnography and linguistics.

In contrast, many archaeologists today receive scant training in the other subfields. Their exposure to ethnology and linguistics are often limited to a required undergraduate course. Native Americans as real live people have faded from their experience. I am embarrassed to admit that in my first five years of fieldwork in the Great Basin, I never met a Native American. Many archaeologists actively distance themselves from cultural anthropology, often because of the excesses of postmodernism, but in so doing, they distance themselves from the descendants of those whom archaeology studies. As we became better archaeologists, we became worse anthropologists. The acrimonious debates that preceded the Native American Graves Protection and Repatriation Act (NAGPRA) showed just how far some had strayed from understanding cultural identity—an issue that is central to cultural anthropology today.

Conversations with colleagues who teach North American prehistory suggest that most teach the subject as a mixture of culture history and adaptive change. But as T. J. Ferguson once pointed out (1996), this often does not mean much to Native Americans. An alternative approach focuses on prehistory as a historical text that reveals the meanings of prehistory to Native Americans and speaks more to the cultural histories of particular tribes.

But the format chosen for prehistory courses depends in large measure on the constraints of academic programs. In the face of low enrollments in anthropology courses, enrollment-based funding formulas leave departments scrambling to wedge their courses into the general education requirements that many universities have enacted. At the University of Louisville, for example, we worked North American prehistory into a historical studies slot because of the course's attention to social change. To teach prehistory as text, the course would have to have been acceptable to a humanities faculty that would have frowned on an interloper and blocked the course's approval, to the detriment of our department's enrollments.

However, I don't regret the course's placement because I find that examining prehistory as a record of adaptive change helps combat the unilineal evolutionary thinking that anthropology abandoned long ago but that remains a major folk-explanation of cultural diversity. While showing the cultural genius of North Americas indigenous societies, I also examine the effects of environmental change and increasing population density, providing an alternative to a racialist explanation of the differences between Native American and European history. For me, then, a scientific materialist approach is a key tool in fighting racism.

But there is always room for improvement, and it is sometimes forced upon us. Changes in permitting processes and the increased control that tribes have over historic preservation have obliged archaeologists to consult with Native Americans. Through NAGPRA, many archaeologists have interacted with Native Americans; without it, relationships between them may never have developed. In small departments, archaeologists may teach North American ethnographic survey courses. These experiences provide academic archaeologists with what many of our predecessors had: real contact with the real issues of real Native Americans. Any archaeologist who has experienced these situations has probably been profoundly changed by their confrontations with unfamiliar ways of thinking and teaching about the past.

The Material World vs. Native American Beliefs

While multiculturalism is the rage on campuses today, anthropology is often excluded. One reason is that other disciplines' approaches to multiculturalism are embarassingly naive; dialogue seems to be all that is needed. Talking is an important first step, but what happens when ideas cancel each other out, as they often do when it comes to human burials?

Science is concerned with evaluating ideas about how the material world works. It cannot address, for example, the truthfulness of religious tenets. I can neither prove nor disprove Hopi beliefs about the afterlife. To be true to my education as a scientist, I must acknowledge that since I cannot prove Hopi beliefs are false, then I must grant Hopis the possibility that they might be true.

If in the process of doing and teaching archaeology we in effect tell Native Americans, "Your religious concerns don't matter," then we are in effect telling them that their religious tenets are wrong—which we cannot honestly say.

Alternatively, if we claim that Native American concerns are simply political issues, and we won't be the whipping boys for 500 years of mistreatment that we acknowledge as immoral, but that we are not personally responsible—aren't we then subverting the very reason for doing archaeology? Archaeologists cannot use archaeology to fight racism if in the process they tell someone that his or her concerns don't matter.

But what about situations where archaeology and traditional histories conflict with one another? For example, did the ancestors of Native Americans come from Asia via the Bering Strait more than 12,000 years ago? or did they originate here, as some Native Americans argue? Honesty compels me to answer these questions in the same way I would respond to a Christian fundamentalist about human evolution. Archaeology is all about things located in time and space. Religion and traditional histories often place things in space and time, and these claims can be subjected to scientific scrutiny, but they fundamentally encode knowledge that is timeless and spaceless. These non-material claims cannot be studied scientifically. This most emphatically does not mean that they are therefore wrong, irrelevant, or uninteresting; it just means that their evaluation lies in some other realm of inquiry.

Assuming that Native American religions reflect some fundamental truths. You will have to make your own decision here, I've made mine—what does it mean when religion or traditional histories and archaeology do not agree? What do things that are rooted in time and space have to say about things that are timeless and spaceless, and vice versa? What is to be the relationship between science and religion? These are the ultimate challenges facing anyone teaching archaeology.

A question of priorities is also raised. Consider this: Archaeologists claim a burial is important for what it says about human colonization of this hemisphere. Don't rebury it, some demand, because the ability to collect new data is our legacy to future generations. But, and I say this as someone who has excavated and analyzed many burials—what if in the process of guaranteeing that scientific legacy we dismiss the concerns of Native Americans and hand down a legacy of racial tension? Is a better knowledge of the past worth it? What are we doing this for, anyway?

If we must return every human burial, every artifact, and in essence, cease being archaeologists, then that may be the sacrifice that archaeology must make for a greater good. But this is not what I think should happen, and it is also not what I think most Native Americans would want to occur. People will continue to reconstruct the past even without archaeology, and a clear investigation of the past that demands evidence and argument open to public critique offers the greatest opportunity to empower people and to learn.

New Opportunities for Collaboration

What of the future? Growing numbers of archaeologists have altered their teaching methods to include discussion of the past's meaning to Native Americans, the permission and consultation process, the issues of burials and archaeological ethics, the adjudication of conflicts between archaeology and traditional histories, and the recognition that Native Americans, like archaeologists, have different ideas about archaeology, the past, and science.

More and more field programs emerge as joint efforts between universities and tribes which simultaneously investigate the past and the present; gather together new groups of people for the first time; and bring intellectual and other benefits to tribal members and archaeologists alike. Examples include Barbara Mills' Silver Creek project in Arizona; George Nicholas' program with the Secwepemc in British Columbia; Keith Kintigh's project with the Hopi; Joel Janetski's project at Fish Lake, Utah; and Cathy Cameron's project in Bluff, Utah. In these projects, Native Americans are equal partners in project definition, fieldwork, analysis, and presentation. As these projects continue, we shall see more Native American archaeologists—a step that promises changes in archaeology as important and exciting as radiocarbon dating.

These projects have worked because archaeologists have approached tribes with genuine interest in the potential for learning and with the understanding that archaeologists' view of prehistory is only one way of looking at the past. The medium is the message. Our methods of doing archaeology is as important and meaningful as the results obtained from research.

This trend will continue in part because legislation forces it, but also because archaeologists and Native Americans alike find this approach fulfilling. For it to continue we must strengthen archaeology's tie to the rest of anthropology. Although Native American identity is at the heart of NAGPRA, the legislation is based on a Western notion of ethnicity. Many archaeologists are unaware of other ways of establishing identity. In southwest Madagascar, where Lin Poyer and I have conducted ethnographic work, identity is based on subsistence, and can change from year to year. Misapprehending ethnicity or other conceptualizations of the past means that some archaeologists will be baffled by the animosity that may follow even a close adherence to NAGPRA. Archaeologists must become better anthropologists.

At the same time, however, archaeologists must become better analysts of material culture and be honest about what can and cannot be inferred from archaeological remains. My experience in ethnoarchaeology has taught me to recognize the difference between using an inferential argument and letting a preconception tell the story. Academic courses need to focus more attention on middle-range theory and formation processes.

Administrators also need a broader education to dispel the Indiana Jones image of the archaeologist. They suppose that to gain tenure, you must do what archaeologists do: Dig! But more archaeologists must link projects to outreach programs to be competitive in academia and in the ever-expanding world of archaeology. Joint ventures with multiple consultations and levels of permission is time-consuming, and faculty may find themselves hard-pressed to conduct sufficient basic research for tenure or promotion. However, adoption of the Carnegie Institute's expanded definitions of scholarship, which place application and service on equal footing with basic research, permit faculty to succeed in academia while pursuing more applied programs, as long as these criteria are accepted by the university.

In closing I would ask that Native Americans understand that while archaeologists may trip over their feet and tongues, most do mean well. Archaeologists don't do archaeology to pursue the imperialistic intentions of a colonial government, at least not intentionally. We are archaeologists because we are in love with the past, with other ways of living and being. We study ruins scientifically, but we also see beauty and elegance in Clovis points, Hopewell pottery, and Pueblo Bonito's crumbled walls.

But if Native Americans need to be more forgiving, non-Native American archaeologists must recognize that Native Americans are individuals, not interest groups; that the interface between Native Americans and archaeology is not a purely political issue; and that we must be prepared to make some sacrifices.

Among others, Randy McGuire (1992) and Larry Zimmerman (1989) point out that an honest dialogue between Native Americans and archaeologists will fundamentally alter the practice of archaeology. This is happening. Archaeology will become applied anthropology or it will become nothing. In so doing, we will create a different, more vibrant archaeology that holds great promise as a way to create unity rather than division.

SAA Bulletin, September 1998

International Implications of the Impact of Repatriation in Nevada Museums

Amy Dansie

One of the greatest impacts of repatriation is the forced confrontation between traditional or spiritual models of reality and the Euroamerican system of beliefs based on science. Of course I cannot resolve such a complex issue here, but how this challenge affects one museum system provides an example of the broader implications of this confrontation. Nevada has collections of international significance and significant repatriation experience.

On the eve of federally-mandated repatriation, over 200 human burials were washed out of their resting place in Stillwater Marsh of western Nevada by the devastating floods of the great 1982–1983 El Niño. Anticipating the change in national human remains policy, the U.S. Fish and Wildlife Service, the Fallon Paiute Shoshone Tribes, and the Nevada State Museum worked together to build an accessible underground crypt to bury the remains, providing the possibility of future research and additional space for reburial. Because the question of affiliation was left open in this pre-NAGPRA agreement, future decisions regarding affiliation could be based on the interpretation of data being assembled and synthesized by the museum's long-term Lahontan Basin Prehistory Project. As the nation's representatives began to address the repatriation issue, the Stillwater Crypt reburial solution—with its ideals of preservation of scientific values while meeting the spiritual needs of the Native American community—was recognized in the Senate Record when the Native American Graves Protection and Repatriation Act (NAGPRA) was being crafted. We thought we were on the right track in the repatriation issue, and apparently so did Congress. Since then, the impact of repatriation on the Nevada State Museum has been immense and complex.

In 1990 the Congress passed NAGPRA (PL 601.101). The requirement to perform an inventory of all human remains and associated objects and to identify those subject to the various provisions of NAGPRA, had wide-ranging impacts in the Nevada Division of Museums and History. Because we receive federal funding, all our collections are included. A NAGPRA inventory requires the accurate identification, reintegration, and well-documented transfer to affiliated descendants of all remains of Native American ancestry. Essential for full compliance with both the spirit and letter of the law, the inventory also requires accurate identification of non-

Indian remains, and of populations that left no living descendants, or descendants now geographically far removed. During our repatriation experiences, the inventory took an unexpected twist of international significance—one that remains unresolved today.

Impact on the Museum

Burials are generally very rare in Nevada, but one area is an exception: the Lahontan Basin of western Nevada. Our original estimate of perhaps 100 burials was, in reality, an unbelievable 550 individuals once the fragments and miscellaneous forensic cases were added to the older Nevada Historical Society and Lost City Museum inventories. Almost none were fully analyzed archaeologically, and less than half are properly documented, but most are of great scientific value. Our small staff is virtually overwhelmed by the actual tasks behind repatriation, because we still have to serve the public and comply with the daily demands of our "real jobs."

The dry caves of western Nevada have preserved thousands of perishable artifacts and many well-preserved, but often displaced, human and dog burials. More than 50 years of ongoing research and various levels of curation have separated the bones from their associated items, and sometimes, from each other. For any given human remains, tracking down all relevant data and artifacts, matching the field notes with the catalog and the various scientific analyses, there is always at least one thing that doesn't match up. Each of these details can take hours of sorting and combing through records. The harder we hit the work, the harder it grabs us, sucking day after day, year after year, out of our careers.

This has resulted in 10,000 hours spent over the past nine years of my life creating a complete inventory of every burial ever excavated in Nevada prior to 1900, with all dates, provenience, and associated artifacts entered into a computerized data retrieval system.

Much of this time has included consulting with tribal officials, studying the law, analyzing the evidence, and trying to understand NAGPRA's finer details for compliance. But the question of affiliation has become the most difficult challenge of repatriation in Nevada. Based on the abundance of unsynthesized data, we concluded that only a thorough scientific analysis could resolve the complexity of determining affiliation with existing tribes. These myriad data will be coordinated for affiliation research by an advanced GIS system, initially funded by the U.S. Navy for cultural resource management expanded with funds from the Nevada legislature. We plan to link the chronometric, geographical, archaeological, and biological data with tribal information on origins, intertribal relationships, and other traditional sources of knowledge about the past to reveal patterns of human population dynamics through time.

This impact of repatriation is a very positive one, because we have a new motivation with adequate funding to synthesize the vast records from the dry caves and the knowledge of living native people of Nevada, using the powerful technology now available. There is great potential for revolutionary new insights into the past, although it will require much time and effort. We have assembled a team of interdisciplinary experts in paleogenetics, Great Basin archaeology, ethnography, and physical anthropology to design, compile, and interpret the results under state and private funding.

Impact on Science, Local Issues

In the Great Basin, the human burials in the museum collections represent a vast time depth, with an almost continuous radiocarbon date series from 100 to 11,000 years ago. Cultural or biological affiliation with the historic tribes in residence cannot be demonstrated from the currently available data. In fact, the opposite is indicated—there is more likely no or a very distant affiliation with most of the ancient remains, and over time there may have been several different groups advancing into and retreating from modern Paiute and Shoshone territory. This conclusion is based on differences in linguistics, biology, genetics, material culture, and lifestyle, and is buttressed by the native oral history that frequently describes battles between the Paiute and other groups in and around the Lahontan Basin.

Furthermore, some prehistoric cultures have no known correlates among ethnographic cultures, such as the Lovelock culture in western Nevada and the Fremont culture in Utah, which although contemporaneous, are apparently unrelated to each other as well. When asked by the tribes to demonstrate our evidence for disputing their affiliation to all the burials from their territory, we can refer to everything ever written on Great Basin prehistory and ethnography, but none of it includes the burial data. It simply hasn't been published or, for significant parts of the collections, hasn't even been analyzed until very recently.

Impact on Science, International Issues

Several recent major discoveries in the museum collections have changed what is known about the ancient people of the Lahontan Basin in the western Great Basin. Research conducted over the past five years has identified the oldest mummy in the New World (9,415 years old), and a total of five individuals over 9,000 years old, four of which are associated with a distinctive plain weave tule and cordage matting previously unrecognized in the New World. A whole new culture is emerging from current research unrelated to NAGPRA, but inevitably affected by it.

The 9,000- to 9,500-year-old Spirit Cave Man, Wizards Beach Man, and Kennewick Man share some distinctive traits not often found in later western Native Americans, but which may be a combination of retained traits of a pre-racial common ancestor of all modern humans, and the emerging proto-Indian. The multiple entry hypotheses, early coastal entry hypothesis, and other models of the peopling of the western hemisphere all can be reexamined in the light of these new data of early Holocene human variation in the New World. Ironically, these windows into the human past have developed just as the burials that could provide the answers are being claimed for repatriation worldwide.

The ancient Nevadans who survived the end of the Ice Age may not have survived the great droughts of the Altithermal, after 7,000 B.P., but then again, they may have. They may have descendants anywhere in the New World, depending on the actual history of their movements and adaptations through time. Only genetic tracking, and perhaps textiles, can reveal the destiny of these ancient ones. Science can reveal these great adventures of the human species on a scale and resolution beyond human memory. But to understand this, information from around the planet will have to be integrated, because it is not an isolated, local problem. Identification of these people is an international issue that can only be explored through careful analysis of facts, including the testimony of human skeletal remains and cultural patterns.

Impact on Human Relationships

Our accumulation and preliminary interpretation of the physical facts is causing tension in the consultation process with some of the Nevada tribes, who claim ancestry with any and all Native American remains from their historic territory. Some deny our right to finish the scientific analysis of the collections, to display artistic facial reconstructions of the Spirit Cave Man and Wizards Beach Man, and demand that we return all the remains immediately, regardless of affiliation. The Native American reaction to discussions of "non-Indian" traits in the early American skeletons is growing into a fierce conflict of spiritual assertions versus scientific questions about reality. If public comments and feedback to our museum are any measure, the harm done to Native American relations may be more serious than they realize. I feel caught against my will in a whirlpool of misunderstanding, misinterpretation, and misapprehensions about my motives. Although I stand accused of living in denial, that my avowed respect for the Native American people is a lie because I value scientific knowledge about their past more than their own religious beliefs, I am not yet ready to abandon this virtually hopeless battle.

Conflicts in Human Models of Reality

One thing I have learned to face is that Indian people who hold to traditional understandings of the universe do not agree with my culture's definition of reality. The physical facts I accept as valid evidence of time, physical appearance, genetic relationship, cultural affiliation, and historic continuity of human populations around the planet are rejected by some

Native Americans in favor of a view that the creator made each group of people independently, and that they never moved from their place of origin. I do not believe it is disrespectful to doubt such assertions that are simply not defensible in the real world of human history.

At a major consultation meeting with the Northern Paiute and Shoshone in November 1997, I tried to ask about the abundant documented evidence of their own oral history which included battles between the Paiute and other people in the Lahontan Basin. I was told that those stories were not the real Paiute history, only lies told to white people. They could not share their sacred knowledge to explain why these stories, steadfastly maintained as fact until nine years ago, were not real anymore. I understand open defiance of science, but not at the expense of factual history.

I never faced this conflict personally until repatriation became federal law. It hasn't been easy because I do care about both human rights and the scientific discovery of lost human history. My personal dilemma in trying to resolve this conflict of values and belief systems is a microcosm of the challenges facing science today in an increasing climate of hostility to rational, objective descriptions of reality. Sometimes I feel that repatriation may be the catalyst that brings such global value conflicts to open confrontation. Scientists can no longer assume they have incontestable rights of inquiry when they conflict with perceived and legislated human rights and opposing belief systems. That doesn't mean science is invalid, but it can no longer be assumed to be an unassailable right of the dominant Euroamerican cultures. However, I still maintain that truth is truth, and some facts about the past will shine in the light of cross-cultural scrutiny.

The gradual accumulation of archaeological facts has lead to many hypotheses of what occurred in the past. In the Great Basin, despite the lack of consensus, there is abundant evidence of major patterns of population replacement throughout the past 11,000 years. According to the spirit of NAGPRA, if the evidence strongly suggests that the identifiable earlier groups would disagree with being identified as ancestors of the Northern Paiute, then it is not right to say they are, despite the feelings of the living tribal people. Political correctness should not require compromising a truth established by facts that all of us can see and evaluate. Most of the possible earlier groups we have identified in Nevada are traditional enemies of the Paiute or have no living representatives; consequently, the best approach to take in standing up for the truth is not clear.

Mitigating the Impact on Science and Human Heritage in Spiritually Sensitive Solutions

I think we did the right thing with the 250 Stillwater burials exposed by flooding in the 1980s near Fallon. An accessible burial crypt allows for respectful reburial, without destroying the scientific potential in case important new research techniques are developed, some of which may be of major benefit to Indian people. It also provides a pre-negotiated reburial process for all newly exposed burials. With such a compromise, the destructive impact of repatriation can be minimized. A similar solution was reached in Utah, where disagreements between tribes regarding prehistoric territories made determination of affiliation for flood-exposed burials impossible.

My job as state museum anthropologist is to help people learn to celebrate our wonderful diversity while discovering how much we have in common. Learning from the ancient ones before they are reburied is now Nevada's official way of mitigating the negative impacts of repatriation. The Nevada legislature and governor have supported explicitly and generously the Nevada State Museum's efforts to establish affiliation through scientific analysis. It is good to know the museum anthropology department is not alone in upholding science and fact in this politically hostile climate. Many other anthropologists are alone in this challenge because administrations avoid controversy.

It is important to stress that our support of science does not mean we disregard the tribal views of reality and spiritual values. In fact, we fully support repatriation to affiliated groups, and have repatriated, or prepared to repatriate, all historic and other identified remains. We are not disputing that disturbance of the dead is a significant issue. This is not an issue of spirit versus science. It has to do with truth and fact. Other tribes with potential affiliation also have rights under NAGPRA, whether they are currently aware of an ancient connection or not.

The impact of repatriation is far reaching, and current proposed changes to the federal law that enhance the capture of scientific information before repatriation, are fully in line with the intent of Congress when the law was originally passed. Accurate identification and classification of the dead is a basic legal principle that should apply to all undocumented deaths to ensure justice, and that includes archaeological analysis of prehistoric human remains.

The common heritage of humankind is at stake in the broader international implications of this issue, such as the efforts to prohibit studying Neanderthal remains in Israel. Furthermore, respecting the rights of Native Americans includes the countless contemporary and future descendants of the Native American people who respect and value scientific facts about prehistory. These Americans with Indian ancestry also have the right to knowledge about their origins, and many of them have been vocal on this subject. The impact of repatriation includes all the legal, personal, moral, spiritual, ethical, intellectual, rational, and emotional turmoil involved in finding a professionally and personally acceptable response to all the human issues arising from the repatriation efforts in America.

Righting the wrongs of our recent past is a noble goal, but there is more at stake than the feelings of Indian people for their generic ancestors represented by these burials. Other cultural and spiritual values are held equally dear by citizens of this world and we can all benefit from learning more about our common origins. These human remains are not just the physical remains of departed persons who deserve respect—they are precious and rare fragments of our human heritage that can provide the most direct understanding of our past. Repatriation of skeletal remains without discovering their underlying messages seems an insult to the wonder of creation that they even exist, and that we are capable, by the grace of our creator, of learning so much from them.

SAA Bulletin, May 1999

Repatriation's Silver Lining

Thomas W. Killion and Paula Molloy

Repatriation legislation has fundamentally altered the treatment of Native American remains and objects held by museums and other repositories in the United States. Passed almost 10 years ago, the repatriation mandate is embodied in two laws: the National Museum of the American Indian Act, which applies to the Smithsonian Institution museums [including our museum, the National Museum of Natural History (NMNH)], and the Native American Graves Protection and Repatriation Act (NAGPRA) which applies to other museums and federal agencies. The laws require organizations funded by the federal government to disclose the nature and extent of their Native American collections and enter into consultation with affiliated tribes over the final disposition of remains and culturally sensitive items identified in the laws. Ironically, the quest for the origins of Native Americans which first brought institutions such as the Smithsonian into being, has now come full circle, and Indian participation in the study of Native American origins and history is rapidly expanding (Echo-Hawk 1997; Minthorn 1997; Swidler et al. 1997; Watkins et al. 1995). This trend is in no small part an outcome of the repatriation mandate.

The passage and initial implementation of Native American repatriation legislation was met with dire predictions for the fate of science and freedom of inquiry (e.g., Meighan 1996; Morell 1995, cf. Jones and Harris 1997). Pitched battles erupted between Indians and museum anthropologists over the identity of remains and their relationship to contemporary tribes (Billeck and Urcid 1995; Bray and Killion 1994; Steinacher et al. 1991[1] mine the repatriation status of remains and objects have landed native and scientific disputants in court (*Na Iwi O Na Kupuna O Mokapu v. Dalton* 1995; NPS 1997). Here we focus on the notion that repatriation represents a loss from the scientific perspective. We contend that while initially daunting to the scientific status quo, repatriation has generally accelerated the pace and scope of research on the origins and history of the aboriginal peoples of North America. We question the a priori assumption of "loss," and instead evaluate the changes that have taken place and their outcomes on the basis of the evidence now available.

Viewed from the outside, repatriation has stirred up controversy, and polarized museums and Native Americans. In spite of this perception, however, potential adversaries engage one another, working ground rules are established, information is shared, decisions are made, and the law is carried out. At the NMNH, the repatriation mandate has yielded unprecedented advances in access to information, and to the collections themselves, by Native peoples and other groups. As a direct result of the repatriation process, Native American participation in the life of the museum has reached an all time high.

Repatriation is sometimes a painful and culturally challenging event. Our experiences include the Cheyenne return, which graphically resurrected a host of tragedies, such as the massacre at Sand Creek and the killings following the Ft. Robinson outbreak (Killion et al. 1992). Other historic period repatriation cases have involved the Apache massacres in Arizona (Speaker et al. 1994), an ambush of friendly Pawnee Scouts in Nebraska (Baugh and Makseyn-Kelley 1992; Riding In 1992), the Nez Perce war (Molloy 1996), and the sorrowful events at Wounded Knee, South Dakota, in 1898 (Smythe 1998). These events require revisitation and evaluation of some of the darkest moments in American history. Our review of the fate of these individuals and the conditions under which their remains were acquired, however, illuminates old history in a new and often profound way. We hope that this effort will challenge our understanding of the past in much the same way that the Holocaust Museum in Washington, D.C., bears witness to the genocide of WWII—by reviewing history in a manner that goes beyond analysis to commemorate the victims and survivors.

Repatriation documentation revisits a pivotal era in Native American history. With a few notable exceptions (Svaldi 1989; Thornton 1990), historical details of encounter, depopulation, and survival among Native American groups are ignored in surveys of Native American demographic change, and are often overlooked as a focus of anthropological research. However, this period is central to both Native and Euro-American history, and is a fertile subject for anthropological inquiry and critical analysis. Furthermore, the events of the Colonial Period were ultimately the impetus for the repatriation movement, and influence its present course.

While repatriation illuminates a critical period in recent history, many anthropologists continue to focus on what they perceive to be its deleterious effects on the conduct of science in general, and the loss of anthropological collections specifically. For brevity, we will address the inventory, documentation, and repatriation of human remains and funerary objects only. There simply are no comprehensive statistics available regarding quantities of human remains returned nationwide. The NAGPRA process is overseen by the Archeology and Ethnography Program of the National Park Service (NPS) in Washington D.C., which monitors the information provided to the tribes by museums, federal agencies, and other organizations. NAGPRA inventories completed to date account for about 200,000 sets of remains, of which almost 10,000 are "culturally affiliated" and presumably available for return if the tribes so desire. There is no mechanism for documenting the actual return of those 10,000 identified remains reported. It also is not clear how many of the reported remains have actually been culturally identified. Some institutions, for example, have reported large collections from the southwest as culturally "Puebloan." In these cases, any or all culturally affiliated tribes may make a claim (McKeown 1998). However, without additional research and consultation with the tribes involved, it is difficult to determine which federally recognized tribe or tribes in the region would receive these remains. In some areas of the country, tribal alliances have formed to take responsibility for the larger, less specific cultural groupings.

Some of the largest natural history and anthropology museums in the country, with collections of human remains in the 5,000 to 15,000 individual range, were given extensions and will not report for another year or more. It is impossible to predict how many culturally affiliated remains will be identified as part of this process or, once identified, how many will be returned. Thus far, the only summary statement possible is that approximately 5 percent of the human remains held by museums outside of the Smithsonian are presently eligible for return. Since there is presently a backlog of intent to repatriate notices awaiting publication, the number is expected to grow.

Because of funding provided by the National Museum of the American Indian Act, repatriation has proceeded much further at the NMNH. Prior to the passage of this legislation, the museum held 18,400 cataloged sets of remains from U.S. proveniences in North America and Hawaii. Since 1992, we have returned more than 3,000 of these to almost 40 individual federally-recognized tribes in Alaska, Hawaii, the Pacific Northwest, and the Great Plains. Another 1,500 individuals are scheduled for return to Plains tribes in 1999.

Documentating the more than 4,000 individuals involved has yielded a great deal of contextual information on the remains that otherwise might never have been widely available. Reports and databases generated by this process reveal information on the cultural origins, circumstances of acquisition, and physical condition of the skeletal remains themselves. Many of these remains have been previously studied, but like most other museums, no permanent, systematic record of this research had been created. Repatriation has provided the first mechanism for pulling together enough information on the remains to answer one of the most common questions asked by tribal representatives and the general public alike—"what have you actually learned over the last 150 years?"

Repatriation has generated the first systematic catalog of remains and objects in the museum ever provided to the tribes. This work has also served to correct errors in the museum's catalog. For example, about 10 percent of the catalog information on cultural affiliation has been found to be in error for the cases completed to date, including information on age, sex, skeletal elements present, and cause of death. In addition to being the Smithsonian's first comprehensive tribal catalog of remains and objects, the documentation record of our repatriation program also chronicles the manner in which the museum complied with the repatriation mandate.

Besides the direct impact on museum collections, we also must consider repatriation's effect on physical anthropology as a discipline. On the eve of the passage of federal repatriation legislation, scientists attempted to evaluate the importance of skeletal studies and how they might be impacted by repatriation. In 1989, Ubelaker and Grant (1989:252) reviewed the previous two years of submissions to the *American Journal of Physical Anthropology* (*AJPA*), and found that 20 percent of manuscripts focused on skeletal anatomy or paleopathology. However, it is not clear if they included papers based on collections not subject to NAGPRA, such as collections from Europe, Africa, Asia, and South and Central America.

To better assess NAGPRA's impacts on research, we reviewed all papers published in AJPA between 1985 and 1996 inclusive, that deal with human remains from the United States. While we expected to see a change in the number of papers focusing on Native American remains in the years following the passage of NAGPRA, this was not the case. From 1985 through 1989, papers dealing with Native American remains represented 6 percent of the total papers published. From 1990 through 1996, such papers amounted to 7 percent.

Based on this, we offer two observations: (1) using *AJPA* as a measure, there is as yet no major effect on published research focusing on Native American remains and (2) physical anthropological studies of Native American remains make up a very small part of physical anthropological research as a whole. Together, these observations suggest not only that repatriation has not yet produced the dire consequences for research that were predicted before the passage of the mandate, but also that the volume of pre-NAGPRA studies focused on Native American skeletal collections may have been overestimated. That said, we must point out that in recent years, fewer researchers have approached the NMNH seeking to perform analyses of our Native American skeletal collections. This is due to a combination of factors, including reduced research funding opportunities, as well as a mistaken assumption that our Native American collections are closed for research—which in fact, they are not.

In addition to physical anthropologists, archaeologists also have been concerned that repatriation would adversely affect research opportunities. To gauge how repatriation might have affected bioarchaeological research, we reviewed all papers published in *American Antiquity* between 1985 and 1996. From 1985 through 1989, only 4 percent of the total papers published focused on Native American human remains; from 1990 through 1996, they total 7 percent. While these percentages are small, there actually appears to have been a slight increase in published studies of Native American remains in the years following repatriation. As with the *AJPA* data, the *American Antiquity* data also suggest that bioarchaeological studies focusing on Native American human remains comprise a very small part of published archaeological research.

While repatriation so far does not appear to have affected the volume of publications, it has led some researchers to be more circumspect in considering research questions and analytical techniques. Certainly destructive analyses, such as isotopic and DNA studies, must be approached more cautiously, and in many cases have been prohibited as a result of concerns over Native American sensitivities. However, the impact of such restrictions should be evaluated in terms of the quality of the lost data, and whether or not other data can mitigate that loss. For example, stable isotopic analysis of human bone can reveal important dietary information. When such studies are not permitted, other methods can be used to fill the gap, such as archaeobotanical and faunal research. As for DNA analysis, its utility for illuminating Native American history and prehistory may be more limited than popular perceptions would suggest. Currently, DNA analysis is limited by the absence of definable, population-specific genetic markers. It is further limited by the difficulty of deriving DNA from skeletal remains, potential laboratory contamination, and the prohibitive expense of the technique (Carlson et al. 1997).

While many of the tribes are strongly opposed to destructive testing, not all are. In 1993, a University of Wisconsin researcher approached our repatriation office with a request to take samples of bone collagen from individuals being readied for return to the Chugach Eskimos of Prince William Sound, Alaska. We recommended that she make direct contact with the repatriation representative for the tribe, explain the importance of the research, and ask permission to take the samples, which she did successfully. Was her success simply a matter of reaching out to the tribe in an honest and meaningful way? Our office also has facilitated repatriation-related osteological studies in collaboration with Native communities from Point Hope and the Seward Peninsula in Alaska (Mudar et al. 1996), and osteologists have recently received support from Great Plains tribes to study pathological conditions to evaluate overall health during the pre- and postcontact periods (Miller 1995). We suspect there are many such examples, and that this kind of engagement is the best way to begin building a solid foundation for Native American community-supported archaeology and physical anthropology in the future.

The repatriation process is providing a clearer understanding of, and perhaps some closure to, a painful period of Native American history. Studies and documentation of the Contact Period can be augmented and revitalized in the context of repatriation, and are of keen interest to many of the Native communities involved. As dialogue concerning the treatment of all human remains continues to evolve both inside and outside anthropology, argument over the rights and privileges of scientists to conduct studies unfettered by public opinion must be evaluated within the context of the research. Data concerning the scope and scale of this research suggest that rather than halting bioarchaeological and physical anthropological research, repatriation has, in fact, generated new opportunities for collaboration. The flowering of these studies in the context of repatriation holds the promise of revitalizing the discipline of anthropological archaeology itself.

[1] Summaries of all NMNH repatriation reports cited can be found on the NMNH Repatriation Office Web site at **www.nmnh.si.edu/anthro/repatriation/repat.shtm**.

SAA Bulletin, March 1999

Postscript

In the time that has passed since we first presented our views on repatriation and its potential for revitalizing anthropological research in Native America, much has transpired. While most of these developments have been positive, some have not, and it is one of these "dark clouds" that is our focus here.

In early 1999, the Smithsonian found itself the subject of newspaper headlines from coast to coast, proclaiming that the institution had refused to return the brain of Ishi, the famous "last Yahi." What wasn't in the headlines was that the claimant in question had no standing under current federal repatriation legislation and was not culturally affiliated with Ishi's people (the Yahi-Yana). Also missing from newspaper accounts was that the Smithsonian was actively consulting with Redding and Pitt River Rancherias, who possess legal repatriation standing, whose people include Yana descendants, and who have indicated their wish to repatriate Ishi's remains themselves. Not long after the first headlines appeared, the Smithsonian was called to testify before the California State Senate and explain its "refusal" to turn over the brain.

How did the repatriation process become so distorted in this instance? Three factors came into play. First, the remains in question were those of a well-known individual, therefore public interest was high. Second, while the Smithsonian played no part in the genocide of the Yahi-Yana, did not conduct Ishi's autopsy or remove his brain, and did not solicit its donation, a bogeyman was needed as an object on which to deflect the public's latent guilt. The Smithsonian fit nicely into this role. Finally, and most importantly, there were individuals outside the repatriation process (academicians, politicians, and the press) who stood to make professional gains by exploiting and distorting the facts of this case.

The difficult lesson learned here is that third parties with political, personal, and professional axes to grind can use repatriation to further their own goals. When outsiders with no legal standing insert themselves into the repatriation process, the relationship between the museum and the involved tribes is disrupted, and the truth of issues of substance can be lost in the ensuing free-for-all. Damage control, rather than consultation, becomes the order of the day.

Based on our experience in this case, we offer three observations:

(1) Know whom you're dealing with. If it is a tribe, does it have standing and is it culturally affiliated with the remains/materials in question?

(2) Know what's at stake. This is particularly important when dealing with those not directly involved in the repatriation process (e.g., scholars, politicians, the press). What is the basis for their self-proclaimed interest? What do they stand to gain (or lose)?

(3) The truth will set you free. The future of collaborative native/scholarly research depends on a foundation of honesty. While institutions have no control over how others might choose to distort the facts, by continuing to deal forthrightly with our Native American constituents, we create the necessary conditions for our continued work together.

III.
Native Peoples and Archaeologists Working Together: Case Studies

The Archaeological Field School in the 1990s: Collaboration in Research and Training

Barbara J. Mills

What is the role of the archaeological field school in the 1990s? How does it contribute to training archaeologists for conducting research in the multifaceted settings we now find ourselves in? Can an archaeological field school conduct research, provide training in field and lab techniques, *and* interface with the many different publics interested in our work?

When I first took over the directorship of the University of Arizona's Archaeological Field School in 1992, I had a chance to think about these questions in the design of my own field program. Over the past four years, I have had several positive experiences in aspects of both research and training that have involved working together with Native American groups, their employees, advisory groups, and tribal members. Some of these experiences were formalized from the outset of the project, some were fortuitous, and still others were planned and carried out after our project had been well underway. Each of these experiences has brought home the fact that research, teaching, and collaboration are not separate tracks, but are necessary components for field schools in the 1990s.

My interest in the archaeology of prehistoric Western Pueblos led me to choose the Sitgreaves National Forest in east-central Arizona as the location for my field project. It was an area that had not seen much excavation in the past 50 years, yet was surrounded by areas that had been well studied—including the Grasshopper area to the south where the University of Arizona had conducted a field school for 30 years and the Homol'ovi pueblos to the north, where the Arizona State Museum, also of the University of Arizona, continues to work.

Our research design includes the study of the changing social, economic, and political organization of prehistoric pueblos in the Silver Creek area, a tributary to the Little Colorado River. Three sites spanning the period of about A.D. 1100 to 1400 are being excavated. The earliest site was constructed within 100 years of a major migration into the area and has a circular masonry great kiva similar to great kivas found at Chaco outliers. The latest site, a 200 room pueblo known as the Bailey Ruin, also is occupied after an archaeologically recognizable migration into the area from the Colorado Plateau, but dating to the late 1200s. Our research is currently being funded by the University of Arizona, the National Science Foundation (SBR-9507660), the Wenner-Gren Foundation for Anthropological Research, and the U.S. Forest Service.

The U.S. Forest Service has been very supportive of the project and has worked hard to help us with the logistics of setting up a field camp at a former ranger station and arranging for special use permits. Although the excavations and camp are on Forest Service land, the project area falls within the traditional use areas of four southwestern tribes: Hopi, Zuni, White Mountain Apache, and Navajo. Before our ARPA permit could be issued, each one of these tribes was consulted by the Forest Archeologist. Our research design was submitted to each of the tribes and we received constructive comments back from their representatives.

Explicit from the outset was our intention to avoid the excavation of human remains. If burials are encountered, our policy is to stop excavations in that unit and leave the remains *in situ* along with all of the associated artifacts. A Memorandum of Understanding (MOU) was signed at the beginning of the project by a representative of each tribe, the Arizona State Historic Preservation Office, the U.S. Forest Service, and the Advisory Council on Historic Preservation. A formal means of review and research dissemination were set up with this MOU: We submit our annual field report to the U.S. Forest Service archaeologist each fall, who then sends it out for review to each of the tribes.

Although formalized from

Figure 1—The author with the White Mountain Apache Cultural Advisors.

the beginning of the project, the process of the review of our annual reports through the stipulations of the MOU has brought only indirect interaction over the past three years. As the Forest Service is the agency responsible for the administration of the permit, feedback has been filtered through the federal agency. In the past two years we have gotten very few comments back from the tribes. While this is an advantage for bureaucratic reasons, it is not satisfying as a collaborative experience. Instead, we have looked to other avenues of communication to supplement the one now legally required by our permit to provide us with more direct interactions.

One alternative is to present the results of our research in the context of meetings of tribal cultural advisory committees. Of the four tribes that signed the MOU, only one of them has a regularly scheduled meeting of their cultural advisors that is open to researchers to present their work and to receive feedback—the Hopi Tribe. However, we were fortunate in having scheduled a trip to Hopi in the spring of 1995 that coincided with a joint meeting between the cultural advisory committees of both the Hopi and Zuni tribes. I discussed our research goals and described our future plans with the representatives of both tribes. From my perspective, the most important result of this meeting was that the cultural advisors got visual images of the sites we are working at and, more importantly, personal contacts were made and/or renewed. I already knew several of the Zuni tribal representatives from five years of employment at the Zuni

Figure 2—The Zuni Cultural Advisory Team at Hough's Great Kiva site.

Archaeology Program. This gave former colleagues a chance to see me in my new role, that of the university professor. I extended invitations to the tribal representatives to visit the project in the field the following summer.

Thus, the second alternative we have turned to is to have members of the cultural advisory committees of their respective tribes visit us in the field to discuss our research. The goal of these visits has been to promote a discussion of common interests in the research we are conducting in the area. Migration, ritual integration, aggregation, and changes in craft and subsistence production are major topics in our research design. These topics are also of great interest to the Native American groups in the Southwest.

I wrote a grant proposal to the Wenner-Gren Foundation for Anthropological Research that specifically asked for funding to support travel by members of the tribal cultural advisory groups to our field project. We explicitly laid out our approach in this research design, which does not assume that oral histories will provide a direct match to the archaeological record. Instead, we emphasize thematic parallels with archaeological interpretations that we can use to construct a dialog about forms of integration following migration that are of interest to archaeologists and non-archaeologists alike. We received our grant last summer and arranged for visits on the part of representatives of two of the four tribes who regularly review our reports: Zuni and White Mountain Apache tribes. This coming summer we hope to have representatives from the other two tribes' cultural advisory committees.

Figure 3—The Zuni Cultural Advisory Team and the author at Pinedale.

Last summer's visits by the White Mountain Apache and Zuni cultural advisory teams were very positive experiences for the tribal representatives, as well as the students and staff of the Field School. At the outset of each visit, we made explicit that any information gained through the visits would be reviewed prior to their use in our research. An outline of topics we are interested in was given to each group at the beginning of their visit.

The styles of interaction of each of the groups was very different. The Zunis used their visit to educate themselves about ancestral sites in the area. They pointed out the similarity of the great kiva we were testing to Village of the Great Kivas on the Zuni Reservation. This visit was tape recorded and photo-documented by both parties. They were clearly using the visit to educate themselves about their ancestral sites as much as we were learning from them.

The White Mountain Apache group were also keenly interested in the archaeological sites, but for other reasons. They made it explicit from the outset that the sites we were investigating were not their ancestral sites, but that the area in general was one that they had used for centuries. They described hunting, plant collecting, and other resource procurement in the area, giving us a window into recent environmental changes. We looked at an historic saw mill that many Apache people had worked in and discussed trails that led from the reservation to Anglo communities along the Little Colorado River. As they were just starting their own heritage center and this was one of the first field consultations made by the cultural advisors, I later learned that the visit was providing a model for how they could conduct future visits to research sites. Their visit was publicized in *The Fort Apache Scout,* the White Mountain Apache Tribal Newspaper, in the context of new directions for their small museum and related activities of their advisory council.

These visits have had several important outcomes. First, they have demonstrated a willingness on the part of both the tribes and the university to establish a dialogue about common themes of interest. Second, the visits have shown the enrolled field school students how actively interested the tribes are in the archaeology of the area—whether descendants of the prehistoric Western Pueblos, as in the case of the Zuni, or as more recent occupants of the same area, as in the case of the White Mountain Apache. Most of our students are not from the Southwest and while a few have participated in constructing NAGPRA inventories in their respective home institutions, most have not had an active role in describing what they are doing to tribal members.

One of our enrolled students last summer was a tribal member from the Gila River Community, a southern Arizona tribe. She was able to see how other tribe's were organized in providing archaeological input.

The advisory team members, in turn, expressed an interest in having members of their own tribe's participate in the field school.

One of the comments that I have heard from tribal representatives in the past is: What does archaeology do for us? The visitors we had last summer expressed a sincere interest in our work, but I know we could be doing more, and doing it more effectively. Every year adds another dimension to collaboration. What I see a need for in the future is having several fully supported Native American students at the field school each year. Indeed, this might be a role for field schools in North America in years to come. We have been very fortunate to have two Native American students. One was recommended to us through academic channels, an undergraduate from the University of Pennsylvania who is now in graduate school at Harvard University. The other is the woman from Gila River Community, who is a full-time employee of her tribe's cultural resources program. Both of these students received full funding to attend the field school through scholarships in their home institutions. Funding for both of these students was key in allowing them the flexibility to attend the field school.

My strategy has been to maximize the diversity of students enrolled and to expose the students to issues through the visits described above as well as guest lectures by American Indian scholars and non-tribal members employed by tribes in cultural and historic preservation. The feedback I have gotten from the tribes has been very positive. However, they would not have been able to participate in these visits without funding. As budgets are continually being slashed, it is more and more difficult for the tribes to fund their own travel. The funding we supplied was

Figure 4—Phillip Tuwaletstiwa setting GPS receiver over permanent geodetic control point at Bryant Ranch, Silver Creek, 1999.

not major, but it made a difference in whether a tribal vehicle could be taken and whether the representatives could afford to miss a day of work.

After this stage of the project is completed, we will be working on a final interpretive report. The information we learned from our brief visits will have to be supplemented with more in depth interviews. To the extent that we are able to publish the results, we will be able to integrate the varying types of information—environmental, historical, and social—into a narrative of the archaeology of the Silver Creek that we hope will be of interest to all who have provided input.

SAA Bulletin, November 1996

Postscript

In the four years since my article was published in the *SAA Bulletin*, the University of Arizona Archaeological Field School has continued to work in the Silver Creek area. Collaboration in research and training also has continued, but has expanded in new directions. Because of this long-term collaboration in one research area, we are beginning to see some patterns emerge in the way that interactions are structured.

We have continued to recruit and enroll Native American students in the field school. However, because of the economic problems of paying tuition and lost wage-earning time that field school attendance necessitates, it has been more difficult to recruit students than we had anticipated. Even with scholarship offerings, we have found that many students cannot afford to attend, even turning down scholarships. The SAA Arthur C. Parker Scholarship and the NSF Scholarships for Archaeological Training for Native Americans and Native Hawaiians, that cover tuition and student expenses, should help alleviate this problem for some Native Americans who wish to attend a field school.

One of the highest enrollments of Native Americans in the University of Arizona Archaeological Field School has been by employees of tribal heritage and preservation programs. These programs have not only paid the students' tuition, but also their salaries during field school attendance. Two Native American employees of the Gila River Community Cultural Resource Program and one from the Navajo Nation Archaeology Department participated in the field school in this way. This training also can fit with the educational goals of the students. Two of the students were enrolled at least part-time in degree programs and could transfer the credit hours to their home institutions. Everyone benefits from this participation and I think this may be one of the most productive ways in which a field school can help in the training of Native American archaeologists.

One new direction has been in conducting more intensive collaborative research with specific tribal programs, in addition to those conducted with tribal cultural advisory committees. Tribal advisory committees have many demands on their time and are more often consulted on large cultural resource management projects in the Southwest to help advise on the proper disposition of human remains and objects of cultural patrimony. Because our excavations do not involve the excavation of human remains, consultation has not been seen as a high priority by some of the committees. Instead, we have begun to build bridges with other tribal programs to more directly incorporate Native American participation in our project.

Our most recent collaboration has been with one of the offices of the Hopi Tribe. Tribes have a tremendous wealth of resources—quite often more substantial than university resources. In the case of the Hopi Tribe, its GIS and GPS technology is much better than what we own and in fact, better than the equipment of most private contracting companies in the Southwest. The director of the Hopi Tribe's Land Information Systems Office, Phillip Tuwaletstiwa, agreed to collaborate with us on our fieldwork during summer 1999. His previous experience includes director of the National Geodetic Survey, geodetic consultant to NASA, and director of the mapping of Hopi traditional cultural properties in the Hopi-Navajo Partition lands. His experience and interest in ancestral Pueblo sites as a Hopi Tribal member all made him uniquely qualified to collaborate on a National Geographic Society grant that we received for summer fieldwork.

Tuwaletstiwa and his staff became part of our field crew for the fieldwork. They used a combination of Trimble Global Positioning System receivers (models 4000 and 4800 series) to establish three permanent geodetic control stations tied to the national Geodetic Control Network. Topographic maps and maps of archaeological features at the site were mapped with a Trimble Total Station (TS 5000). The GPS data and Total Station data were then processed with Trimble's GPSurvey and TSOffice software and exported to ESRI's ArcView GIS software. ArcView was used for the topographic analysis and cartographic printing, which included two- and three-dimensional maps of the site as well as viewshed calculations from the highest point of the site. This collaboration provided access to the best mapping and positioning equipment available, the expertise to run the equipment, final products of the highest quality, and demonstrations for the students in state-of-the-art equipment and the potential for joint projects with tribes.

Two general patterns have emerged from our collaborative projects. First, funding is a constant challenge. This is true for both field schools and tribes; finding the resources to combine the two is not an easy task. Second, it often is difficult to predict the most fruitful way to pursue collaborative projects. By keeping our program flexible, we have been able to incorporate new activities in constructive ways as they cross our path.

Involving the Caddo Tribe during Archaeological Field Schools in Texas: A Cross-Cultural Sharing

James E. Bruseth, James E. Corbin, Cecile E. Carter, and Bonnie McKee

Each year the Texas Archaeological Society (TAS) conducts a weeklong field school in the State as an opportunity for Society members to gain hands-on experience with archaeological field and laboratory work. In 1991 and 1992 the senior author served as the project archaeologist for field schools along the Red River of northeastern Texas. This portion of the state was once part of the homeland of the Caddo people, and as part of the 1991 and 1992 field schools several sites relating to their cultural heritage were investigated. Most attention was devoted to the Arnold Roitsch site, a prehistoric and early historic civic-ceremonial center with two earthen mounds (one of which had washed away in a flood in 1991). This site was targeted for most of the field school activity since erosion was actively destroying portions of the site, and because looting of Caddoan cemeteries at the site had been rampant. The field school was an attempt to gain important archaeological information before the site was totally destroyed, and to salvage human remains that had been vandalized by looters.

Prior to the 1991 season, the TAS leadership and the senior author agreed on the need to contact the Caddo Tribe, present the field school plans, and seek their advice. Consultation with the tribe was especially important since human remains would be encountered during the field school. Although all fieldwork was conducted on private land and statutory requirements for tribal notification were not applicable, we felt it was nonetheless imperative to obtain the views of the Caddo Tribe on how human remains should be treated.

We visited the Caddo in the winter of 1990–1991, and gave a presentation to the elders. Our reception was extremely cordial, and a good exchange of ideas and comments occurred. The elders were very interested in the project, and asked to visit the field school. They indicated that human remains, obviously, must be treated with respect for the deceased, but could be examined by a specialist before *reinterment*. Although earlier contacts have occurred between Texas archaeologists and the Caddo Tribe, in retrospect our interaction about the field school was the beginning of a new, and hopefully long-lasting, relationship between Texas archaeologists and the Caddo people. We should add that building this relationship was long overdue since archaeologists have been conducting investigations in the Caddoan archaeological area for nearly a century.

During both field schools, 25 to 35 members of the Caddo Tribe visited the excavations. They attended evening presentations, dined with the archaeologists, and visited the fieldwork. Special tours were given at each of the sites, and the Caddo were shown how we use archaeology to learn about the past. Quite understandably, a few elders had difficulty visiting some areas—especially those near human interments. We deferred to their judgment on what and how much archaeology to show them. Nonetheless, the experience was extremely rewarding, both to TAS members and to the Caddo people. Some members of the tribe even participated in the excavations, and in fact one member of the tribe, who is also a coauthor of this article (Carter), worked with us during the duration of both field schools.

Several particularly memorable events occurred as part of our interaction with the Caddo Tribe. During both field schools, the Caddo performed dances for the archaeologists. Some dances were performed entirely by the tribal members, and the field school participants were invited to join others. At one point during the 1991 field school, nearly a third of the TAS members were dancing with the Caddo. This was quite remarkable when one considers that the 1991 field season had over 500 participants.

During the 1992 field school, a grant was secured from the Texas Committee for the Humanities by one of the authors (McKee), offsetting the expenses of the Caddo Tribe to visit the field school. The grant also enabled the development of special activities to make their visit more rewarding. Particularly noteworthy was a ceramics manufacturing workshop. Prehistorically, the Caddo made some of the finest pottery in the Southeastern United States, but today they have lost all knowledge of their once-great ceramic tradition. The workshop began with a breakfast and introductory session by one of the authors (Corbin) on ceramics manufacturing techniques, clays, and firing. After breakfast Corbin and several Caddo toured the Museum of the Red River. Here the group was allowed to peruse the Caddoan ceramics in the museum's collection. The Caddo were fascinated by the sophisticated vessel forms and the variety of decorative techniques and design elements. Traditional Caddoan pottery is coiled, yet many vessels exhibit a regularity of form that belie this hand-forming technique. There was much discussion about the obvious skill of many ancient Caddoan potters, not only in terms of vessel production, but also in design layout and execution. Engraving and incising were the primary techniques used by these potters to execute a number of design elements. The seminar participants expressed obvious pride in the artistic skill of their ancestors, particularly in the execution of various scroll designs using delicate, fine line engraving techniques.

After the museum tour, the group proceeded to the field school campground to observe an open firing demonstration and to participate in a hands-on pottery making workshop. Unfortunately, a tremendous surprise thunderstorm the night before had thoroughly soaked the fuel supply and the ground. While the group was visiting the museum, the TAS had located a supply of resin-rich lathes from a nearby wood-drying kiln. We had fuel, but the wet ground and gusty wind made conditions anything but ideal. We explained to the seminar participants that the ethnohistoric records generally indicate that traditional open firing of pottery was an early morning affair (when there was little or no wind) and that most potters insisted on absolutely dry ground before firing. Nevertheless, we built a roaring fire in an attempt to dry the ground somewhat and constructed a makeshift wind break. After preheating several Caddoan style vessels which had been provided by the seminar instructor, the vessels were placed in the coals and the fire rebuilt. The pitch-soaked fuel and the wind conspired to provide a very fast and very hot fire. During the firing, dull explosions from within indicated that this activity was not to be a complete success.

While the fire and pots were cooling, the hands-on pottery making session was begun. Everyone—women, men, and children—enthusiastically joined in the wedging of the clay to prepare it for pot making. It has been the instructor's experience that the wedging, coiling, and shaping of clay into pottery vessels is a relaxing experience. As the work in the seminar proceeded, the group, composed of Caddo Tribal members of all ages and gender, some TAS members, and the instructor, became voluble as the pounding and shaping of the clay removed any remaining doubts and inhibitions. Clearly, pot-making could be a social affair. In this case, it became a means for two cultures and different ideologies to see that there was a common goal for the Caddo and archaeologists. Although the resulting pots—instructor's included—were hardly comparable to the prehistoric Caddoan works of art, the level of understanding and camaraderie achieved by this remarkable event was significant. Even if that was all that was achieved, then the seminar was a success. We also hope that further sessions in the future may kindle a resurgence of interest in ceramic manufacture so that the Caddo may reclaim another part of their long and rich history.

Overall, our interaction with the Caddo Tribe during the archaeological field schools turned out to be one of our most rewarding accomplishments. Although much important archaeological information was obtained and will appear in print during coming years, both field schools were greatly enhanced by the involvement of the Caddo people. New friendships were established and new lines of communication were opened. Both will undoubtedly help us as we address future and potentially difficult issues such as working with provisions of the Native American Graves Protection and Repatriation Act. We have also learned that the Caddo are very interested in the results of our archaeological efforts, but that we need to develop more effective ways to share our results with them. Our standard technical reports, copies of which have been provided to them in the past, are not an effective means of communication. Many members of the tribe have been attending the Caddo Conference, an annual meeting of archaeologists working on Caddoan archaeology. These meetings are a step in the right direction, but we believe our efforts with the Caddo people during the field schools show that personal interaction is the best method of sharing ideas and information.

SAA Bulletin, January 1994

Collaboration at *Inyan Ceyaka Atonwan* (Village at the Rapids)

Janet D. Spector

In my 30-year career as an archaeologist, the first occasion I ever had to work with Indian people was in fieldwork at Little Rapids, a nineteenth-century Wahpeton Dakota summer planting village located in south-central Minnesota. Our collaborations began somewhat late in the project, in 1986, the fourth and final year of fieldwork. The effects were nonetheless dramatic, transforming the character of our field program and my perception of the nineteenth-century Wahpeton community.

Why did it take so long to become involved in a collaborative project? Nothing in my disciplinary training at the University of Wisconsin (1960s–1970s) predisposed or prepared me to work collaboratively. On reflection, I see that there were many disincentives for doing so—few of them deliberate but powerful nonetheless. My training was fairly conventional for a specialty in the history and culture of Indian people in the Upper Midwestern United States—in my case, during the period of colonial expansion. This apprenticeship discouraged me from even imagining productive collaborations between Indian and non-Indian people in archaeology. These are some of the messages I absorbed:

Message 1: I learned that Indian people did not participate in archaeology as teachers, authors, or excavators. I had no models—positive or negative—of non-Indian archaeologists working with Indian educators, spiritual or community leaders.

Message 2: There is very little connection between contemporary Indian people in our region and the people we study archaeologically even in fairly recent time periods. "Contact" with Europeans quickly led to acculturation, dislocation, cultural disintegration, and a breakdown of cultural distinctiveness and vitality. Our training implied that modern Indian people had little knowledge about the past. Too much time had elapsed; too much had been lost.

These presumed ruptures between past and present are reinforced in the ways our discipline is sub-divided, our majors are organized and courses taught, and our research designed. Anthropology fragments our knowledge about Indian histories and cultures by breaking the field into cultural anthropology and archaeology. The former conventionally studied "traditional Indian cultures" in the timeless, "ethnographic present"; while the latter studied groups known primarily through the archaeological record, and neither showed much interest in contemporary people, or, until recently, the period of colonization. Archaeological "cultures" are very distinct from those known ethnographically. We define cultures taxonomically, on the basis of characteristic material objects and we name groups after geographic or time periods (Mississippian, Woodland, Archaic, and Oneota) rather than ancient Winnebago, Dakota, or Anishinabe, in our area, as if these groups had no relationship to one another.

Message 3: Indian people today are interested in archaeological sites artifacts for "political" reasons, not because of cultural or historical interests. This cynical view is reinforced by the general absence of courses about local colonial history and the lingering legacies of those distressing times, particularly from the Indian perspective. In our region, transcripts of nineteenth-century treaty negotiations document a 150-year history of Indian concerns about the desecration of burial and other sacred sites. These protests predate by just a few decades the extensive archaeological surveys and later excavations of mounds and other earthworks which laid the foundation for regional archaeology—projects done without Indian participation or consent. Archaeology students would be well served by knowing about this history of relations between Indians and archaeologists.

These are just some of the messages I received during my enculturation into archaeology and they created real barriers against imagining active, mutually respectful relationships with Indian people. These barriers began to diminish for me only after becoming involved in feminist anthropology and archaeology. Over the last two decades, feminist, third world, African-American, Chicano, and American Indian scholars, activists, and their allies have seriously challenged many academic disciplines including anthropology and archaeology. What are the ramifications of the fact that until fairly recently academic knowledge has been produced almost exclusively by white, middle-class men of European descent, socialized in cultures that discriminate on the basis of race, sex, and class? How has this domination by a rather narrow segment of the population determined the curriculum and the content of courses we teach? our research priorities? the projects that get funded? the manuscripts that get published?

Across the disciplines we have exposed pervasive androcentric and eurocentric (less delicately put sexist, racist, heterosexist, and classist) portrayals of human life, past and present. We have shown that who we are—our gender, cultural background, social and economic position, and personal histories—shapes the character of our work in significant ways. And we have called for more responsible academic work, acknowledging that those of us who produce public knowledge about other people hold a powerful and privileged position.

As my own criticisms of archaeology became increasingly pointed with respect to the treatment of women as subjects of study, I also became acutely aware of the exclusion of Indian people from the creation of archaeological knowledge about their histories and cultures. For some time, the dissonance between my critique of archaeology and its exclusions, and my lack of contact with Dakota people on the Little Rapids project became almost unbearable. At that point I became more active in pursuing a collaboration.

Collaborations at Little Rapids

Initiated in 1979, the goal of the Little Rapids project was to learn about the Wahpeton community life during a turbulent and poorly known period—a time of rapidly accelerating Euroamerican settlement and escalating tensions between cultures as U.S. government officials and Protestant missionaries pressured Dakota people to give up their lands and ways of life. I was particularly interested in understanding more about how these pressures affected men and women and how gender roles, relations, and beliefs shaped the character of encounters between Dakota people and Euroamerican colonists.

Though I was unsure of how to begin, I was committed to making contact with Indian people. In the process of securing permission to excavate at Little Rapids from the landowners and the state archaeologist, I sent my project proposal to the (now) Minnesota Indian Affairs Council. Within a few weeks, the Council's Executive Director Donald Gurnoe sent me a copy of his letter to Norman Crooks, then chairman of the Prior Lake Sioux Community, the Dakota community geographically closest to Little Rapids. "Many times in the past," Gurnoe wrote,

> the scientific community has run afoul of Indian people through failure to communicate and their insensitive approach to the concerns of the community. This, apparently, is not the case in respect to this project, as Professor Spector has made every effort to enlist the support of Indian people through our offices (Gurnoe to Crooks, April 7, 1980).

This response encouraged me to pursue direct contacts with Dakota people. Chris Cavender, now professor of American Indian Studies at SW State University in Marshall, Minnesota, was referred to me as a well known Dakota educator. He was not available at that time and I began the project without further Indian participation.

We excavated at Little Rapids from 1980 to 1982 through the University of Minnesota's archaeological field school program, then suspended excavations to complete the analysis of those materials. In 1984–1985, while on sabbatical, I felt I could no longer, in good conscience, continue doing Dakota archaeology without their involvement.

I tried again, this time successfully, to reach Cavender. Our initial conversation was awkward. It seemed late to be consulting him about a project designed several years earlier without any Dakota input. Chris had never heard of Little Rapids, and although he was cordial, he was distant, and I suspected, suspicious. Candid about his views of "anthros" as he calls us, Chris was quite open in his cynicism about the motives of academics, including me.

In our initial conversation I mentioned that nineteenth century written records consistently named Mazomani as a prominent leader at Little Rapids. Chris said nothing about this at the time, but later he asked if we could visit the site together. Mazomani, it turned out, was related to him through his mother, Elsie Cavender, who was raised by her grandmother, daughter of Mazomani and Blueberry Woman. Over the next few months Chris and I made a number of trips to Little Rapids, often bringing other family members along. We had long conversations about the tensions between archaeologists and Indian people. I learned a good deal about Chris's family history. His mother was a well known oral historian, particularly knowledgeable about the 1862 conflict between some Dakota people and some of the newly arrived American settlers and U.S. soldiers that ultimately led to the forced exile of Dakota people from Minnesota.

Being at the site with people having a direct kinship link to it was a profoundly moving experience. We shared a deep respect for the place that, unlike many Indian sites in our area, had been shielded from plowing, construction and other modern destructions. The only major disturbances there had been done by decades of amateur archaeologists drawn to Little Rapids by the burial mounds at the southern end of the site, their activities permanently etched into the landscape. Though Indian visitors knew we were not digging in or near the cemetery, it was excruciating to walk near the scarred, sacred mounds with them.

As the 1985–1986 school year began, Chris and I planned to teach together at Little Rapids. We secured university funding and recruited other instructors for the field program: Carolynn Schommer, a Dakota language instructor at the University of Minnesota and also a descendant of Mazomani, introduced crew members to the Dakota language, tailoring her lessons to our specific work. Ed Cushing, a university ecologist, led students on environmental field trips teaching them about the natural history of the area. He, Chris, and Carolynn compared Dakota and non-Dakota names for and ideas about the local plants that were—and still are—important to Dakota people. Sara Evans, a history professor, helped us critically evaluate nineteenth-century written records, and Chris shared what he knew from Dakota sources about the people and events described in those documents.

Finally, a project felt right to me. We worked as an interdisciplinary, multicultural team. Every day Chris and Carrie talked about Dakota family, community, and spiritual life; about Dakota philosophy, place names, and the Dakota council fires; and we talked about the Conflict of 1862 and its tragic aftermath. We also talked about racism—nineteenth century and contemporary—including incidents that erupted during the field season.

Before we began to dig, Chris spoke briefly in Dakota, expressing our collective respect for the spirit of the place and our hopes to be guided by wisdom and sensitivity in our treatment of the people who once lived there. A pipe ceremony was conducted by Amos Owen, a Dakota elder and spiritual leader who communicated in words that had been spoken at Little Rapids for centuries before the voices were silenced there in the 1850s.

Those of us with previous field experience appreciated the 1986 season even more than the novice crew members who had no basis for program comparisons. We found it extraordinary to work with people who had direct family ties to the place and history we were studying; extraordinary to hear Dakota spoken there after the silences of more than a century and a half; extraordinary to share the pipe with a Dakota spiritual leader. The student apprentices could not imagine archaeology being done any other way.

It was hard to resist romanticizing our Dakota colleagues. Just as we sometimes fantasized about finding an ideal archive or a key artifact that would reveal elusive aspects of the past, most of us also hoped that Chris and Carrie would have special insights about the site or the recovered artifacts. Though they connected us to the past in very tangible ways each day, neither was particularly interested in the archaeology or the materials we unearthed. This was true of most of the Indian visitors to the site. Given the long history of tensions between Indians and archaeologists, I was grateful that Chris and Carrie had agreed to participate in the project at all. I know it was not without considerable ambivalence.

Writing About Little Rapids

In 1987 I began to write my book *What this Awl Means: Feminist Archaeology at a Wahpeton Dakota Village* (Spector 1993). I wanted to produce an accessible, human scale portrayal of the community; a rendering that would give readers an empathetic sense of the times as well as a feeling of the connections between that past and the present. I wanted to claim my own voice and authorship while simultaneously introducing other voices, visions, and perspectives. But each time I began to write I found myself tethered by the conventions of archaeological writing—the dull, lifeless, distanced, detached, and taxonomic rhetoric of our field—a rhetoric that subordinates the people we study.

I turned my attention to an artifact we had discovered in 1980 in a garbage dump, a 3″ antler awl handle, delicately inscribed with a series of dots and lines. The handle would have held a short, pointed, iron tip for perforating leather hides to be made into tipi covers, clothing, bags and other accessories.

In response to this evocative find, after discovering the meaning of the inscriptions—they were tallies women kept marking their hide-working accomplishments—I wrote a short interpretive narrative encapsulating a good deal about what we had learned about the Little Rapids community. This story sets the scene and the tone environmentally, culturally, and historically; it introduces some of the people associated with the site; it reveals what the awl might have meant to the woman who used it and to her community; and it suggests how the awl handle might have been discarded. The rest of the book unravels the narrative, layer by layer exposing what we learned through excavations, documents, and Dakota sources. I discuss how awls are traditionally treated by archaeologists (typologically if at all) and describe the history of relationships between Dakota and non-Dakota people including fur traders, military men, missionaries, and archaeologists. Mazomani's nineteenth-century family and their contemporary descendants are prominently featured throughout the book. The book is partly a critique of archaeology, partly a professional memoir and story of the dig, and partly a community study, all presented with as little archaeological jargon as possible.

The collaborative relations continued throughout the writing and publication process. I presented early versions of the interpretive narrative to Chris and his family members and to Indian studies classes on numerous occasions. These were important facets of revising the manuscript. Editors at the Minnesota Historical Society Press continued consultations with Indian people. The manuscript was sent to both archaeologists and Indian educators for review. The Indian readers urged me to write more about the damages done by amateur archaeologists at Little Rapids, more about Indian criticisms of archaeology and about repatriation issues and laws, and to say more about the ethics of digging one part of the site that might have been a Medicine Dance area.

Conclusion

The collaborative work on the Little Rapids project was an entirely rewarding experience. My relationships with members of Mazomani's family have broadened and deepened since I first worked with Chris and Carrie, enriching my work and life. Regretfully, there are still major barriers against collaborative work in archaeology in our area and in a university setting: it is very costly to support team-taught field programs; few Indian faculty resources or students are at the University and potential colleagues are more likely found outside of the academy and often without the credentials required for staff appointments; and many archaeologists are still resistant to sharing the power and privilege of setting archaeological priorities and standards involved in serious collaborative work. Nonetheless, I can't imagine doing the archaeology of Indian people without their active and vital participation. An inclusive archaeology will entail more than simply adding the voices of so-called "others." It will transform the ways we practice archaeology and the way we view and portray the past, enriching our discipline. Our future depends on it.

SAA Bulletin, June 1994

The Integration of Traditional and Scientific Knowledge on Leech Lake Reservation, Cass Lake, Minnesota

Rose Kluth

When asked to submit an article for the Working Together column, I experienced the same reactions that I always do when asked to represent the reservation on tribal issues—apprehension followed by a sense of responsibility. The reason for this is simple—I am a non-Indian archaeologist who believes that Indian people should represent themselves regarding these sensitive issues that are very close to their heart. However, the reason that I was employed by the reservation was to do exactly this—bring their opinions and ideas directly to the archaeological community by using my acquired training and skills. For this reason and because they have entrusted me with their knowledge, I feel a responsibility to bring this information to you through this forum.

Traditional vs. Scientific Knowledge

Integrating scientific and traditional knowledge on archaeological projects is an attainable goal. However, there are inherent challenges in combining these approaches. We have been successful in incorporating traditional and scientific research in the Leech Lake Heritage Sites Program. While this approach may not work for all tribes due to differing perspectives on archaeology, our program has served the needs of the Leech Lake Reservation well. I will first present a discussion of the mission and objectives of the Leech Lake Heritage Sites Program, offering examples of integrating traditional knowledge into Section 106 compliance and tribal archaeology projects.

The Leech Lake Heritage Sites Program is a part of the Division of Resource Management of Leech Lake Reservation in north-central Minnesota. The objective of our program is to provide cultural resource management services from a Native American perspective. These services are provided to federal and state agencies, and include all facets of Section 106 compliance. We exclusively hire Native Americans to participate in this program, and provide training supplemented with on-the-job education. What sets our program apart from others is that the employees provide us with a unique perspective about prehistoric cultural materials, as well as how to deal with sensitive sites and objects in a manner that is acceptable to their cultural beliefs.

Typically, Native Americans have not been encouraged to participate in the preservation process. Traditional beliefs have led some Native American people to avoid the field entirely. In the past, most archaeological fieldwork was performed by non-Native Americans, and the resulting reports were reviewed by non-Native Americans, even if the project involved tribal lands. At no point in the process was there a mechanism for Native American review or consultation, even if burials were involved. This process has changed dramatically within the last decade, with the implementation of federal legislation such as NAGPRA and the 1992 amendments to the National Historic Preservation Act. At last, the time has arrived for Native Americans to play a primary role in the preservation process.

Before discussing the integration of traditional and scientific archaeology, we must define both. *Traditional knowledge* is a compilation of the knowledge of tribal culture history, past and present lifeways, language, spirituality, rituals, and ceremonies. This knowledge is gained by living the culture and by listening to the stories and oral histories of elders, parents, and grandparents. *Scientific knowledge* is knowledge that is obtained through testable and reproducible data. Archaeological data, and the means employed to obtain that data, are, for the purposes of this discussion, an example of scientific knowledge.

Incorporating Traditional Knowledge in Section 106 Compliance Work

To accurately convey the process of integrating traditional and scientific knowledge within our program, I will first discuss the incorporation of tradition on a daily basis. Following this, four projects will be presented. Each project is an example of what we consider to be the successful integration of both traditional and scientific knowledge.

Daily Traditions

When the cultural resources management program was created, the employees were consulted about their concerns regarding archaeological fieldwork. Several individuals mentioned that their grandmothers had told them never to work on or near burial sites, and that they should smudge themselves with sage or cedar every morning before work. They were also instructed to place tobacco on the ground before excavating. This was to be done as a sign of respect to Mother Earth for the disturbance that was about to take place. They were warned that if they did not do these things, they or their families might be hurt. Also, they expressed concern about the use of alcohol on the job—this must be avoided in order to maintain respect with the spirit world and Mother Earth. After hearing their concerns, we assured them that an ample supply of cedar, sage, and tobacco would be on hand for them to complete these functions before beginning fieldwork, and any necessary ceremonies should be completed as they saw fit. By doing this we have created an atmosphere that is comfortable and respectful to the needs of the crew without in any way affecting contractual needs or specifications.

The Ogema-Geshik Site

In summer 1993 we were asked to investigate a possible archaeological site disturbance in the northwestern corner of the reservation. A survey to determine site limits was initiated, as was an evaluation of the level of site disturbance.

Shovel tests were placed on a 10-m grid in order to determine the horizontal and vertical extent of the site. During shovel testing, four bear claws were found in a single shovel test. The bear claws were removed and bagged for transport back to the lab, along with the other artifacts located that day. Later, one of the crew members, speaking with the field director, said that he was a member of the Bear Clan and requested that the field director place the bear claws back where they were found. The field director complied, and the bear claws were reburied in their original location. The crew member placed tobacco near this location. This individual was satisfied with the resolution, and felt comfortable with our reporting the information in the final archaeology report.

Fieldwork continued at the site, and the crew located human remains. These remains were immediately reburied by the same crew members. They then placed tobacco near the area where the remains were found, as well as a dish with food for the spirit of that individual. They spoke to the spirit, asking the spirit to understand that they meant no harm, and that they would move away from the area. The crew members discussed the situation with the field director and requested that they move their shovel tests back at least 200 ft from this area, as they felt that it was a very sacred area that must not be disturbed. We complied, continuing our survey, and were able to delineate site limits without further disturbance to the sacred areas. We uncovered the remains of an important prehistoric wild ricing site, obtained the information needed to make an assessment of the site, and the crew felt comfortable working in the area because proper respect had been paid to the sacred areas.

U.S. Tribal Highway (USTH) 169 Project

In summer 1995 we completed an archaeological survey for the Minnesota Department of Transportation along a portion of USTH 169 in north-central Minnesota, near the Mille Lacs Reservation. We maintained daily contact with Mille Lacs Reservation staff, informing them of our progress. Before excavating test units, an intact catlinite pipe was found eroding from a bank located above an old roadbed. When the pipe was discovered, we immediately contacted Mille Lacs Reservation staff, who met us at the site. The crew members did not remove the pipe from the ground, but rather left it in situ for the Mille Lacs staff to observe. The Mille Lacs staff wanted the pipe reburied immediately as they felt that it indicated the presence of an Ojibwe burial site. They reburied the pipe out of the proposed right-of-way, west of the area where it was found. Our crew was instructed to place our test units away from the area where the pipe was originally located. We respected their concerns and completed our excavations away from this area. As a result of our fieldwork, we determined that this site was eligible for listing in the National Register of Historic Places. We were able to complete the archaeological fieldwork, yet respect the concerns and traditional beliefs of the Mille Lacs Reservation representatives.

NAGPRA

In fall 1993 we received more than 200 museum inventories of sacred objects, unassociated funerary objects, and objects of cultural patrimony that may have been associated with the Leech Lake Anishinabe people. In order to begin the NAGPRA process, the Leech Lake Tribal Council created an elder council, called the Leech Lake Advisory Council on Cultural Resources. The council was to work with the heritage sites program director in deciding whether these objects should be repatriated. After many prayers, meetings and discussions, the elder council determined that the way to proceed was to combine oral and written histories regarding these objects. The council asked me to visit all museums in Minnesota in order to determine if their collections contained items that could be attributed to the Leech Lake Anishinabe people. If so, these objects would be brought back to the reservation and dealt with in the proper traditional manner. All of the meetings to date have involved much prayer and a great deal of discussion regarding the old ways and the proper and respectful disposition of these objects. However, the council has chosen to rely on existing museum records to determine which objects came from the Leech Lake Anishinabe people and has combined both written and oral histories in its work with NAGPRA.

Pug Hole–Klein Lot Site

In summer 1995 we completed an archaeological survey on Leech Lake Reservation tribal lands before leasing a lakeshore lot. A previously recorded site was relocated, and the site limits were expanded to include the lot in question. Severe erosion was noted on the lake side of the lot. Later that summer, human remains were found exposed within the eroded area. A representative of our elder council was contacted, and he came with us to the site to rebury the remains. He instructed us to remove only those remains that were actually visible. We were not to displace any soil to remove any of the human remains still located within the bank. These remains were reburied on the lot farther inland from the shoreline.

A meeting was held to discuss possible methods to halt the erosion. Because an archaeological site was located on this lot, I was consulted regarding erosion control methods. Would it be possible to plant trees on the lot, or should the bank be shored with large stones? I contacted our elder council for advice. One of our elders said that the shore should be left to erode, as it was a natural process that should not be fought. He said that the spirit of the human remains that were still buried there either wanted to move to the water in order to be near the water spirits or they were on the next step of their journey. He said that if we placed rock on the eroded area it would not stay put, as the spirits in that area would be much more powerful than any stones. He said that it would be dangerous for a heavy equipment operator to drive over this site, as he might be injured or killed because of his actions. His decision was respected, and the site was left alone. Although it was difficult for me to allow the site to erode, I felt that we must heed the traditional knowledge of the elders. There was no alternative once we understood. It was a decision that respected the elders' traditional knowledge.

Discussion

These examples are specific to our reservation and tribal archaeology program. We understand that it may not be feasible for archaeologists to access traditional knowledge in many settings. However, I strongly encourage communication between archaeologists and Native Americans in a manner that is appropriate and respectful to tribes and amenable to archaeologists.

I read again with interest previous Working Together articles. There is a commonality in approaches between tribal archaeology programs, with a strong reliance on oral histories and a respect for traditional knowledge. After reading these articles I was proud to have been asked to participate in this forum. However, I hope that we do not suggest that archaeologists cannot work with tribes regarding archaeological issues. John Allison's 1996 submission was somewhat unsettling to me for this reason. Allison states that "I tend to get a little impatient . . . reading articles by archaeologists who still don't get 'it'," and "There are lots of jokes among tribal people about the ignorant anthropologists asking ridiculous questions and getting ridiculous answers from people who don't trust them" (1996:14). These types of statements have undoubtedly angered and frightened archaeologists away from the tribal consultation process for years, and I believe they have also hampered the NAGPRA process. If we tell archaeologists that their questions and process are ridiculous, why will they bother to consult with tribes except when they absolutely must? We have to encourage dialogue between the archaeological and tribal communities rather than inflaming both sides.

Archaeologists have to be informed as to what the "rules" are when working with tribal people. On the other hand, they must understand that a lack of trust exists because, in the past, archaeologists have not consulted with Native Americans regarding their projects, and they have not trusted their oral histories when presented as evidence. This has been made clear to me through the NAGPRA process—if we can find a written history documenting cultural affiliation between human remains or sacred objects, this serves as evidence for the proof of cultural affiliation. In the current climate, traditional knowledge simply does not carry the weight that a written history does.

There has to be an outreach from the Native American community as well as from the archaeological community in order to share perspectives. We are all a part of our own culture; my culture places a strong emphasis on scientific research and data. Native American culture places a great emphasis on oral histories and traditional beliefs. Neither is wrong. We must come together and try to understand the other. If we do not, we will be battling the same issues over and over again with bad feelings on both sides. I believe that we can work together because we have the same goals—site protection and a knowledge of past lifeways. Through frank communication, we can work toward those goals.

SAA Bulletin, September 1996

Postscript

Much has changed in the field of historic preservation since this article was published. Tribes are now active, recognized participants in the Section 106 process, not only through the establishment of Tribal Historic Preservation Offices, but also through the new Section 106 regulations that became effective June 17, 1999. These new regulations recognize the unique role of tribes in the Section 106 process by acknowledging tribal sovereignty and recognizing the government-to-government relationship between tribes and the federal government. Although these regulations do not please all parties, I believe that they are a dramatic step in the right direction for opening the doors, or perhaps forcing the door open, to communication between federal agencies and tribes.

Recent meetings regarding the new Section 106 regulations revealed that many federal agency personnel are fearful of the potential problems in having to work closely with tribes on historic preservation issues, both on and off-reservation. This is an attitude that escapes me, as it has been my experience at Leech Lake Reservation that our historic preservation staff work overtime to ensure that the Section 106 process runs smoothly. I also believe that coming to the table with an attitude of reluctance and anger will do nothing to move the preservation process forward. However, I will not lay all of the problems on the tables of the federal agency representatives. What has become clear to me is that tribes must take the lead in providing federal agencies with guidance regarding the most puzzling issues for preservation professionals, including:

- What are Traditional Cultural Properties (TCPs)? How can they be located and documented in a respectful manner during the Section 106 process?

- What is the difference between historic properties with religious or cultural significance and TCPs? What is the role of the federal agency in documenting these sites?

- What is adequate and respectful consultation with tribes? How should consultation be initiated and continued through the Section 106 process to ensure that adequate consultation has occurred?

- Which tribes should be consulted regarding an upcoming federal undertaking? Where can information be obtained regarding which tribes to contact regarding an upcoming undertaking so that no one is inadvertently omitted from the process?

Federal agency representatives are quite concerned about these issues and tribes are the only ones that can help answer these questions. Tribes must show federal agency personnel the correct procedure to respectfully open dialogue. Federal agencies must recognize the validity of oral information provided by tribes and that trust between both parties must be established before effective communication can take place. These new changes are an opportunity for all for positive dialogue and a chance for open communications rather than as hurdles to overcome.

Archaeology and Alutiiq Cultural Identity on Kodiak Island

Rick Knecht

The Kodiak Archipelago covers an area the size of Massachusetts, and lies in the Gulf of Alaska on the northern edge of the Pacific. Six native villages, reachable only by boat or air taxi, cling to the coastal fringe that surrounds the mountainous interior of Kodiak Island. The Alutiiq people survived successive occupations by Russian fur hunters and American settlers. By the end of the nineteenth century there was too little left of the culture to attract anthropologists; as a result, no traditional ethnography exists for the Alutiiq. Collectors have long since scoured the villages for remaining Alutiiq material culture on behalf of museums in the "lower 48" and Europe. Elders, with childhood memories of being beaten in BIA schools for even speaking Alutiiq to each other, were sometimes reluctant to teach the young people. Others simply were unable to speak above the noise of television sets. Archaeological publications were technical and found in journals that still remain inaccessible to most people. As late as the 1980s, Alutiiq students in village schools were told that theirs had been a simple "stone-age" culture. Perhaps more than anywhere else in Alaska, native culture had been erased from the landscape.

In 1983 Richard Jordan, then at Bryn Mawr College, began a long-term research project on Kodiak, near the village of Karluk. We began the project in the usual fashion, asking permission from Koniag Inc., the regional native corporation, and the Karluk Village Council. Some elders had bitter memories of Ales Hrdlička, a physical anthropologist working out of the Smithsonian Institution, who in the 1930s had removed hundreds of human skeletons from a site in Larsen Bay, still known locally as the "bone yard." In an effort to allay any lingering doubts about our intentions, we regularly invited our neighbors in Karluk over to see our finds, and increasing numbers of people came to watch us excavate. As we puzzled over the past together, it became clear to both archaeologists and the native community that neither had a monopoly on knowledge; we needed each other to truly understand the culture history of the island. An exchange that began as professional etiquette became a mainstay in research.

In 1984, when Jordan's proposal to the National Science Foundation was turned down, the native community came to the rescue. The Kodiak Area native Association (KANA), a regional nonprofit corporation administering health, education, and economic development projects, was then headed by Gordon Pullar. An Alutiiq leader with undergraduate training in anthropology and a deep interest in cultural preservation, Pullar encouraged us to return to Kodiak, and helped by providing crew members through a youth employment program. The village of Karluk donated the use of a house, and residents often stopped by with freshly caught salmon and halibut.

I directed the field school composed of eight native high school students from Karluk, who, to our mutual delight, quickly became superb field technicians. Together we excavated the first complete Alutiiq dwelling, recovering more than 2,000 artifacts. Their families got daily updates on our discoveries, and the interest of the native community in archaeology continued to grow. We finished the project three weeks ahead of schedule, and joined Jordan's crew on a prehistoric wet site where we found a wealth of wooden artifacts and artwork. At the end of the season Karluk invited every village on the island to attend a potlatch, along with a day-long workshop on archaeology, site tours, and a display of the season's finds.

Plane loads of visitors arrived from around the island. The level of interest and enthusiasm was intense. During the question and answer period we were asked what would eventually happen to the artifacts after study was completed. Faces fell when we replied that the only available repository for archaeological material in Alaska was at the University of Alaska Museum in Fairbanks, some 800 miles to the north. A consensus was quickly reached that a local museum dedicated to Alutiiq culture, with the needed climate controls and secure facilities sufficient to house the Karluk One collection, was needed. Other collections and objects long absent from the island could also be returned. As archaeologists, we pledged to join the native community in making the project a reality.

KANA established a Culture Heritage Committee, which visited museums around the country and met with their staffs. Nancy Fuller of the Smithsonian's Office of Museum Programs offered sound advice: "Don't wait for your museum building to begin your cultural preservation programs." Accordingly, I was hired in spring 1987 as a coordinator for KANA's newly formed Culture and Heritage Department. Resources were admittedly scarce at first; I wrote the first grant on a chair in the hallway, on a borrowed clipboard. By 1990, however, KANA had established the Alutiiq Culture Center to house programs, equipment and a rapidly growing collection.

The 1987 season was the last of five field seasons undertaken by KANA and Bryn Mawr; Jordan moved on to University of Alaska-Fairbanks, working with KANA on joint research projects until his untimely death in 1991. KANA continued to support archaeological fieldwork, both independently and in cooperation with universities and museums. At least one and often multiple archaeological field projects have been underway on Kodiak every summer.

Amy Steffian directed excavations at Hrdliçka's old site in Larsen

Bay, this time with Alutiiq crew members and support from the village and KANA. Human remains encountered in this and other projects are studied and reburied in accordance with the wishes of the native community closest to the site. In 1991, after a long battle with the Smithsonian, and the help of the native American Rights Fund and KANA Larsen Bay residents prevailed in their request to have the remains removed by Hrdlička returned. More than 700 individuals' remains were returned for reburial, opening a new era in relations with the Smithsonian. KANA also helped support important prehistoric excavations by Philomena Knecht in Chiniak, Chris Donta in Monashka Bay, and Neal Crozier in Larsen Bay, as well as numerous research efforts by other anthropologists and ethnohistorians.

In 1990 KANA, the University of California-Berkeley, and the Sakhalin Regional Museum, USSR, conducted a joint research project at Three Saints Bay, the first Russian settlement in Alaska, which was directed by Aron Crowell. More than 40 field school students from Berkeley and the native community on Kodiak participated, as well as five Russian archaeologists.

In summer 1991 I accompanied three Alutiiq college students to the then Soviet Union. Valery Shubin had invited us to join him in excavating a site in the Kurile Islands, where some Kodiak and Aleut peoples were settled by the Russian-American Company in the early nineteenth century. We uncovered the remains of house pits and artifacts identical to those we knew from Kodiak.

In recent years, village and regional native corporations of the Kodiak Island area have begun to assess the archaeological resources on their lands. In 1992 the Old Harbor Native Corporation sponsored excavations on the Awa'uq Refuge Rock, a fortified sea stack, which was the scene of an attack by Russian fur hunters on an Alutiiq group in 1784. This was the first excavation of an Alutiiq refuge rock, and it provided data on a tragic event absent from school history books.

Site survey supported by Akhiok-Kaguyak Corporation yielded the discovery of a site nearly 3 km long on the upper reaches of the Ayakulik River, where we mapped about 150 prehistoric housepits. We also investigated the Alitak petroglyphs, and at Russian Harbor, located and mapped the site of the first recorded contact between Russians and Alutiiq people in 1763. In 1992 and 1993, with the support of Afognak Joint Venture, Inc., and Afognak native Corporation, we conducted a large-scale excavation at Malina Creek, a large prehistoric midden in danger of being lost to erosion. Site surveys near the village of Old Harbor, directed by Ben Fitzhugh, were partially supported by the Old Harbor Native Corporation. At least 80 new sites were recorded during the 1993 and 1994 seasons. Rescue archaeology this spring sponsored by Koniag, Inc., resulted in the recovery of 5,000 mostly wooden artifacts from the Karluk One Site, which is rapidly eroding.

In an effort to continue archaeological field work on a meaningful scale, Afognak native Corporation in the summer of 1994 began an ecotourism program, called "Dig Afognak." Paying participants joined archaeologists as they excavated sites and conducted surveys. It is hoped that this three-year pilot project will spread to other regions, particularly where sites are threatened by erosion or development. In addition, Afognak native Corporation annually donates a percentage of its profits to support the Alutiiq Culture Center.

Archaeological research, combined with oral histories shared by the elders, has been integrated into a wide variety of programs aimed at preserving and sharing Alutiiq culture as a whole, and has evolved into a grass-roots Alutiiq cultural renaissance on Kodiak Island. Training in cultural resource management has been provided for native land managers, and a site watch program helps prevent losses from vandalism and erosion. The Lost Village Project documents villages abandoned since 1900, integrating site survey, historic archives, and oral histories. In other projects, traditional meeting houses were constructed in villages, and the Kodiak Tribal Council established an Alutiiq dance group. Native artisans, drawing inspiration from artifacts and from KANA's slide collections of museum collections, began mask carving, and relearned the lost arts of making bentwood hats and skin-covered kayaks, An Alutiiq studies curriculum for village schools was developed, featuring detailed lessons in Alutiiq prehistory and language. Alutiiq heritage weeks are annu-

Sven Haakanson Jr. examining an artifact at the Malina Creek Site, Kodiak Island, Alaska. Photo by Rick Knecht, Alutiiq Museum archives
Photo courtesy of Alutiiq Museum

al events in village schools. Alutiiq culture has become part of the Kodiak landscape once again.

In 1988 KANA, with support from the Alaska Humanities Forum, sponsored the first Kodiak Cultural Heritage Conference, attracting 40 speakers from eight countries and native elders to celebrate the richness of Alutiiq culture. Within the island community, non-natives gained new insights and respect for native heritage. Many Alutiiq people also gained a sense of renewed respect for their heritage and, ultimately, themselves.

Last spring, ground-breaking ceremonies took place for the Alutiiq Archaeological Repository and Culture Center, an 11,000 ft^2 facility with state-of-the-art climate control and security. A $1.5 million grant from the Exxon Valdez Oil Spill Trustee Council was given to the Kodiak Area native Association to help restore archaeological sites damaged or vandalized in the wake of the 1989 oil spill. Joining the construction project is yet another village corporation: natives of Kodiak, Inc. The project succeeded because of heavy support by both the native and non-native residents of Kodiak Island.

An archaeological project has thus grown into a research effort undertaken by the Alutiiq people themselves, so that they, their children, and non-natives would better understand their history and cultural identity. Some former native field school students are now pursuing graduate degrees in anthropology. Others staff the archaeological laboratory at the Alutiiq Culture Center. The Alutiiq now plan, fund, and staff archaeological field and laboratory research, and are in a position to be in control of the preservation and interpretation of their own history.

The Alutiiq people have learned that there is a reason why governments worldwide invest in preserving their cultural heritage. Cultural identity and a sense of shared heritage are what binds a society together, and gives them power as a people. In this sense archaeologists have an opportunity to make their discipline meaningful to the lives of Native Americans; and in turn Native Americans can make archaeology more meaningful for all of us. As we have learned on Kodiak Island, archaeologists and native Americans have a shared interest in the past, and an attempt at a synthesis of these two bodies of knowledge is needed if we are to know it truly.

SAA Bulletin, November 1994

Postscript
Using the Community Archaeology Model Elsewhere in Alaska

In May 1995, some six months after this article was published in the *SAA Bulletin*, the Alutiiq Museum and Archaeological Repository opened its doors. The newly formed Alutiiq Dancers lined the entranceway resplendent in fur parkas, beaded headdresses, and elaborately painted bentwood hats. The ribbon was cut amidst a thunder of drumming and song. In the exhibit gallery were the artifacts that had been excavated over the past decades, along with family heirlooms, photographs, and artwork. For the communities of the Kodiak archipelago, the Alutiiq Museum was the culmination of a long-held dream.

The 4,500-ft^2 facility was built with the latest climate control, security, and storage equipment. The name "artifact repository" was appended as a reminder to government agencies and larger museums that the new institution was now one of two museums in Alaska that was ready and willing to curate archaeological collections. About one-third of the floor space was dedicated to compact storage systems for artifacts and archives. Another third of the building is a laboratory designed to process large numbers of incoming artifacts, for rescue archaeology on sites threatened by erosion and development is an unfortunate, but necessary, priority. The Karluk One wet site, described earlier, has since been completely lost to erosion. With a fully equipped local repository, the community has been able to respond quickly to these emergencies, saving artifacts and data that otherwise would have been lost.

Annual archaeological digs continue to include large number of local residents as crewmembers. The Afognak Native Corporations Dig Afognak eco-tourism project continues to flourish and has produced three dissertation projects in prehistoric and historic archaeology. Artifacts and data from the annual excavations help nourish the role of the museum as a regional culture center. The collections provide new inspiration to native artists. Alutiiq motifs and artists are now a highly visible and dynamic part of the Alaska artistic scene. The museum works with language preservation efforts and hosts an Alutiiq word-of-the-week program on public radio. Workbooks and other curriculum materials produced for local schools focus on archaeology as well as Alutiiq traditions and language. The museum also has just received a major grant for an exhibit of ethnographic material from Smithsonian collections, "Looking Both Ways," which is a cooperative effort between the museum and the Smithsonian's Arctic Studies Center in Anchorage. Local artisans have studied the parkas and other materials in the collections and produced replicas, reintroducing forgotten skills. Large portions of the long-eroded cultural landscape of the Kodiak Archipelago have been restored in recent years.

Perhaps the most significant outcome has been the pivotal role now played by the Alutiiq community in the stewardship of archaeological resources, not as a consulted party by a federal agency, but as the major funder, planner, and repository for archaeological work in the region. Aluttiq scholars who began as field school students on archaeological projects on Kodiak are now in the final stages of graduate training. Mark Rusk entered the Ph.D. program in anthropology at Brown University in 1999. Sven Haakanson Jr., from the village of Old Harbor, is completing his dissertation in anthropology at Harvard University and has just been hired as executive director of the Alutiiq Museum and Archaeological Repository.

Shortly after the museum's completion in 1995, I left Kodiak and moved to the Aleutian Islands to direct the planning for a regional museum to be built in Unalaska. We utilized the same model that had been successful in Kodiak, beginning with the involvement of residents in the planning and staffing of a community archaeological project. Rick Davis (Bryn Mawr College) and I directed two years of excavation at the Margaret Bay site which yielded more than 10,000 artifacts as well as data from a poorly-known period of Aleut prehistory. Professionals, students, and long-time residents worked side by side in both the field and laboratory. Interest and involvement with the museum project intensified. A proposed museum site was located within 100 ft of the Margaret Bay site.

A Museum Planning Committee was formed from representatives from the Qawalangin Tribe, the village, regional native corporations (Ounalashka Corporation, the Aleut Corporation), the City of Unalaska, and the public at large. It was the first time that all the local native entities and the city had met together for any reason and the successful working relationship that evolved has helped bring our community together. On August 28, 1999, the Museum of the Aleutians opened its doors to hundreds of residents from throughout the Aleutian and Pribilof Islands. It is a 9,400-ft^2 facility and fully equipped to preserve the archaeological and cultural heritage of the region. Located on land provided by the Ounalashka Corporation, it was constructed with $4 million from the City of Unalaska and displays collections held in trust for the other Aleut corporations and tribal entities of the region. The nearest comparable facility is 750 miles away—on Kodiak Island.

Archaeology, Education, and the Secwepemc

George P. Nicholas

When I completed my Ph.D. at the University of Massachusetts-Amherst, I had the usual expectations of obtaining a faculty position at a prestigious university. A year later, following a move to British Columbia, I was indeed teaching archaeology and anthropology in a university program, but one located on an Indian reserve. I have not once regretted this change of venue for it has led to my ongoing involvement with aboriginal peoples from across North America. Worldwide, the relationship between archaeology and indigenous peoples is now undergoing substantial change, and we are reaching the point where it may not be possible, nor desirable, to do archaeology without their involvement and collaboration. I thus feel privileged to be where I am and doing what I'm doing with the Secwepemc and other native peoples in such interesting times.

Secwepemc and Secwepemc Archaeology

The Secwepemc, or more commonly the Shuswap, are an Interior Salish people of south-central British Columbia. Their territory centers on the Fraser River and the North and South Thompson Rivers. Of the 17 bands that comprise the Secwepemc, the largest in population and land base is the Kamloops Band whose reserve is located adjacent to the city of Kamloops. The Kamloops Reserve has been a center for Secwepemc affairs for thousands of years and today includes both the Kamloops Indian Band and Shuswap Nation Tribal Council offices, and other agencies and programs. This reserve was also the location of a residential school in which traditional cultural and language was replaced with a Catholic/European Canadian equivalent.

In 1989 a collaborative educational program was initiated between the Secwepemc Cultural Education Society and Simon Fraser University (SCES/SFU) to establish a native-administered, native-run, postsecondary educational institute on the Kamloops Indian Reserve. The program would enhance the quality of life of native people; preserve, protect, interpret, and promote their history, language, and culture; and provide research and developmental opportunities to enable native people to control their own affairs and destiny.

Currently, the program offers a bachelor of general studies and bachelor of arts degrees, with majors and/or minors in anthropology, sociology, archaeology, First Nations studies, and linguistics, among other subjects, and several certificate programs. Over 100 lower- and upper-level university courses are offered each year, as well as several graduate courses. The program continues to expand and now has over 250 registered students. In 1993 the program was awarded the Canadian Association of University Continuing Education's Award for Excellence.

Virtually from the start, archaeology has been an important component of the SCES/SFU program. Degree-related options include both a major and a minor in archaeology, and a joint anthropology/archaeology major. Fifteen archaeology courses are currently offered, most on a regular basis, ranging from introductory courses on method and theory, to regional overviews, to such advanced courses as lithic technology, prehistoric human ecology, and archaeological theory. In addition, we try to customize standard courses or develop news ones pertinent to our students and the larger native community, as the following examples illustrate:

ARCH 386-Archaeological Resource Management introduces students to an in-depth and globally oriented examination of the problems of, and solutions to, the management of archaeological and cultural resources. Case studies on the management of archaeological resources in Africa, for example, or on such culturally sensitive issues as reburial and repatriation in Australia, can provide new ways of solving problems in North America. Guest speakers have included Chief Manny Jules (Kamloops Indian Band) and Brian Apland (B.C. Provincial Archaeologist).

ARCH 334-Archaeology for Educators is oriented to students who have a strong interest in archaeology, but plan to pursue a career as teachers at all grade levels. This course allows them an opportunity to integrate archaeology into their teaching: the earlier the values of the past are passed on to children, the greater their appreciation of archaeology will become. Such a course thus represents a type of cultural resource management that will prove very effective in the long run, providing it can be offered widely and regularly.

In 1994 we hosted the 4th B.C. Archaeology Forum where over 120 archaeologists, academics, and provincial and First Nations representatives gathered to discuss current events and issues affecting archaeology in the province. Since 1994 we have also administered the Alvin Jules Scholarship for First Nations Students, which is funded by contributions from consulting archaeologists throughout the province.

SCES/SFU Archaeology Field School

In addition to course work, additional training in archaeology is available through our archaeology field school, now entering its seventh consecutive year. The field school has focused on site survey, testing, and evaluation—skills clearly important to First Nations as they become increasingly involved in resource management. Much of our fieldwork has been directed to three important areas of research that complement and extend previous archaeological research in the region:

- Systematic survey and testing for early postglacial prehistoric sites, dating to between about 10,500 and 6,000 years ago, on high glacial lake terraces along the Thompson River valley—work that will contribute to a better understanding of the poorly known Early period in the southern interior of British Columbia;

- Investigation of long-term patterns of land use to determine how prehistoric peoples utilized the different landscapes that developed within the Thompson River valley in different ways over the last 10,000 years; and

- Examination of non-pithouse archaeological sites. The archaeology of the southern interior is dominated by the pithouse villages of the late Holocene; fieldwork directed to other types of sites provide a more representative view of the range of lifeways once present.

Our field studies have also been integrated into a three-year interdisciplinary study funded by Social Sciences and Humanities Research Council project on Traditional and Prehistoric Secwepemc Plant Use and Ecology. The project investigators, Nancy Turner, Marianne Ignace, Harriet Kuhnlein, Chief Ron Ignace, and myself, are examining:

- traditional ecological knowledge and its influences on sustainable plant harvesting;

- nutritional and pharmacological properties of traditional Secwepemc plant foods and medicines;

- botanical and linguistic evidence for the origins of prehistoric movements of Secwepemc peoples; and

- the archaeological evidence of the antiquity of these sustainable practices and the role of plant resources in the development of the Plateau culture. Project personnel include Secwepemc elders, students, and community members whose involvement may help to identify traditional use sites that are archaeologically invisible. Projects such as this represent an important link between cultural and natural resource management.

Along with its research orientation, the SCES/SFU Archaeology Field School has also been involved with cultural heritage projects on behalf of the Secwepemc people. For example, we are working with the Kamloops Band to mitigate the impact of a large housing development and golf course on and around a location where we had previously conducted extensive field studies. We also have conducted work on behalf of the Secwepemc Cultural Education Society and the Secwepemc Museum. These projects allow us to help the Secwepemc people balance current land use plans with heritage preservation, as well as to introduce our students to the very real demands of mitigative archaeology and to the rewards and frustrations that are part of cultural resource management.

Archaeological Problems and Prospects

The SCES/SFU Program and others like it have accomplished a great deal in terms of meeting the educational needs of First Nations. For our part, we are confident that our graduates, whether they go on to careers as farmers, educators, or band council members, carry with them knowledge that will someday be used as tools by their home communities and nations. This is especially so for those in the archaeology program, many of whom have gone on to full- or part-time employment with various aboriginal organizations, provincial agencies, and consulting archaeology companies. SCES/SFU alumni also are pursuing graduate studies in archaeology and anthropology.

Naturally, there are growing pains. Some relate to cultural differences that we, as educators, need to be sensitive to. Certain problems stem from the fact that First Nations peoples historically have been educationally disadvantaged, a problem only seriously addressed in recent years. Despite the apparent degree of acculturation in many native communities, there remain some important

Figure 1—John Jules (Kamloops Band) now oversees archaeological projects on the Kamloops Reserve.

cultural distinctions. For example, native students may miss classes not only when there is a death in their immediate (or more distant) family, but also when a relative is ill and needs their care, or when they need to spend time with the family of a recently deceased relative. The death of a community elder means that many students will be absent. Cultural differences also arise in the field; during the 1991 field school, several students would not touch any bone they found during site survey, even if it was obviously animal, although they would bring it to my attention.

It is important to expose archaeology students to many different value systems. To this end, in both 1993 and 1995, the SCES/SFU field school was run as a joint venture with the University College of the Cariboo and college anthropologist Catherine Carlson. This cooperative approach was designed both to allow aboriginal and non-aboriginal students to work together and to rotate them through two very different projects. Carlson has been investigating the contact-period native settlement associated with one of the first Hudson Bay trading posts in the area to explore native accommodation or resistance to European Canadian influences, while my work has focused on past human ecosystems, as outlined above. Two teams were formed to work on these projects, each containing students from both institutions; halfway through the field season, the students changed sites.

In terms of some of the larger issues relating to archaeology here, we would like to see an integrated approach to cultural heritage develop between SCES/SFU, the Kamloops Band, the Secwepemc Museum, and the Shuswap Nation Tribal Council. Many of the components are in place, and these organizations interact a good deal, but we still lack a formal structure to pull everything together in a ongoing, consistent manner. There are still too many gaps for sites to fall into, as illustrated in 1994 when a newly discovered site on the Kamloops Indian Reserve was threatened and later destroyed by road-widening work. To address these and other issues relating to heritage preservation, the Kamloops Band, working with several archaeologists, has recently developed a comprehensive archaeological resource policy.

In many places, the success of archaeology projects and cultural resource management strategies may be adversely influenced by band politics. This has not proved a noticeable problem on the Kamloops Indian Reserve. While there is naturally some dissension over certain issues within the community, our archaeology program continues to receive strong support from the Band Council and the Secwepemc people. However, there will always be those who remain wary of archaeologists, and unconvinced of their contributions. Some native interest groups are also openly opposed to any archaeology perceived to threaten their interests.

The importance of involving First Nations people in archaeology is derived from their different perspectives of the past and the role that archaeology can have illuminating that past. We encourage students in the SCES/SFU Program to think about issues and look forward to their innovative responses to this challenge. Non-native archaeologists also must learn to look at the past in different ways as well. Continuing a tradition begun by Eldon Yellowhorn, my teaching assistant in 1992, each year we now leave a tobacco offering before backfilling a site. Although my worldview is different from the Secwepemc's, the offering is given as an expression of respect for these people, both past and present, and of a continuing commitment to their heritage.

Training Native Archaeologists

Today, cooperative ventures, earning trust, advocacy, and the presentation of the past have become as much a part of archaeology as are locating sites and measuring artifacts. Archaeologists, for their part, need to recognize that they are dealing with members of a different culture and be flexible accordingly. How we discuss the peopling of the New World with native students is one area requiring a balance between scientific evidence and beliefs of an in situ creation.

Issues relating to the discovery of human remains and reburial and the preservation of sacred sites will always be sensitive ones. But even here there is much potential for innovative approaches. For example, native students with training in archaeology and physical anthropology,

Figure 2—Nola Markey (O`chi`chak`ko`cipi Crce) in foreground overseeing a Secwepemc Museum trainee.

and experience in different value systems, would serve an important role as cultural brokers between archaeologists and native communities to resolve problems relating to human remains and sacred sites.

As aboriginal archaeologists increase in number, they will confront a variety of moral and spiritual issues relating to animal and human bone and to spiritual or secret-sacred sites, especially within the context of archaeological heritage management, and will have to make decisions on their own or in consultation with elders and community members. In this context, non-aboriginal archaeologists may be able to offer little advice, since they may not be sensitive to, or knowledgeable about, belief systems and perceptions of the landscape different from their own. With the SCES/SFU program, we encourage our students to think about and discuss how they would approach such problems as these.

Conclusions

The collaboration between Simon Fraser University and the Secwepemc Cultural Education Society has made it possible to offer a university-based archaeology program directly to aboriginal people in a setting they are comfortable with. This has not only made such educational programs available to interested students, but has increased awareness in archaeology within the aboriginal community. And, on a personal note, it has enriched my life immeasurably.

Worldwide, indigenous peoples view archaeology with both apprehension and promise. Our task as archaeologists is to make what we do more accessible and understandable and to promote our field's various applications. Archaeology, after all, has a vital role is such areas as: nation (rebuilding); pursuing land claims; identifying and preserving heritage sites of local significance; verifying oral traditions; writing one's own history; and offering employment opportunities.

We must keep in mind, however, that it is not simply enough to teach indigenous peoples to do our version of archaeology. We need to recognize that cultural diversity does not apply only to lifeways and languages. There are other stories to hear about the past, told in voices that we may be unfamiliar with, largely because these people have not spoken before. There are other ways of knowing the past, other ways of interpreting the archaeological record, that we may be very uncomfortable with because they stem from different cultural traditions. The archaeologies that will emerge as indigenous people become archaeologists themselves will undoubtedly have a positive effect on the discipline. And these potentially different views of the past represent another type of cultural diversity—one that we, as anthropologists, have much to learn from.

SAA Bulletin, March 1997

Postscript

Things are seldom boring when it comes to archaeology and indigenous peoples. The past several decades have witnessed a long-overdue change in the way archaeologists have gone about their business, and even more profound changes are likely to appear in coming years. Throughout North America and elsewhere in the world, aboriginal people have begun to request a say in what happens to their own past. For a long time, when ethnographers and others entered the traditional territory of a society to spend time living among them, there often was a period of negotiation to obtain permission to conduct their studies. The ethnographers more often than not also took the time to learn as much of the language and customs as they could beforehand. Archaeologists, on the other hand, have grown accustom to conducting research with only minimal contact with the descendants of the societies they study, in part because those people have been largely invisible. In both Canada and the United States, the practice has become antiquated.

In British Columbia, consultation with the appropriate First Nation is now a prerequisite for obtaining an archaeological permit. This requirement occurred in response to demands for greater aboriginal representation, and overall, has had a positive impact on the discipline as it makes archaeologists more responsive to contemporary needs and their work more relevant. On the other hand, requests to Band Councils to review permit applications may sometimes strain the ability of those communities to evaluate them in both a timely and knowledgeable fashion. Not surprisingly, archaeology is generally of low priority in communities where health care, employment, access to resources, and land claims make more immediate demands. It is in helping First Nations balance their commitment to the present and the past that the SCES/SFU Archaeology Program may have its greatest utility.

The SCES/SFU Archaeology Program, now in its tenth year, continues to prosper. We continue our commitment to offering not only the basic field skills to aboriginal people by which they can obtain archaeology crew positions, but also the academic credentials necessary to become archaeologists themselves. To this end, we now have graduate students in both archaeology and anthropology who split their time between Kamloops and the main campus in Burnaby. Another development that provides new opportunities for our students is involvement in archaeological resource management projects. Since 1997, over 20 current and former students, all of whom had taken the Archaeology Field School, have been employed on CRM projects, and an equal number have received research grants. The experience gained in these projects adds significantly to the student's knowledge, to their "hireability," and to their potential contribution to their nation. A number of our former students is now working for their bands, helping them to make more informed decisions about current land use and cultural resources.

Our program's recognition by First Nations both in British Columbia and across Canada has been rewarding. On the other hand, there are occasional disappointments and frequent challenges. For example, I am surprised that so few aboriginal organizations are actively encouraging members to take advantage the opportunities we provide in archaeology. Not only is there a real need in Native organizations for people with an understanding of archaeology, but Aboriginal students with degrees or other qualifications in archaeology can virtually write their own job ticket. There are bands who recognize the need for aboriginal archaeologists, and those who strongly support archaeology in general, but even they sometimes appear not to follow through. There also is the challenge of "a little archaeology being a dangerous thing." I have met representatives of several bands who were under the impression that completion of an introductory course to archaeology would enable them to become the band's archaeologist. Finally, archaeology, a relatively complex discipline, may have a high attrition rate even in large university classes when it comes to such important courses as archaeological theory; small educational programs will have a harder time ensuring that all necessary courses are offered without resorting to a "dumbed-down" version.

Despite these stumbling blocks, I see aboriginal people assuming a significant role in how archaeology will be performed in the future. For now it is critical that we provide opportunities for Native Americans to understand more completely why archaeology is done in the first place, obtain the necessary skills to do it themselves, and have the knowledge required for informed decisions about their archaeological heritage. For their part, archaeologists need to make the effort to understand the position of aboriginal people. There are significant cultural differences that sometimes get lost in the politics. It also is important that we earn each other's trust; there may be times when archaeologists are forced to jump through hoops to demonstrate our commitment to working with tribal personnel. Patience is a hard lesson learned, but one of lasting value.

Finally, an important element in teaching archaeology to aboriginal people is knowing when to let go and to let them use the tools we offer as educators to explore their world. This is when we stop teaching and begin learning from them. That time has come for archaeologists and aboriginal people.

Time, Trust, and the Measure of Success: The Nevada Test Site Cultural Resources Program

Colleen Beck, M. Nieves Zedeño, and Robert Furlow

The Nevada Test Site Cultural Resources Program, under the direction of the Department of Energy, Nevada Operations Office, is broad in scope, encompassing the agency's work, archaeological and historical research, and ethnographic studies and consultation with American Indians. The integration of goals and views of the Department of Energy, American Indians, ethnographers, and archaeologists is an ongoing process with its roots extending to the 1970s. Each journey along this road demonstrates the complexity of multicultural relationships and the rewards of concerted effort. The following overview of past, present, and future developments of the Nevada Test Site Cultural Resources Program shows what can be accomplished by working together.

A Historical Retrospective

In the 1970s the program began, as most have, as a basic Section 106 compliance endeavor. The Nevada Test Site's mission was to test nuclear weapons during the Cold War. In the early days archaeology was viewed as counterproductive, costing time and money, and interfering with national security projects. Mythical stories, such as archaeologists demanding that projects be moved around discarded toilet bowls, had spread across the country. At the same time, archaeologists were struggling with the fundamentals of the Section 106 process, trying to set up frameworks that validated statements of archaeological significance in a national climate of general unease with the process.

The Department of Energy, like other agencies, had to meet its mission, the needs of the users, the cultural resources' requirements, and in addition, go through external review of its compliance by way of consultations with the Nevada State Historic Preservation Office (NSHPO) and the Advisory Council on Historic Preservation (ACHP). Understandably, the formalization of cultural resource programs for implementing the National Historic Preservation Act of 1966 was a slow process that took almost 20 years to develop and laid the foundation of ongoing government-to-government consultation between American Indians and this federal agency.

The American Indian Consultation Program

Throughout the Cold War years, American Indian tribes were forthright about their claims to the land under the jurisdiction of the Department of Energy and critical of the Nevada Test Site's mission. This area had originally been withdrawn in 1940 for a practice bombing range and in 1950 was transferred to the Atomic Energy Commission. Therefore, only a few decades had passed since the tribes could have access to the region; elders still remembered coming to this area to hunt or gather native plants. The passage of the American Indian Religious Freedom Act (AIRFA) in 1978 gave all Indian people hope of gaining access rights to their ancestral lands in the near future. However, cultural resources still were viewed as archaeological sites, not as places and natural resources of traditional significance to these Americans.

By the late 1980s the Department of Energy began to plan its American Indian Consultation Program at the Nevada Test Site and was one of the country's leaders in developing a comprehensive consultation process. This program emerged from the establishment of a 10-year archaeological study, the Long-Range Study Plan for Negating Potential Adverse Effects on the Archaeological Resources on Pahute and Rainier Mesas, Nevada Test Site, Nye County, Nevada, directed by Lonnie Pippin of the Desert Research Institute. Pahute and Rainier mesas contain the densest archaeological remains found on the Nevada Test Site, and the mesas were an area critical for the underground testing of nuclear weapons. In a programmatic agreement between the Department of Energy, the NSHPO, and the ACHP, the Department of Energy agreed to conduct consultations with American Indians regarding resources of importance to them on the mesas.

The first consultation program begun by the Department of Energy did not occur at the Nevada Test Site, however, but at Yucca Mountain, the site of a planned nuclear waste repository that would occupy a small portion of the southwest corner of the Nevada Test Site and extend onto adjacent lands outside this facility. The consultation occurred in compliance with AIRFA. Richard Stoffle and his ethnographic team determined that 17 tribal groups representing three ethnic groups—Western Shoshone, the Southern Paiute and the Owens Valley Paiute, and the Las Vegas Indian Center, representing all Indian people in the Las Vegas Valley—had ancestral ties to the region, and were those whom the Department of Energy should invite to the consultation table.

Participating in consultation with a federal agency can be a difficult decision for a tribe and its members. Uncertainty revolves around numerous concerns, such as whether participation could negatively affect ongoing land claims, and questioning whether the consultations would be fulfilling events or only be compliance procedures without the opportunity for substantive tribal input to the Department of Energy. In the end, all but one group agreed to participate in the consultations. The first meeting between the Department of Energy, the Desert Research Institute's archaeologists, the ethnographic team from the University of Arizona, and the Indian groups was memorable in that 34 official tribal representatives, federal agents, archaeologists, and ethnographers set aside differences and uncertainties to plant the seeds of a successful long-term program. At this crucial meeting, representatives of 17 tribes and three pantribal organizations decided that they could be most effective by working as a group rather than as separate entities. They established the Consolidated Group of Tribes and Organizations, elected a chair, and, as in all subsequent meetings, were given time to meet privately for discussing and making decisions about resource preservation issues and for formulating recommendations to the Department of Energy. All decisions and recommendations were then submitted for review and approval by the tribal councils.

Thereafter, the consultation program proceeded systematically and entailed semi-annual meetings held at the Nevada Test Site and visits to locations of interest to the Consolidated Group. Through the meetings and trips, long-term friendships developed among all participants. Over time this group of people learned to work through their differences toward a common goal, practiced compromise, and adapted to the limitations of conducting such work at the Nevada Test Site. In turn, the Department of Energy responded by examining all and following most of the Consolidated Group's recommendations and by granting additional support for research and consultation. All of the research and consultation activities are funded and organized through the Department of Energy's Nevada Operations Office.

Figure 1—Paiute elders respond to the ethnobotany questionnaire during a field trip to Pahute Mesa, Nevada Test Site.

Beyond Section 106: An Integrated Approach to American Indian Cultural Resource Preservation

A key to the success of the Nevada Test Site Cultural Resources Program has been its emphasis on a "broad-spectrum" approach to American Indian resource preservation and its responsiveness to concerns and recommendations expressed by American Indian elders and official representatives. At the recommendation of the Consolidated Group, the Department of Energy implemented a tribal archaeological monitoring program to keep the tribal councils informed of archaeological activities and assist archaeologists if excavations uncovered human remains or other sensitive materials. Monitors were trained before the field season and had to write a field report for the tribes.

From the initial stages of consultation, the Consolidated Group emphasized the importance of field-based consultation with full participation of Indian elders. Thus, the first large-scale ethnographic project at the Nevada Test Site under AIRFA, the Native American Cultural Resources on Pahute and Rainier Mesas, Nevada Test Site (1994), directed by Richard Stoffle, entailed a systematic ethnobotanical and ethnoarchaeological inventory. Three tribal elders from each of the 17 tribes came to the site for a three-day field visit, were interviewed individually by an ethnographer, and responded to a detailed standardized questionnaire. A mail survey of every adult member of each tribe produced an additional 1,233 (22.7 percent) responses. Such a systematic approach to consultation was viewed by the Consolidated Group as the only means toward establishing productive relationships between the agency and the tribes.

The Formation of Task Groups

Following the success of this project, the Department of Energy entered into consultation on the Native American Graves Protection and Repatriation Act (NAGPRA). This consultation proceeded as systematically as the previous one, with the Consolidated Group representing the culturally affiliated tribes and organizations. The NAGPRA process, however, introduced a new consultation procedure that met with enormous success: the formation of task groups or "subgroups." The Consolidated Group designated a subgroup of six representatives, two from each of the ethnic groups, and entrusted it with the task of viewing the archaeological collections under consultation. The NAGPRA subgroup, with assistance from the ethnographic team and the archaeologists, reviewed the archaeological sites, site reports, and collection in the Department of Energy curation facility. At the end of this process, they chose the items to be viewed by the tribal elders and other knowledgeable representatives.

Through the series of individual interviews with tribal elders and representatives, the archaeologists learned the validity of the Indian people's perspective on the artifacts. The Shoshone and Paiute Indians were semipermanent hunting-gathering societies with cultural items that frequently served multiple purposes, including in ceremonies, a context rarely identified by archaeologists in the Great Basin. While archaeologists easily see the significance of archaeological sites and artifacts in terms of potential data, the cultural experts could see the significance of artifacts in terms of their sacredness because of the context.

The tribal elders and representatives identified 267 NAGPRA items and recommended that these be reburied at the Nevada Test Site. The Consolidated Group reviewed these determinations and forwarded this recommendation to the Department of Energy, while also asking to rebury human remains and associated artifacts from the Nevada Test Site that were curated at the Nevada State Museum. The Department of Energy agreed with the recommendations and facilitated the repatriation and reburial procedures both financially and organizationally. A number of items left in the Department of Energy curation facility now belong to the member tribes of the Consolidated Group, and the agency cares for them on their behalf.

The integration of the Consolidated Group into the Department of Energy's programs and the performance of the task groups have been so successful that the group was asked to participate in the development of the Nevada Test Site Environmental Impact Statement (NTS-EIS) in 1995. The ethnographic team assisted the American Indian writers subgroup in the preparation of its own section for the NTS-EIS, an unprecedented development in the country. By involving the Consolidated Group in this

Figure 2—
An American Indian monitor participates in the Rock Art archaeological survey in upper Fortymile Canyon, Nevada Test Site.

planning document, the tribes were kept well informed of Department of Energy's plans for the uses of the Nevada Test Site. The NTS-EIS presents American Indian views and concerns on Department of Energy's plans at the earliest stage possible for consideration by the department, a situation benefiting all parties involved.

After completing the NAGPRA consultation and the NTS-EIS, the Department of Energy agreed to fund a second large-scale ethnographic and archaeological study, which integrates a systematic archaeological recording of over 3,000 petroglyphs and an ethnographic inventory of these and other rock art sites in the Nevada Test Site. Tribal monitors participated in the archaeological fieldwork and produced a field report to familiarize the tribes with the 1997 ethnographic field season. The Nevada Test Site Rock Art Study, coordinated by Colleen Beck, Richard Stoffle, M. Nieves Zedeño, and the rock art subgroup, has the potential to strengthen the working relationships among the ethnographers, the archaeologists, and the tribes, while expanding everyone's knowledge of these resources.

Expanding Consultation:
The Future of the Program

The fact that the American Indian Consultation Program can look into the future is a reflection of its past. Thus far, the Consolidated Group has included tribes with cultural ties to the Nevada Test Site; cultural resource assessments have been conducted within the boundaries of this facility. However, consultation is expanding to include other tribes and off-site resources. A direct outcome of the NTS-EIS is the Department of Energy's Nevada Operation Office decision to fund the ongoing American Indian Low Level Radioactive Waste Transportation Study, codirected by Diane Austin and Richard Stoffle, in which the Consolidated Group, through the transportation subgroups, is helping contact other tribes whose lands are located along transportation routes. Similarly, the American Indian writers subgroup is involved in the evaluation of cultural resources in the Central Nevada Test Area and other off-site locations. Also in the future of the Nevada Test Site American Indian Consultation Program is the study of Traditional Cultural Properties, as defined by the National Historic Preservation Act of 1966.

The success of the American Indian Consultation Program has been due to several factors. The Department of Energy has continually funded and facilitated the program for almost a decade, creating consistency in the participation of involved tribes and organizations and a sense of commitment and mutual trust. The Department of Energy, Nevada Operations Office Environmental Protection Division, has been the program coordinator since its onset in 1990. The Desert Research Institute has been working on the Nevada Test Site Cultural Resources Program for almost 20 years, has taken responsibility for curating the Nevada Test Site collection, and has subcontracted to the University of Arizona's ethnographic team for seven years. The members of the Consolidated Group have varied slightly through time, as have personnel at the Desert Research Institute and the University of Arizona. However, by far the majority of people have remained the same, facilitating the development of a program that has not had to backtrack to accommodate new organizations or people. Most of all, the success of these endeavors reflects the commitment of the participants to working together.

Perhaps the greatest measure of this success is the current movement of other federally managed facilities, such as Nellis Air Force Base, toward implementing other American Indian consultation programs that include the participation of the Consolidated Group and are modeled after the Nevada Test Site Cultural Resources Program.

Original research reports are available from the National Technical Information Service, the Desert Research Institute, and the Bureau of Applied Research in Anthropology, University of Arizona.

SAA Bulletin, May 1997

Postscript

In 1998 the American Indian Low Level Radioactive Waste Transportation Study and report were successfully completed. This project was followed by another off-site study, the American Indian Intermodal Transportation Study (1999), directed by Richard Stoffle who worked with the Consolidated Group's transportation subgroup. Also a product of the earlier work on the NTS-EIS was the participation of the American Indian writers subgroup, which prepared the American Indian Resources section for the NTS Resource Management Plan (1998), with the assistance of Richard Stoffle and M. Nieves Zedeño. In 1999, the Department of Energy began NAGPRA consultations with the Consolidated Group regarding a recently identified artifact collection from an off-site location and two smaller collections from the Nevada Test Site. These three collections were made prior to the inception of the Nevada Test Site's Historic Preservation Program in the late 1970s and Colleen Beck, Robert Furlow, Richard Stoffle, and M. Nieves Zedeño are facilitating the recent consultations. These current and completed projects have continued to further solidify the established working relationships.

Original research reports are available from the National Technical Information Service, the Desert Research Institute, and the Bureau of Applied Research in Anthropology, University of Arizona.

IV.
Native Peoples and Archaeologists Working Together Beyond the Borders

Working Together on the Border

Randall H. McGuire

When Kurt Dongoske asked me to write for the Working Together column of the *SAA Bulletin*, I agreed with some apprehension and misgiving. My uneasiness springs from the fact that the project under discussion is ongoing. Although we have gone out of our way to consult with Native Americans, and so far this process has gone well, there remains the chance of misunderstanding, unanticipated events, or differences of conviction to destroy the existing good will. This process of consultation involves people from three different cultures, and two different nation states, further increasing the chance of something going wrong. I was reluctant to write this article both because of this uncertainty, and because of a fear the article itself might jinx or compromise the process. Kurt argued that I should go ahead, pointing out that even when all participants approach the process with good will, uncertainty, apprehension, and the possibility for misunderstanding are an ever-present aspect of archaeologists working together with native peoples. And, he is right.

Elisa Villalpando of the Centro del Instituto Nacional de Antropología e Historia (INAH) of Sonora and I are currently conducting excavations at the site of Cerro de Trincheras. The site is located about 110 km south of the United States–Mexican border, by the town of Trincheras, Sonora, Mexico. The project is funded by the National Science Foundation (SBR9-320224) and sponsored by both Binghamton University and the Centro INAH de Sonora.

Cerro de Trincheras is one of the most spectacular and largest archaeological sites in Sonora. It is a late prehistoric Trincheras Tradition village (A.D. 1300 to 1450) built on an isolated volcanic hill. The hill rises more than 150 m from the flat desert plain, and covers about 100 ha. The prehistoric inhabitants of the site built over 880 terraces on the hill, and then constructed brush and mud houses on these terraces. Very little archaeological research has been done in Sonora, and our project is the first archaeological excavation at Cerro de Trincheras.

Historically, Tohano O'odham people lived in the region around the site, and they claim the site as an ancestral village. Today, the vast majority of Tohano O'odham people live in the United States, but a few hundred still live in several villages to the north and west of Trincheras. The Tohano O'odham consider themselves as one nation divided by the European-imposed United States–Mexican border. The border is a harsh reality of Tohano O'odham life that creates very different social relationships and living experiences for the people on opposite sides. The United

States and Mexico, however, regard the Tohano O'odham as citizens of the respective nation states where they live.

The modern cultural, social, and political context of our project is complex. Archaeologists and Native Americans come to the process of consultation with very different conceptions about the past and very different cultural and political interests. Our attempts to work together in this project necessarily involve three cultures, at least two languages, and the laws of two nation states. The history that created this complexity also created complex power relations. In 1848 the United States seized one-third of the state of Mexico and in 1854 negotiated the Gadsden Purchase to acquire southern Arizona. Today, Mexico exists in the shadow of the United States, and this power relationship tints all social relations. The Tohano O'odham regard both the United States and Mexico as colonial invaders. Yet, an O'odham from the Tohano O'odham Nation in Arizona is treated in Mexico as a citizen of the United States.

In Mexico all archaeological materials are legally the heritage of the Mexican people. All archaeological sites and artifacts are property of the national government, regardless of the ownership of the land that they are found on. INAH is the Mexican government agency that administers, researches, and preserves the national archaeology. Any negotiations concerning the disposition of burials and sacred goods must be made with INAH, and only INAH has the authority for repatriation to Native American nations or communities.

Repatriation and reburial have not surfaced as highly visible indigenous issues in Mexico. Although I suspect that many Native American communities in Mexico hold similar feelings about these issues as their U.S. brethren, they have not expressed their feelings in a high profile national debate. Mexican archaeologists are generally untroubled by the repatriation and reburial debates that have dominated U.S. archaeology over the last decade. They also are highly suspect of any attempts to import the conflict to Mexico.

Since the passing of NAGPRA and a state reburial law, archaeologists and Native Americans in southern Arizona have developed fairly regularized means and procedures for consultation on archaeological research. All of the Native American nations and communities of southern Arizona have either a committee or a designated individual within their governmental structure to handle this consultation. Over the last five years relations between archaeologists and Tohano O'odham people in southern Arizona have ranged from bitter conflict to cordial cooperation. The Tohano O'odham have generally allowed the nondestructive analysis of skeletons and mortuary goods before their return to the nation and reburial.

Elisa Villalpando and I have been conducting archaeological research in northern Sonora since 1985. Up until the current project, this research has been survey, surface collection, and mapping, with no excavation. Before each previous field season we sent copies of our proposals and our reports to the O'odham communities of southern Arizona (Tohano O'odham Nation, Gila River Indian Community, Salt River Indian Community, and Ak Chin Indian Community). In the spring of 1988 a delegation from the San Xaviar District of the Tohano O'odham Nation visited our survey project in the Altar Valley of Sonora. Except for this visit we had received very little response to our efforts.

In 1984 the French Center for Studies of Mexico and Central America launched an ethnoarchaeolgical project at Quitovac, Sonora. The French researchers obtained permits from INAH's Consejo de Arqueología in Mexico City, but did not contact the traditional authorities of the local native communities. The project ultimately ended in bitter conflict with the Tohano O'odham.

Quitovac is one of the most sacred places in the O'odham world, and one of the handful of surviving Tohano O'odham villages in Sonora. The O'odham creation story says that at Quitovac the cultural hero, I'Itoi, killed a monster that threatened to destroy the people. To celebrate this event Tohano O'odham from Sonora and Arizona gather at Quitovac each year for the *Wikita* ceremony. In 1989, after the ceremony, the French researchers systematically mapped and collected the ceremonial ground. They also excavated some graves and in the blessed cave where the Tohano O'odham kept the sacred eagle feathers for the *Wikita* ceremony.

Tohano O'odham people objected to these excavations claiming that the individuals who had given the French permission to excavate were not Indians, and that recent burials had been disturbed. The Tohano O'odham cultural affairs committee from Sells, Ariz. took a leading role in the negotiations that followed. The Centro INAH de Sonora, in Hermosillo, obtained the skeletons and artifacts from the French Center for Studies of Mexico and Central America, and in 1993 transferred them to the Tohano O'odham cultural affairs committee, who then arranged for their reburial at Quitovac in April of that year. This was the first time in the history of INAH that archaeological materials legally in INAH's possession were reburied.

In designing the excavation project for the spring of 1995 we felt that we had to make a greater effort at consultation with the O'odham than we had in the past. We came to this position both because we would be excavating, and because of the changing relations between archaeologists and Native Americans in the region.

Excavation, as opposed to surface survey, greatly increased the chance that we would disturb burials, or sacred objects, or both, in our research. In 1991 we had mapped the site and identified a large, badly looted, cremation cemetery. Hoping to avoid burials, we proposed to not excavate this cemetery. However, we realized that we might encounter burials in the other portions of the site.

The experience of the French was foremost in our minds as we wanted to avoid the misunderstandings and abuses that had happened at Quitovac. The Centro INAH de Sonora had played a leading role in returning the burials and sacred objects to the Tohano O'odham. The organization was also involved in negotiations with the Tohano O'odham cultural affairs committee about plans to develop the Sierra Pinacate as a Mexican national park.

Finally, we felt that it might be easier now than in the past to initiate and maintain a process of consultation. The cultural affairs committees and offices of the Native American nations and communities of southern Arizona made it easier for us to contact key individuals in those communities. Once initiated we also thought it would be easier to maintain the process with standing committees or offices that would survive changes in tribal governments.

We initially contacted the Tohano O'odham cultural affairs committee by sending it a copy of our grant proposal for the project. A meeting, arranged for September 1994 in Trincheras, included a committee representative, an Anglo lawyer working for the Committee, and representatives of the local community and INAH. The meeting concluded cordially; we agreed that if we did encounter any burials, we would excavate them so they would not be looted, and then contact the cultural affairs committee.

The Tohano O'odham were pleased we had consulted with them concerning a project in Mexico, and suggested that we also contact other indigenous nations and communities in Arizona such as the Pasqua Yaqui Indian community and the Hopi Nation. We subsequently sent all of the O'odham groups, the Yaqui, and the Hopi copies of our proposal. Only the Ak Chin community and the Hopi Nation responded to our query. Both indicated that we should deal directly with the Tohano O'odham Nation.

We began fieldwork at the beginning of February 1995. Within the first few weeks we had located several possible cremations, one definite cremation, and two inhumations. We left the cremations in place. They did not contain ceramic vessels, and we did not think they were obvious enough to attract looters. Our workers, however, immediately recognized the bones in the inhumations as human, even though none of them contained extensive grave offerings. We excavated the inhumations immediately in fear they would be looted if we did not.

On March 4, we met with two members of the cultural affairs committee and their attorney in Caborca, Sonora. It was agreed that we would be allowed to do nondestructive analysis on the inhumations and the remains would be reburied afterward. The only point of contention was how long we would keep the bones before reburial. Because we had not yet spoken with a physical anthropologist about doing the analysis, we wanted a year to get the work done. The Tohano O'odham clearly wanted the work done more quickly.

On March 13, 1995, a delegation from the cultural affairs committee visited us in the field. Four members of the committee and their attorney came. The visit was quite cordial, for the most part. Based on conversations at this meeting it was decided to back fill the known and possible cremations without excavating them.

At the present time the consultation process between the Cerros de Trincheras excavation project and the Tohano O'odham nation appears to be going well. Relations remain cordial, and we have so far been able to come to mutually satisfactory agreements. After analysis, the skeletons will be turned over to the Tohano O'odham. The few artifacts found with the burials will also be turned over to the Tohano O'odham at the same time.

We hope that consultation will continue to go well when we start our second field season in February 1996. Given the complex social, cultural, and power relationships working among three cultures and two nation states, the chance of misunderstandings remains high. We also have some concern that all of our dealings have been with the Tohano O'odham nation in Sell, Arizona. We have not talked to the various Tohano O'odham communities in Sonora, in large part because they are not as well organized on this issue as their Arizona brethren, making it difficult to know whom to contact. But, as Kurt pointed out when he convinced me to write this article, uncertainty, apprehension, and the possibility for misunderstanding, are an ever-present aspect of working together with Native Americans.

SAA Bulletin, November 1995

Postscript

At the time we published the original article for the Working Together column in November 1995, the consultation process between the Cerros de Trincheras excavation project and the Tohano O'odham nation was going well. During the next excavation season in spring 1996, we located several more inhumations and arranged for physical anthropologists to analyze all of the inhumations from the site during 1997. Relations remained cordial, and the project, the Centro INAH de Sonora, and the Tohano O'odham Cultural Affairs Committee seemed to have arrived at mutually satisfactory agreements.

We concluded the article by noting that the possibilities for misunderstandings and problems remained high. Given the complex social, cultural, and power relationships working among three cultures and two nation states, we worried that things could change for the worse. Unfortunately this is exactly what happened: All of these ambiguities added to events transpiring on the other side of Mexico, came into play to create the problems we had feared.

The ambiguities were manifested when the Tohano O'odham sent a letter to INAH's Consejo de Arqueología in Mexico City requesting permission to follow the precedent established by the repatriation at Quitovac in 1993. The letter was written in English and signed by the chairman of the Tohano O'odham Nation in Sells. The Consejo responded that the materials could not be exported to the United States and the site of Cerro de Trincheras did not lie in the traditional territory of the Tohano O'odham. The Centro INAH de Sonora replied with a letter clarifying that Quitovac was in Sonora and that Cerro de Trincheras was in the traditional territory of the Tohano O'odham.

The Consejo rebutted that because of the Sandanista (EZNL) revolution that had begun in Chiapas in 1994, the policy of the Consejo was to not return archaeological materials to indigenous communities. Ignoring the precedent set by the French excavations at Quitovac, it argued that if this repatriation were allowed, indigenous communities throughout the nation would request return of archaeological materials. (Mexican law does not give indigenous communities any autonomy or even partial sovereignty, as is the case with tribes in the United States. Indigenous communities are simply civil associations. The law also makes archaeological materials the property of the Mexican nation and not that of individuals or communities within the nation.) The fact that the petition had come from the Tohano O'odham Nation, located in the United States, and not from Mexican citizens, made the request doubly problematic. The Consejo also stated that DNA testing of the skeletons would be necessary to prove that they were indeed Tohano O'odham before a request from any O'odham living in Mexico could be considered.

Currently the inhumations from Cerros de Trincheras still reside at the Centro INAH de Sonora. The project and the Centro INAH de Sonora had entered into negotiations with the Tohano O'odham with the good-faith expectation that the precedent established at Quitovac would be followed by the Consejo de Arqueología in Mexico City. Given the massive assertion of indigenous rights in Chiapas, the Consejo had chosen to make explicit policy rejecting the precedent. Needless to say, this turn of events has compromised relations between the Tohano O'odham and both the project and the Centro INAH de Sonora. As we concluded in our original report of this situation, uncertainty, apprehension, and the possibility for misunderstanding are an ever-present aspect of working together with Native Americans. This is especially true when we are working across international borders.

Making History in Xaltocan

Elizabeth M. Brumfiel

In the June 1994 issue of the *SAA Bulletin*, John H. Jameson, Jr. (1994), encouraged archaeologists to promote public education and outreach. The institutional reforms he calls for are essential, but ethical and legal mandates should be accompanied by practical discussions of how to implement public education and outreach successfully. My own attempt at communicating archaeological research results to the public led me to define a number of principles that might be broadly applicable. Below, I describe my efforts to improve communication and mutual understanding in a Mexican village; ongoing discussion of outreach techniques can be found in *Public Archaeology Review*.

My efforts at public communication resulted from a bargain I made with the people of Xaltocan, Mexico. At the beginning of my fieldwork in 1987, about 60 people gathered in the town square to ask why they should let me work in their town. What was in it for them? Well, I replied, Xaltocan has an illustrious history, and if you let me work here, I can learn more about it and tell you, and you can tell your children. The people accepted this answer, and the fieldwork proceeded. But when I tried to fulfill this promise, I found that telling people about their prehistory is not something that professional archaeologists do easily or well.

What Is a Popular Prehistory?

I began my efforts at public education by asking what meanings prehistory could have for contemporary, rural Mexicans. Searching for prehistories aimed at the Mexican public, I found three examples: the social studies textbooks issued by the Mexican Secretaría de Educación Pública and used in all public grade schools in Mexico, including Xaltocan; a municipal history of the Valley of Mexico community of Tlahuac, written by a local, amateur historian; and a comic book history of the Xaltocan region written in Nextlalpa, Xaltocan's *municipio* capital. Each of these works interprets the prehistoric past: in each "something foreign, strange, separated in time, space or experience is made familiar, present [and] comprehensible" (J. P. Dumont, 1978:4, *The Headman and I: Ambiguity and Ambivalence in the Fieldwork Experience*. University of Texas Press, Austin). Let us see how this is done.

In the social studies textbooks (México 1988, Secretaría de Educación Pública, *Ciencias Sociales*. Grados 3°–6°. México, D.F.), Mexican prehistory is tied to the ideas of community and progress. Prehistory is presented as the achievement of greater material comfort, which results from technological development and a more complex division of labor.

Beginning with Paleolithic hunters and gatherers, humans learned to make tools, use fire, create symbols, harvest crops, care for animals, make pottery, nets and baskets, and record the passage of time. With a more complex division of labor came more numerous laws and formal leadership, which promoted social order. The texts present focused discussions of the development of maize agriculture, the rise of regional civilizations in Mesoamerica, and the Colombian exchange.

These textbooks do a lot of things right. They have a clear narrative structure: Through expanding knowledge and cooperation, humans transform their lives from harsh misery to higher levels of leisure and comfort. Present and past are linked by explaining the origins of everyday things (fire, maize, cows, and sheep) and by drawing from past human experience generalizations to guide contemporary action (a better life can be gained by acquiring technical knowledge and participating responsibly in the social division of labor).

González-Blanco Garrido's (1988) municipal history embodies some of these same strategies. It focuses upon the fate of Tlahuac under Aztec rule. The author doesn't dwell upon the town's defeat and subordination; rather, Tlahuac and other subject city-states are said to have been brought into a larger, unified political body, better able to pursue its common interests. The narrative is ultimately tragic because the social unity under which these communities prospered was shattered by Moctezuma's lack of resolve in dealing with the Spanish. The moral for modern Mexicans is clear: well-being is dependent upon the unity of the nation which should not be ruptured by either ethnic strife or class struggle.

Archaeology appears only briefly in this work. Two Formative sites in the Tlahuac area are described as a prelude to the main narrative. But some effort is made to link past and present, listing artifact types and their presumed functions. Thus some connection is made between unfamiliar objects and daily activities familiar to the reader.

Varela and Varela's (n.d.) comic book history of Nextlalpa follows the structure of prehispanic central Mexican migration myths: Yaotl, a leader of the Toltecs, leaves the failed Tollan, founds the town of Nextlalpa, and teaches his people to exploit the local lacustrine resources. However, the narrative is satirical: the potbellied Yaotl replaces the heroic Toltec leaders of Aztec mythology; Yaotl's wife, not the chaste, demure Indian princess of legend, is voluptuous and demanding; Yaotl's people are a straggly band of lazy, contentious refugees, incessantly critical of Yaotl's leadership, and unappreciative of the innovations and progress he offers.

This work ties past and present in several ways: (1) continuity of place is summoned; Nextlalpa's location on an ancient lakebed is recalled by detailed descriptions of past techniques of lacustrine exploitation; (2) a clear analogy is drawn between the politics of progress in Yaotl's band and contemporary Nextlalpa, with the implication that apathy and wrangling obstruct beneficial change; and (3) contemporary tension between Nextlalpa and neighboring Xaltocan is rooted in the past: the comic book explains that Yaotl's band settled Nextlalpa only after agreeing to pay a heavy tribute to Xaltocan. Now the tables have turned, and Nextlalpa is a *municipio* capital with authority over Xaltocan. Perhaps, the narrative suggests, this is just, after Xaltocan's past treatment of Nextlalpa.

Again, archaeological material occupies a marginal place in the narrative. In the final pages of the comic book, Yaotl orders the people to learn to manufacture and use various artifacts. As in the Tlahuac history, the comic book explains the functions of artifacts, making a connection between unfamiliar prehistoric objects and continuing contemporary activities.

What Is a Good Popular History?

Which of these narratives should we prefer? We can judge them by standards of evidence, comprehensiveness, and relevance.

Evidence

If it is true, as Hodder (1984) and Gero (1991) have argued, that an infinite number of narratives can be constructed from a single set of "facts," it is also true that there are an infinite number of narratives that are *not* compatible with the tangible evidence yielded by archaeological excavation and interpreted according to the rules of stratigraphy. The social studies textbooks, for example, claim that all the domestic arts had to await sedentism and food production. However, this is contradicted by baskets from the dry caves in highland Mexico that predates village life by 4,000 years.

Comprehensiveness

If, as the textbooks suggest, prehistory is the unremitting triumph of human progress, then interludes of regress (e.g., the collapse of Maya civilization and the fall of highland regional centers at the end of the Classic) are inexplicable. Indeed, these interludes are barely mentioned in the textbooks. Similarly, if social stratification arises from a natural division of labor, with the consent of the governed, then the existence of power and exploitation in complex societies cannot be comprehended. In fact, the textbooks omit any reference to the use of coercion in securing or maintaining social advantage. Human sacrifice and militarism are mentioned only as particularistic culture traits: as the Olmec are noted for their giant head sculptures, so the Mexica are known for their militarism.

Relevance

Prehistory can be relevant in three ways. First, prehistory can have political relevance, such as archaeology confirming a people's claim to particular resources (Trigger 1980), or when artifacts provide evidence of a group's particular contributions to the national patrimony, justifying its claim for equal standing within contemporary society (see Williams 1989). The comic book's reference to Xaltocan's extraction of tribute from Nextlalpa constitutes a trivial example of historically based political claims. But where prehistory has been used to fan the flames of ethnic, nationalist, and imperialist struggles, the political implications of archaeology are very serious (Kohl 1990, McCann 1988, Trigger, 1984). Second, prehistory might be relevant in teaching beneficial lessons about nature, culture, or human behavior. The textbooks and the Tlahuac history both contain narratives where the state affairs described at the beginning are transformed by the story's end (see Terrell 1990, on the structure of archaeological narrative). The cause of the transformation provides the cautionary lesson of the narrative, for example, "Progress is achieved through technological development and responsible participation" or "Well-being is achieved through social peace." Third, prehistory might be relevant by endowing the past with content and meaning. Without myth or history, the past is a void that leaves the present unaccounted for. And yet, according to Shanks and Tilley (1987:103), the past becomes meaningful only in relation to the present, implying that prehistory cannot be meaningful without a politically or didactically relevant narrative. For example, both the Tlahuac history and the comic book attempt to create meaningful pasts, discussing everyday uses of artifacts. Both efforts fail because the discussion of artifact function is marginal to the historical narratives where political claims and didactic generalizations are made.

Based upon these considerations of evidence, comprehensiveness, and relevance, I developed some guidelines for the exhibit I wanted to develop for Xaltocan.

First, the exhibit was organized around a didactic generalization, introduced by "What is the value of knowing the past?" It emphasized that the Xaltocan people had always lived in complex natural and social worlds that had required continual collective problem solving. The exhibit implied that that inventiveness, collective effort, and determination to survive characteristic of the ancient Xaltocamecas provided an excellent model for their living descendants.

The choice of this generalization was dictated by pragmatic and ideological considerations. In terms of pragmatics, it can be sustained by archaeological data. Artifacts are used to implement subsistence and social strategies; thus they lend themselves to narratives of transformation through goal-directed innovation. In terms of ideology, this generalization counsels collective problem solving and self-determination as opposed to passivity and deference to bureaucratic elites. This counsel contradicts the didactic morals of many other presentations of Mexican prehistory, for example, those in the textbooks and in the Tlahuac history, which seem to counsel a naive and passive social peace.

With its emphasis on continuous cultural change within a local community, my narrative attempted to counter the essentialism of many contemporary interpretations of prehispanic cultures. In the social studies texts especially, prehispanic cultures are defined in terms of a set of unchanging culture traits, implying that culture change is a consequence of one people replacing another. I am frequently asked in Xaltocan whether a particular local artifact was produced by the Toltecs, Chichimecs, or Aztecs, to which I reply that it was made by the ancestral Xaltocamecas. My goal is to create a sense of continuity of place and to highlight the possibility of internally generated culture change. Again, these ideas are needed because they are often discounted in official texts that seek popular demobilization. Thus, my focus narrative reflects my assessment of the political situation in contemporary Xaltocan.

Second, I focused on artifacts and place as physical links between past and present. I chose to focus on artifacts because most Xaltocan households have collections of prehistoric curiosities, and I thought people would become engaged in matching their pieces to the illustrations and discussions of ceramic chronology, craft production, and household ritual. I described formal and stylistic variation in artifacts over time, interpreting this variation by reference to archaeological evidence that documented changing needs and world views of the ancient Xaltocamecas (following Gero 1991). I also compared the artifact forms and frequencies of Xaltocan to other contemporaneous sites in the Valley of Mexico, establishing the unique identity of Xaltocan among the many Late Postclassic settlements and trying to communicate a specificity of place.

But Isn't This Science?

My exhibit sounds a lot like a site report. Its descriptions are acceptable, if elementary, Mesoamerican archaeology. Why, then, did the gap between professional discourse and popular prehistory loom so large in my original efforts to communicate with the people of Xaltocan?

The largest gap between popular prehistory and professional archaeology occurs in the area of relevance. Most professional archaeologists judge reports by their theoretical relevance. Work becomes significant as it confirms or alters our understanding of human nature or our ability to explain the archaeological record according to general laws of culture change. In contrast, popular prehistory lacks any explicit attempt to test general theories of human nature or cause and effect.

In popular archaeology, theoretical relevance is replaced by didactic generalization, which is likely to cause professional archaeologists some discomfort. In professional archaeology, such generalizations are considered unnecessary or even presumptuous. However, absence of didactic generalization from professional work is more apparent than real. Terrell (1990) argues that most professional presentations of the data in archaeology assume a narrative form, and many contain implicit didactic generalizations. In addition, a growing body of literature calls attention to the ways in which archaeological language, models and theories imply generalizations about nature, culture, or human behavior which advance specific political agendas (Conkey and Spector 1984; Gero, Lacy, and Blakey 1983; Shanks and Tilley 1987:46–67; Trigger 1980). It now seems apparent that, whether addressing a professional or popular audience, archaeologists habitually endow the past with didactic generalizations that serve as a basis for contemporary action. Thus, it may be useful for professional archaeologists to be consciously aware of the didactic implications of their writing, both popular and professional, and to consider its political and moral implications.

What archaeology will be meaningful to the public? Archaeology that embodies the following characteristics:

(1) It should contain a clear narrative structure, where the conditions at the beginning of the tale are transformed by the end. The long-term cultural changes defined in the course of archaeological research offer a natural basis for narrative structure.

(2) It should link past and present by establishing a continuity of place, or by describing how familiar tasks in contemporary life were accomplished in the past, or by documenting the origins of artifacts, customs, or features of the landscape that are familiar to the public.

(3) It should make the past meaningful by presenting a didactic generalization, concerning, for example, the preservation of the environment, the maintenance of social harmony, the fostering of individual initiative, or whatever else seems to speak to contemporary concerns in a way that is factually correct, politically relevant, and morally responsible.

Making History in Xaltocan—The Exhibit

The exhibit itself consisted of 24 sheets of poster board, each addressing one aspect of the research with text and illustrations, including maps of the prehistoric region and the site (showing the locations of excavation units), photographs of features and artifacts, and copies of drawings from sixteenth century Mexican codices. Each aspect of research was introduced with a question; I hoped that this would cause people to continue reading to find the answer.

In the first two sections of text (*Why did we produce this exhibit?* and *Why is it important to know the past?*) I introduced the theme of progress through local initiative and collective action. The next sections correlated events at Xaltocan with events in Mexican national history, to establish the importance of events in Xaltocan. (For example, Xaltocan was conquered by the Aztecs in 1430; everyone has heard of the Aztecs. Xaltocan was attacked by Cortés prior to the conquest of Tenochtitlan;

everyone has heard of Cortés). This was followed by a map of the region during the prehispanic era and a map of the town showing where we had excavated. Thus, people would be able to link the photos that followed to particular places in the town.

Next, the exhibit dealt with the founding of Xaltocan. *Who founded Xaltocan?* was a question that the Xaltocamecas, themselves, had asked me early in my research project. My answer established a continuity of place by showing how Xaltocan's population included many different groups of people drawn to the community over the course of time. Discussions of how the ancient inhabitants altered the local environment, *How was the "island" of Xaltocan made?* and *How were the "chinampas" of Xaltocan made?*, extended the theme of the exhibit, progress through local initiative and collective action.

A description of fauna remains linked past and present, since most of these animals still play a role in the village economy. Illustrations of each species from the Florentine Codex put meat on the bare bones of archaeological research. In some cases, the role of a particular species had changed; the suggestion that the ancient Xaltocamecas had eaten their dogs stimulated a lot of comment!

The unique identity of Xaltocan was evoked by discussion of *Symbols of citizenship*, a particular form of obsidian lip plug that may have served as an ethnic marker.

A discussion of ceramic chronology, illustrated with photos of sherds from our excavations, enabled people to learn something about the pieces which they, themselves, had gathered over the years. In Xaltocan, almost every family has a small collection of sherds, figurines, spindle whorls, and obsidian tools that they have found. Informing people about artifacts in their possession was also the goal of the section *Spinning and weaving*, which described the kinds and uses of spindle whorls, and *Obsidian working*, which described the methods of obsidian tool-making and the functions of the tools produced.

Help us solve a mystery! was an effort to draw viewers into the research process by asking them to help us think of the function of a problematic artifact type, obsidian eccentrics.

Burials exploited the curiosity that most people have about human skeletons. We could comment upon several interesting features of burials at Xaltocan: all the burials were children, and all were buried very near domestic structures. These features were explained by reference to Aztec ideas of the soul, established by current ethnohistoric scholarship.

To deal with religion, the exhibit distinguished between "state" ritual and domestic ritual. The discussion of domestic ritual examined the varieties and functions of figurines (objects of much local interest), of musical instruments (and the symbolic importance of song and dance in Aztec ritual), and censers and braziers (and the meaning of fire in Aztec thought). Since we found many images of the Aztec god Tlaloc at Xaltocan, we discussed why this particular deity, a god of rain and water, might be found at the Island settlement of Xaltocan. Finally, with reference to *State religion*, we described the stone platforms which were the most interesting architectural feature which we encountered at Xaltocan.

Finally, we asked, *Who were the first archaeologists in Xaltocan?* We explained that we had found figurines dating from the Terminal Formative and Early Classic periods in deposits of much later occupational debris. We concluded that the ancient inhabitants of Xaltocan found these figurines at other more ancient settlements in the Basin of Mexico and brought them home as objects of curiosity or veneration. This established continuity between the activities of the ancient inhabitants of Xaltocan and its current inhabitants. It was also a concession to the priority and authority of local inhabitants when it comes to matters archaeological, while simultaneously establishing a long-standing community interest in the past, legitimating our own research project.

We supplemented this exhibit of research results with a home video documenting the research process. The video showed test pit excavations; sherd washing, weighing, and classifying; and flotation sample processing. All members of the project (local workers, American students, and professional Mexican and American archaeologists) briefly described how the work was carried out and why certain procedures were followed, for example, why we dug with trowels instead of shovels, why we screened, how flotation samples were processed, what information they yielded, etc. The video was a big hit! Xaltocamecas loved seeing their relatives and neighbors on the screen.

Both the exhibit and the video were warmly received. Although we were unable to provide any advanced publicity about the exhibit, more than 100 people viewed it over the two days it was installed in the plaza of Xaltocan. It seemed to hold people's interest; people who came to the exhibit spent quite a long time looking at the pictures and reading the text. Sixty-five free copies of the text were available for people to take home; all the copies were taken and were acknowledged with thanks. I stored the exhibit with a village resident with instructions that it should be lent out to the schools or the *municipio* administration for further public use. However, I don't think that any use has been made of the exhibit in my absence. I hear that there is a new government-built museum in Xaltocan; in the future, it may be possible to integrate parts of my exhibit into a permanent display in the museum.

Finally, I do feel that I made good on my promise to inform the people of Xaltocan about their prehistory. But I would like to publish the exhibit as a small book. If I find a source of funding, I will probably undertake a publication project.

SAA Bulletin, September 1994

Postscript

Our Xaltocan exhibit in 1992 was a big success in terms of public relations. When we returned to Xaltocan in 1997 and 1999, the town council cited the exhibit and other contributions to the public understanding of Xaltocan's history (e.g., the use of some of our information in the primary school curriculum, our donation of publications about Xaltocan to the municipal archives) as reasons for allowing our research to continue.

However, the public archaeology program has taken some ironic twists, particularly in terms of the political goals that I had envisioned for the program. My goals were to strengthen the Xaltocamecan sense of agency and to increase Xaltocan's solidarity with other towns in the region in order to increase resistance to Mexico's powerful, centralized state. To achieve these goals, the exhibit emphasized that: (1) people, on their own, changed their culture to adapt to their lakebed habitat, (2) Xaltocan had long resisted the rule of centralized states, including the Aztecs, and (3) Xaltocamecas could feel pride and self-confidence because of the achievements of their ancestors.

However, recent research by ethnohistorian Frederic Hicks indicates that Xaltocan received a large influx of population from Tenochtitlán after the Aztecs conquered the town. Nahuatl may have replaced Otomí as the native language in Xaltocan at this time. Thus, the history of Xaltocan looks more like successive waves of peoples and cultures than it used to. Moreover, this information makes it possible for the people of Xaltocan to think of themselves as Aztecs, to identify with the conquerors rather than the conquered, and to take pride in dominance rather than resistance. In fact, some Xaltocamecas have used what they have learned about local prehistory to claim a higher status than people in surrounding towns. An unexpected outcome of this status competition is that neighboring towns are now clamoring for archaeologists of their own.

The exhibit increased the demand for information about Xaltocan's past. The Xaltocamecas are impatiently awaiting the publication of a bilingual report on our 1990–1991 excavations. Since this is a professional report, they are bound to feel frustrated by the lack of attention to individual artifacts (as esthetic and historical pieces) and by the apparent lack of relevance to the research question we chose to address (how resource use is affected by political change). I will have to redouble my efforts in developing an exhibit for Xaltocan's new archaeological museum to compensate for the disappointment. There also is some talk of my developing an "archaeological park" for Xaltocan on an empty lot near the center of town. This lot appears to contain elite architecture, but excavating elite architecture would require a shift in my research skills and interests. I don't know if I will agree to do it.

I have found that working together in archaeology is an ongoing process. Public archaeology has marshaled support for archaeological research in Xaltocan, but it has not created a consensus about what is interesting and politically valuable about the past and how archaeological research should proceed. The existence of these tensions seems to be an integral part of public archaeology.

Archaeology in the Middle of Political Conflict in Yautepec, Mexico

Michael E. Smith

Many professional discussions of archaeology and the public describe ideal settings in modern industrialized nations. These sound naive and out of touch to those of us who have faced the complexities of fieldwork in the Third World. The traditional accounts of archaeologists "working together" with local peoples describe settings where there is basically a single community and a single local public to deal with. Those of us who work in other countries, however, must deal with multiple publics that often present conflicting demands to the foreign archaeologist. In 1993 my field crew and I found ourselves in the middle of a violent political struggle in Yautepec, Mexico, that exerted a strong influence on both our research design and our community interactions. The concept of "working together" took on complexities that illustrate some of the problems of doing fieldwork in other countries today. One of the lessons from the 1993 season is that there is no single "public" for archaeology. We are responsible to numerous publics, and positive interactions with one public may be viewed as harmful by another.

Yautepec, a town of 40,000 in the central Mexican state of Morelos, has a reputation for deeply divided political allegiances. It has a long history of conflict, often violent, extending at least back to the Mexican revolution of 1910 (the revolutionary general and hero Emiliano Zapata was from a town not far from Yautepec). Archaeological fieldwork in Yautepec began in 1989 with excavations of a large palace—the only extant Aztec royal palace building—by Hortensia de Vega Nova of the Morelos Instituto Nacional de Antropología e Historia (INAH) state office. When my wife, Cynthia Heath-Smith, and I visited that year, de Vega and other archaeologists (including the director of the Morelos INAH office) urged us to come excavate Aztec houses at Yautepec. We agreed that the open fields adjacent to the palace were a promising place to dig; this was the downtown area of a major Aztec city, and the ground surface was covered by dense artifact scatters. The Sociedad Cultural Yautepec, a local organization of citizens interested in the history and culture of the town, was helping to support the INAH excavations and invited me to speak at one of its meetings and also encouraged us to dig in Yautepec.

We obtained funding (from the National Science Foundation and the National Endowment for the Humanities) and permits (from the central INAH office in Mexico City) and began fieldwork in summer 1992. De Vega was still excavating at the palace, but the Sociedad Cultural

Yautepec had split into factions. One faction withdrew and formed the new Patronato Pro-Restauración de la Zona Arqueológica de Yautepec, Morelos. This became the primary organization helping the INAH excavations; members did modest fund-raising and helped with various logistical matters. Our 1992 season was devoted to an intensive survey to define the extent of Aztec Yautepec under the modern town, and we spent a lot of time knocking on doors and requesting permission to root around in peoples' yards. The Patronato provided considerable help during the first season, including funding one of the local workers we hired, securing a letter of permission from the municipal president, running public service ads on the local radio station asking people to cooperate with our project, and making lemonade for the crew.

There were no overt political problems that season, although we did notice graffiti on public walls indicating conflict over the water situation. The major political cleavage in Yautepec today is between the dominant party, the Partido de la Revolución Institucionalizada (PRI), and the leftist opposition party of Cuauhtemoc Cárdenas, the Partido de la Revolución Democrática (PRD). The federal government had proposed a decentralization of the water supply whereby control would pass from the federal government to local authorities. The party in power, the PRI, was in favor of this change, whereas the PRD party was opposed, and there has been at least one death over this issue. During the summer 1992 season, we made plans to begin excavations the following January in the open fields across from the palace (Figure 1). This area had been desig-

Figure 1—Vacant lot adjacent to the Yautepec royal palace. In 1992 we made plans to excavate Aztec houses here.

nated an INAH Archaeological Zone; it had been surveyed, with property markers set up.

In fall 1992, however, the open fields of the archaeological zone—but not the area of the pyramid itself—were taken over by a planned squatters invasion (Figure 2). The squatters, whose shacks literally appeared over night, were affiliated with the PRD. They claimed to be poor landless people who were simply looking for a place to live. They immediately petitioned the state and municipality to provide utilities such as electricity and water for their tarpaper shacks. Other residents of Yautepec told us, however, that most of the squatters owned land elsewhere, and this was simply an organized grab for more land. The PRI-controlled municipal government and INAH immediately began legal actions to evict the squatters. The Yautepec government did not want this new PRD block in town, and INAH wanted to reclaim its registered archaeological zone. For a variety of reasons (many still unknown to me), these efforts were unsuccessful, and the squatters remained in place.

The situation was at a standoff when we arrived in January 1993 to excavate. We looked for alternative places to dig, and received permission to work in the large walled yard of a secondary school several hundred meters from the pyramid and archaeological zone. It seemed likely that the squatters would be evicted soon, and we would be able to dig where we had originally intended. After a month, it became obvious that no progress was being made, and we abandoned plans to excavate in the affected area.

We avoided the squatters' settlement as much as possible, fearing possible violence against the U.S. archaeologists and students. The squatters invasion and the attempts to evict them became news in the national media. Newspaper and television reporters were regular visitors to

Figure 2—Shantytown of squatters established in fall 1992 in the fields shown in Figure 1. This photo is taken from the Yautepec palace.

Yautepec to follow the story of the dispute, and I was interviewed numerous times. I avoided making statements about evicting the squatters; this was not our responsibility, and I did not want to provide the opportunity for misleading stories about "gringo archaeologists trying to throw people out of their homes." At one point, the squatters became very active and belligerent, picketing the statehouse in Cuernavaca and staging marches and protests in Yautepec. Several protesters jumped over the wall of a lot adjacent to the squatters' settlement where we were excavating an Aztec house and threatened our workers. One worker, a PRI member, complained to the local PRI office, and word soon reached the governor, who sent a contingent of state troopers in bright blue uniforms with shotguns to guard the excavation crew. There were no further threats and the troopers soon grew bored, so we put them to work at the screens. When we completed the excavation adjacent to the squatters' settlement, we declined further protection, and there were no more incidents of this type.

During the 1993 excavations, my university would not let me employ local workers directly unless they became New York State employees, drawing biweekly checks in Albany and paying U.S. and N.Y. income tax. We had to subcontract out for the labor, and the Patronato in Yautepec agreed to be the subcontractor. The subcontract forged an even closer relationship between the project and the Patronato. It turned out that all of the officials of the Patronato were also active PRI members, who endeavored to use our relationship for the benefit of the party. For example, the PRI wanted to use our hiring to reward party activity, and prospective workers were told that they couldn't be hired on the project unless they joined the PRI. We resisted this, however, and ended up hiring whom we wanted (even a few PRD sympathizers). We were invited to various party functions, and the PRI used our relationship for their own propaganda: "The PRI supports work on the history of Yautepec while the PRD destroys Yautepec ruins." We were thus aligned politically whether we liked it or not. We also benefited from this PRI connection; we used a telephone and fax machine in the PRI office, party workers helped with some of our negotiations with landowners, and one student rented a room above the office.

Landowners in Mexico are often wary of letting archaeologists dig for fear that their property will be seized if anything interesting turns up. There were rumors around town that we were going to tear down the secondary school because we had found buried pyramids there; in fact, we had uncovered domestic structures and burials (Figure 3) and the school was in no danger. This general fear, coupled with the very public struggle over eviction of the squatters, made many landowners hesitant to let us excavate. We did manage to get permission to dig in about 13 modern properties (including two schools and two sixteenth-century church yards), and these served as sampling frames in our search for buried houses.

It proved a very successful excavation season, despite having been prevented from digging where we had originally planned. We uncovered the first set of Aztec urban houses ever excavated and recovered sufficient data to reconstruct the activities and social conditions of their inhabitants.

We returned to Yautepec for more fieldwork in 1994 and 1996. These seasons were devoted to a regional survey of the Yautepec Valley. Although our lab and housing were based in town, most of our time was spent in the countryside, where we did not encounter any problems of a political nature. As the 1997 field season begins, the squatters are still in place, and by now they have seriously damaged the archaeological remains with their house construction, latrines, trash pits, and looting.

Just who constitutes our host community in Yautepec? To which of the many publics are we responsible and in what ways? Table 1 lists 16 distinct publics in Mexico that are relevant to the project, but this is a great simplification of a complex situation. Many of the categories in Table 1 are composite groups, often with conflicting interests and roles. For example, the municipal government included two relevant factions: The PRI-controlled municipal president's office supported the project, while the PRD-controlled public works department tried to stop the fieldwork.

In the context of Yautepec politics, it is tempting to view the PRI as the "good guys," helping us and promoting archaeology and preservation of the archaeological record, and the PRD as the "bad guys," who block fieldwork and contribute to looting and site destruction. Many personal friends are active PRI partisans. It is not a difficult decision to continue to work with the PRI in the future, although this ensures the continuing alienation of the PRD faction in town. But maybe the members of the PRD have a greater need for public education and attention from archaeolo-

Figure 3—Excavation of an Aztec structure in the yard of a secondary school in Yautepec. Note our audience of students on the balcony.

Table 1. Relevant Publics at Yautepec, Morelos.

Category	Public
Archaeological Publics:	1. Consejo de Arqueología, INAH, Mexico D.F.
	2. Centro INAH en Morelos, Cuernavaca
	3. Local archaeologists and historians
Governmental Institutions:	4. Municipal government, Yautepec
	5. State government, Morelos
Community Organizations:	6. Sociedad Cultural Yautepec
	7. Patronato Pro-Restauración de la Zona Arqueológica de Yautepec, Morelos
	8. PRI, Partido de la Revolución Institucionalizada
	9. PRD, Partido de la Revolución Democrática
	10. Primary and Secondary Schools
	11. Yautepec Catholic church
Local Residents:	12. Excavation workers and families
	13. Landowners
	14. Squatters
	15. Other Yautepec residents
	16. The Mexican public

gists. Perhaps our efforts would make the greatest impact if directed at the opposition party. On the national level, the PRI-controlled government has long supported archaeology, including research, education, and conservation. But what if the PRD were to win a presidential election? Would this have a negative impact on archaeology and the archaeological record? Any efforts directed at PRD partisans in Yautepec, however, would surely alienate the people and organizations of the PRI.

My solution to this dilemma is to continue to work with the PRI for logistical reasons and to concentrate public education efforts with the schoolchildren of Yautepec. The students and teachers at the public schools constitute one of the major publics for our work in Yautepec. We conducted several excavations in the secondary school near the pyramid and one excavation in a primary school in another neighborhood. These became major foci of public education. All of the students got to see the excavations, and we lectured to more than 1,000 students throughout the course of the season; I also gave some lectures at the secondary school in subsequent seasons. We began excavation of an elite residence in the schoolyard but were not able to complete the work before the end of the field season. Later, an INAH team completed the work and consolidated the architecture to serve as an open exhibit for the secondary school.

We also cooperated with a program run by the Sociedad Cultural Yautepec designed to teach fifth- and sixth-graders about archaeology and the archaeological heritage of their town (this project was funded by a grant from the PRI-controlled federal government). A group of these students toured the excavations each week, and we talked to them about

Yautepec's history. These students and our project were subjects of a television documentary made by the state public television station.

We will be working in Yautepec for several more years, mostly conducting laboratory analysis. I have given public lectures and written articles for local newspapers, and project members are planning to produce one or more exhibits along the lines suggested by Elizabeth M. Brumfiel (1994:4–7, 15). Many project activities, both research and community interaction, will continue to involve project members in unintended factional affiliations. We don't have much choice in this, given the nature of local conditions in Yautepec. Our landlords, for example, are involved in the Patronato, the PRI, and the local schools. The bulk of our work in public education will continue to focus on the students in Yautepec's primary and secondary schools. These children are the future adult citizens of Yautepec, and at least they have not yet joined a political party.

Acknowledgments

This paper is a revised version of "Which of Many Publics Do We Serve: Archaeology in Morelos, Mexico," presented at the session Descending the Ivory Tower: Maximizing the Involvement of Benefits to our Host Communities at the 13th Annual Northeast Mesoamerican Conference, University of Massachusetts, Amherst, Mass., December 2, 1995. I want to thank Sharon Swihart for the invitation to participate in that session. Funding for the Yautepec excavations was provided by the National Science Foundation, the National Endowment for the Humanities, and the University at Albany, SUNY. I want to thank Hortensia de Vega Nova and other archaeologists and officials of the Centro Regional Morelos, INAH, for their support and help during a difficult field season. I also thank the many students who have worked at Yautepec for their assistance with the project and for their contributions to the improvement in community relations.

Note: Information about our excavations can be found on the Web at **www.albany.edu/~mesmith/yaucity.html.**

SAA Bulletin, September 1997

The New Role of the Ancient Lovers of Sumpa

Karen E. Stothert

The Museum and Cultural Center of the Lovers of Sumpa (Museo Los Amantes de Sumpa y Centro Cultural) was inaugurated in April 1997, in Santa Elena, coastal Ecuador. The concept of the new museum—the goal of which is to teach and celebrate the unique indigenous cultural tradition of the Santa Elena Peninsula—grew out of a collaboration between archaeologists and the community. The museum was built thanks to an extraordinary cooperation among private and public institutions in Ecuador.

The museum was opened after a 20-year drama involving the serendipitous recovery of a pair of human skeletons, their popularization as an emblem of cultural identity, and the transformation of an archaeological site into an interpretive center and focus for the development of heritage resources. During those years, the writer, an archaeologist trained in investigation and the preparation of scientific reports, progressively developed new roles in heritage education and the promotion of Native American culture in coastal Ecuador. But it never would have happened without the Lovers of Sumpa.

The story began in 1977 when the late Olaf Holm, then-director of the Anthropology Museum of the Central Bank of Ecuador, asked me to excavate a preceramic site on the Santa Elena Peninsula. This work resulted in the description of the Las Vegas preceramic culture and the recovery of the remains of 200 individuals buried in the site between 8000 and 6700 B.P. The site is the oldest well-documented preceramic camp in Ecuador. During that first season we discovered a tomb containing two embracing skeletons, the remains of a woman and a man who died some 7,000 years ago. Because values in Ecuador do not impede the public display of human remains, the double burial known as the "Lovers of Sumpa" (los Amantes de Sumpa) became the focus of media attention, and Holm encouraged use of the find to attract public attention to archaeology. I began to give slide lectures—strategically using the figures—to inform people, especially schoolchildren, about the value and richness of their cultural patrimony and to foster its protection and scientific study.

By 1979 plans were circulating in the Central Bank of Ecuador to construct a site museum in Santa Elena, to protect the Lovers and the unexcavated portions of the archaeological site, and to allow public visits. Regrettably, as the price of oil fell in the 1980s, the project was never funded, although funds were allocated for guards to be posted at the site

24 hours a day for at least 20 years. Demographic and ideological changes occurred during those 20 years. Initially, archaeology was considered a pastime of the well-to-do. Narratives about ancient peoples and cultures did not figure into the worldview (or political discourse) of the majority of the people, and the prehistoric past was largely ignored by educators.

When I first began to work in the Santa Elena region in 1970, the popular view was that the local people were deculturated remnants of an ancestral past, to which they had little connection. However, conversations with Jorge Marcos, Olaf Holm, and others, and my observations of *campesinos* (rural people), revealed to me the continuities between the cultural adaptations of the prehistoric and colonial periods and the way of life of rural people today. These people had abandoned their native languages and dress early in the Colonial period, and they have not been called Indians since the last century. Nonetheless, communal ownership of land is part of their political focus, and they maintain a body of traditional knowledge and customs appropriate to their unique environment that distinguishes them from other Ecuadorians. The modernization process, however, evident in the abandonment of the land and the traditions of the past, is accelerating as the people who grew up before World War II age and die.

The workmen who excavated at the Las Vegas site continued to work with me at other, ceramic-stage archaeological sites in the 1980s, and I grew more appreciative of their knowledge of the environment and their skills in transforming its resources to human use. These men, as well as

Figure 1—Built at the edge of the archaeological site, this traditional house is the focus of living history exhibits, including cooking and craft activities. Photo by Roberta McGregor.

their relatives and friends, helped me to interpret the archaeological record, and soon I began to combine ethnographic and archaeological studies. This strategy had been characteristic of the work of Olaf Holm and was employed fruitfully by Silvia Alvarez, Jorge Marcos, and others in their studies in coastal Ecuador. Documentation of the living traditions of Santa Elena is as important as the archaeological studies; much of the information one can gather from elderly people today has not been transmitted to the younger generations, and thus, customs traceable to the Colonial and prehistoric periods are disappearing daily. Artisans frequently say "Write this down, *señorita*, because when I die nobody will pay any attention to this profession." Working together with elderly informants, we have created a body of information that not only pleases people, but is educational and stimulates pride.

In the late 1970s and 1980s the indigenous movement in Ecuador and the ideology of the left contributed to the development of the connection between the existing *campesino* communities of the coast and their aboriginal and archaeological past. For example, in the town of Valdivia a celebration of "6,000 years of Valdivia" became, the next year, a celebration of 6,001 years, and then 6,002 years. A small museum celebrating the ethnic identity of the people of the Valley of Chanduy with ethnographic, historical, and archaeological materials was opened at an important Valdivia archaeological site. In the town of Agua Blanca archaeologists Colin McEwan and María Isabel Silva began working together with the residents in an integrated program of archaeological research and community development, making it possible for the community, which once survived by making charcoal from the forest and digging up ruins to sell ancient artifacts, to find a new, sustainable economic focus in ecocultural tourism.

By the mid-1990s the Santa Elena Peninsula had become a regional economic center with a population that had doubled four times in 20 years, but the proposed site museum was still under discussion. Meanwhile, a new generation of socially engaged professionals, such as archaeologist Ana Maritza Freire of the Central Bank Museum, began to publish illustrated archaeological reports for popular distribution. I continued to give lectures in rural churches and schools, combining the results of archaeological and ethnographic studies, and I delivered some motivational lectures as part of community development projects. In these slide talks I expressed my admiration for the people of rural coastal Ecuador as I described the skill of their elderly artisans and farmers, their knowledge of the environment, and their long history and prehistory, filled with achievements comparable to those of the ancient peoples of Mexico and Peru. As a foreigner, I apologized for lecturing to them about their own ancient culture, but the information about prehistory was new to them, and people were impressed that a foreign professional was interested in their traditional crafts and customs. One man shook my hand after a lecture and said that he felt proud to be a *cholo*. This term, often applied in a deprecating sense, is now being adopted by people who value the unique identity and aboriginal heritage of the people of the southwest coast of Ecuador.

In 1993 I worked with Clarice Strang, director of the community development programs of Pro-Pueblo Foundation, a dependency of a private cement company (La Cemento Nacional del Ecuador), and we presented the idea for a site museum in Santa Elena to the general manager of the company. A year later, La Cemento decided to build a museum building, and we were launched into the roles of promotors and entrepreneurs. With the commitment of the cement company, Fredy Olmedo, director of the Anthropology Museum of the Central Bank in Guayaquil, agreed to install the proposed exhibit; the City of Santa Elena donated land for the museum; and the Fulbright Commission offered to sponsor a scientific consultant. In addition, we formed a private foundation (Fundación Los Amantes de Sumpa)—made up of natives and residents of the Peninsula of Santa Elena, including educators and community activists of various political stripes—the role of which is to administer

Figure 2—Upstairs in the traditional house, Ulberta Filomena Soriano Laínez weaves cotton textiles on a vertical loom using techniques that have persisted since the prehistoric period.
Photo by Ralph Howell

the new museum, raise funds, and make it serve the community. Together we developed a museum philosophy, and in 1994, with the president of Ecuador presiding, the cooperating institutions signed an agreement specifying their participation. Shortly thereafter commenced an unprecedented cooperation between La Cemento and Fulbright, the Museum of the Central Bank, local government, and a private foundation.

As the project began in earnest, it was clear that both a museum and cultural center were desired by all. By working together with the members of the foundation, my ideas about how to interpret the past evolved rapidly; we developed a new rhetoric and hammered out ideas about how to celebrate ethnic identity, teach children pride in their roots, and protect the environmental and cultural resources of Santa Elena. This kind of creative activity seems to be associated with societies at a developmental stage where older community-based traditions are in crisis. Similarly, a focus on the protection of archaeological and environmental resources in Santa Elena has materialized in the course of economic development just when the destruction of those resources has reached an advanced state. Our mission successfully attracted support from both private and public sources because it satisfied a variety of political, personal, and institutional needs: The new museum generated publicity for the cement company and for the mayor of Santa Elena; the opening of the museum was perceived as beneficial for the growing tourist industry; and neither the Lovers of Sumpa nor the foreign archaeologist who played focal ceremonial roles in the process were politically aligned.

Today, on entering the Museo Los Amantes de Sumpa you are invited to visit the archaeological site that is protected so that future study can result in a more complete interpretation of the early people who lived there from 10,000 to 6700 B.P. A small building on the hill shelters three burials, displayed in situ in glass cases, surrounded by giant photos of the excavations and interpretive texts. Here, in the oldest cemetery in Ecuador, Ecuadorians marvel at the depth of their history and the success the Las Vegas people had over a period of 4,000 years. The remains of the Lovers, named for the region that once may have been called Sumpa, seem to communicate across time the importance of human affection, and the burial has become an emblem of the first inhabitants of Santa Elena, the people who may have originated the great cultural tradition of coastal Ecuador. The image of the Lovers has inspired poets, musicians, sculptors, and choreographers in Ecuador and beyond. On Sundays, schoolchildren bring their families to see the Lovers.

Your visit to the museum continues in the main building where there are 15 colorful, thematic exhibits, including eight large-scale dioramas and walk-in environments, which explain how history is written in the ground, the value of archaeology as compared to *huaquerismo* (looting), what archaeological analysis reveals, the nature of the environment before recent deforestation, and the way of life of each of the prehistoric peoples/cultures of the region with emphasis placed on the great achievements of each prehistoric group. The museum is alive with inspirational texts and other audio-visual devices, and visitors are given opportunities to converse with guides, participate in activities, and enjoy live performances.

The origins of the modern petroleum industry are shown in an exhibit of colonial tar boiling, and then five rooms are designed to represent the ethnographic present (ca. 1935 to modern times). First there is the workshop of *campesino* bronze casters and blacksmiths, and you then enter a house in which spinning, weaving, and dyeing activities are explained. A colorful storefront display shows that while the *campesino* ceramic tradition is virtually extinct, a new industry produces replicas of ancient vessels for sale to tourists. Through the windows of an old house you can see a mannequin laid out in an old-fashioned coffin, wearing handmade white clothing, and bearing a *cordón*, a kind of belt fabricated during the wake for the protection of the dead individual. This exhibit celebrates a special custom, characteristic only of the people of this part of Ecuador, which has roots in both the Precolumbian past and in the Colonial period. Finally, one sees a replica of the food offerings set out on a table for enjoyment by dead relatives on the Day of the Dead, celebrated every year in Santa Elena. This custom is another disappearing aspect of the local ethnic identity.

Outside the main building are several exhibits, the most important of which is the reconstructed *campesino* house, furnished as it might have been in 1935. Here, elderly workers perform traditional activities and converse with the public. Bronze casters fabricate metal artifacts in the workshop below the house, and a cooper makes wash tubs. Upstairs, women spin, weave, and grill plantains and roast sweet potatoes to serve visitors. An elderly gentleman makes hats from palm fiber (so-called Panama hats, which used to be the principal cottage industry in Santa Elena). Our museum guides report that sometimes older visitors to the house exclaim, with tears in their eyes, that this is just like their grandmother's house and they remember!

The theme that unites the entire museum is the celebration of dead ancestors—the skillful and knowledgeable people who merit our admiration because they successfully confronted the challenges of life and made this history. The most important contribution of the project is that the museum now functions as an educational resource in a region where few facilities serve thousands of schoolchildren. Working together with educators and community development specialists has raised my consciousness about the value of making the results of anthropological research available for children, the community, and tourists. I had once worried that most Santa Elena residents did not know what a museum was and had never wished for one. I now believe that the museum and cultural center was a good use of scarce resources because the exhibits serve to communicate ideas that educators value. Furthermore, the people with little education who work in the living exhibits are pleased to tell curious visitors about their crafts and the old days. The experience makes the near past accessible to people who have been accustomed to deprecate it. Also, the deep past is accessible for the first time. People enjoy the museum and return when they can.

The foundation is now working to bring a full-time educator onto the museum staff and to integrate museum visits into school curricula. Visitors may acquire a guidebook to the museum, as well as other related publications. Currently we are producing a film celebrating ancestors, and we hope to build a library and commercialize the production of local crafts in order to contribute to the economic development of the most disadvantaged sector of the population.

As this project developed, and as we planned the museum displays and outlined the texts, I worried whether the content reflected community thought, or my own, derived from my understanding of the importance of roots developed in my own society. I had verified the contents of the ethnographic exhibits with elderly informants, but *campesino* informants did not ask the question, "Who are we?" Museologists and educators ask this question and it appears on the walls of the museum; we answer the question using evidence from the past and from the *campesino* present. I cannot be sure that the museum speaks for *campesinos* and nonprofes-

Figure 3—In a workshop below the traditional house, Adela Borbor and Rosa Camatón, the last campesino bronze casters of Santa Elena, cast metal for visitors to the museum. Photo by Ralph Howell

sional people, but because those people generously told me their stories, showed me the tables for the dead, and explained the use of funerary belts, I felt that they were telling me who they were. Natives of Santa Elena consistently have voiced their pleasure with what is expressed in the Museum.

The most difficult part of this project has been finding the financial support to build and, more importantly, to operate the museum long term. A few conflicts arose as we struggled within our budget to design appealing, didactic, and enjoyable exhibits suitable for sophisticated urban viewers, native and foreign tourists, schoolchildren and the less-educated public. Today the museum expresses eloquently the mission of the members of the foundation, chiefly educators. These people donate their time to a degree beyond expectation, and act as guides themselves in order to maintain contact with their audience. They are proud of the excellent educational facility which we have built, and its content meets their expectations, serves their purposes as educators and as members of a community that has found few ways to express its being and its history. I am no longer concerned that we are distorting anyone's view: Rather, we have created a viewpoint where one did not exist, and no sector of the public has been disquieted. Recently the National Congress of Ecuador officially recognized my collaboration in the museum project, and in investigating and promoting the cultural heritage of Ecuador.

In the course of my association with the Anthropology Museum of the Central Bank, I have taken on that institution's educational mission and have worked with Ecuadorians to apply the results of anthropological and archaeological research to the educational and social needs of the community in Santa Elena. Archaeology can play a big role in the modernization process. In the new Museum of the Lovers of Sumpa it is wonderful to listen to volunteer guides, including members of the foundation, local high school students, and some of the former workers who excavated the archaeological site, as they teach and share with visitors the museum's message.

SAA Bulletin, March 1998

Postscript

The Museum of the Lovers of Sumpa began its third year of life with a series of educational workshops and cultural programs organized in conjunction with the Anthropology Museum of the Central Bank of Ecuador (Guayaquil). These events attracted a new public and generated some much-needed income. Attendance is rising now, but during the disastrous El Niño phenomenon (late 1997 through 1998), torrential rain devastated the region, leaving in its wake unemployment, economic stagnation, slowed tourism, and reduced income for the museum.

During the 1998 emergency, the foundation, composed of 10 committed volunteers who manage the museum on a part-time basis, had to focus its attention on immediate concerns rather than develop a long-term strategy. The chaotic conditions currently found in Ecuador continue to impede the resolution of the museum's problems. Nevertheless, by August 1999, I saw busloads of children and tourists crowded the museum campus on weekends and holidays. Recently the dean of one of the Peninsula's largest high schools was so impressed by the museum that he now plans to require visits by his students and faculty. Groups of students of tourism from various universities visit the Lovers of Sumpa regularly.

With increased attendance, the prognosis is brighter, but the museum depends upon the good-will of the National Cement Company and the Central Bank of Ecuador for its continuing operation. The future of this support is unsure. In 1999, exhibit repair and improvement was accomplished with capital funds, depleting the foundation's bank account. Neither staff nor funding exists for the purpose of maintaining the exhibits. Currently foundation members are searching for ways to manage the museum more effectively, seek substantial donations, and broaden the support base. The museum is accomplishing its immediate mission, but requires a dedicated executive. Unfortunately, there is no funding for such an individual.

To help resolve management problems, the foundation is working with a new Peace Corps volunteer experienced in a small business operation, who already has sent letters to English-language tourist guidebooks so that the museum will be included in their new editions. He has arranged for the donation of a bilingual web page for the museum (**www.geocities.com/TheTropics/Harbor/1619/LosAmantes/index.htm**; also some of the contents of the museum may be found on the web site of the Anthropology Museum of the Central Bank at **www.webnexus.com/users/vlp/mssumpti.htm**).

Relief may come from the Ministry of Education which is still processing the foundation's 1997 request for a full-time teacher to be assigned to the museum to develop programs for the 50,000 schoolchildren of the Peninsula, coordinate school visits, and promote the training of teachers and the integration of the museum into school curricula. Today, class groups from the more well-to-do schools visit the museum, but poorer public schools do not have the resources to support such field trips.

Despite severe economic and political problems in Ecuador, there is an unceasing struggle both within national institutions and at the local level in Santa Elena to promote the use of museums as important cultural and educational resources. The museum of The Lovers of Sumpa and the

Real Alto Museum are two examples of how community-focused institutions are responding positively to crisis. In a recent experiment, leaders of the rural town of San Marcos worked with volunteers from the Anthropology Museum of the Central Bank and the National Institute of Cultural Patrimony to install an exhibit in their regional school. Community funds, a generous check from the mayor of Santa Elena, and donations from several other institutions made the installation possible. As a result, archaeological materials which I recovered during salvage excavations in San Marcos were returned to community custody in the form of a handsome teaching exhibit which also has potential as a tourist attraction.

Since writing the original article, I have become discontented with my own use of the term *campesino* because it fails to name the unique, native people of the region, some of whom participate actively in the Ecuadorian indigenous movement (CONAIE), and many of whom are proud to be called *cholos*. The Museum of the Lovers of Sumpa is playing a growing and much-appreciated role in the celebration of *cholo* ethnic identity.

Working Together—Archaeological Research and Community Participation

Charles Stanish and Chapurukha M. Kusimba

In a recent edition of *Current Anthropology*, two social anthropologists debated a central question in anthropology: To what degree, if any, should an anthropologist act as an advocate for the community that he or she studies? On one side, Roy D'Andrade (1995) argues that the anthropologist should be as objective as possible. In contrast, Nancy Scheper-Hughes (1995) argues that, since objectivity is impossible, we should conduct "a politically committed and morally engaged anthropology."

The two articles by D'Andrade and Scheper-Hughes, plus the 10 comments and two responses, raised a number of epistemological, theoretical, and practical issues. One of the core issues of this debate is epistemological: to what degree do the activities and values of an anthropologist affect and/or compromise the data under study. The postmodernist position is that all data are inherently biased and objectivity is impossible. Therefore, according to Scheper-Hughes, the anthropologist should take an advocacy stand, based on an "explicit ethical orientation to 'the other'" (1995:418). The empiricist or neopositivist position, in contrast, is that while individual observers are biased, the scientist should maintain the most objective position as possible and then construct falsifiable models that can be tested by other scientists. Any factor that biases the observer should be avoided. The anthropologist should dispassionately follow a replicable methodology and record the relevant data. From this position, taking a moral position, as suggested by Scheper-Hughes, would represent an inappropriate bias in the methodology.

Archaeology was mentioned only once in this debate, and merely as an aside to the main arguments. However, as we read these articles and focused on the debate of anthropologist as objective observer versus active moral participant, we were struck by one of the great ironies of contemporary anthropology. The subdiscipline of anthropology historically most associated with cultural imperialism—archaeology (e.g., going to foreign lands, pillaging the cultural heritage, and then locking that heritage up in dusty natural history museums)—was now in the best position to act as an advocate for those whom it studied while at the same time maintaining the scientific integrity of the data. A number of historical factors that have occurred over the past few decades both within and outside the discipline make this possible. These factors include the rise of processual archaeology in the 1960s and 1970s that shifted the archaeologist's interest away from objects to information, the dramatic rise in society's awareness of environmental and ecological issues, the increasing importance of cultural and biological assessments in development projects around the world, and the rise in the number of indigenous archaeologists in many nonwestern nations.

In a word, archaeologists who work in developing nations can, in many instances, act as advocates for the politically and economically powerless without compromising their database. Even the most adamant postprocessualist would not argue that an object in the ground is somehow altered by the culturally bound and subjective values held by an archaeologist, be they submerged, hegemonic values or truly saintly impulses. Of course, the collection and interpretation of those objects is conditioned by those values, and they represent an important biasing factor to be controlled by explicit methodologies and sophisticated model building and testing. The point is that wherever one falls on the postprocessualist/neopositivist debate in contemporary archaeology, it is certain that cultural values will affect the interpretation and collection of data. However they will not alter the archaeological database itself, as the artifacts in the ground and the sites on the surface are a priori to any existing culturally constructed world of meaning. It is only the interaction of the archaeologist with those data that the epistemological problem of the effect of cultural values and structure (or "production") of the empirical world becomes problematic. In this one sense, archaeology is profoundly distinct from ethnography in that the actions and values of the observer are irrelevant to the nature of the database. A morally based ethnography changes the cultural context and actions of the subject(s) and therefore remains problematic from a neopositivist, scientific perspective, but an archaeology that seeks to achieve moral goals alongside scientific ones only biases the collection and interpretation process, but not the data themselves.

We offer two cases in which we, as archaeologists, have taken an advocacy role in the area of our research expertise. The first case is the Island of the Sun in Lake Titicaca, Bolivia. The second involves a legal land dispute in Kenya.

The Island of the Sun is divided into three Aymara communities, the dominant indigenous ethnic group in Bolivia. During the course of two seasons of settlement survey and excavations, Stanish negotiated with one of the communities to build a complex on community land that is to serve as an educational, recreational, political, cultural, and tourist center. The community center is completely owned and run by the local residents in common. Stanish, the archaeologist, provided the funds (through private donations) to purchase nonlocal materials (cement, paint, wood, etc.) while the community provided the local materials (adobe brick, sand, rocks) and provided the labor and expertise to construct the complex. A democratically elected committee ran the entire process and continues to maintain the buildings. They will continue their work and finish the community center complex when additional funds are available.

The construction of this center has several important implications for the community. First, it disabuses negative stereotypes of rural peoples by Bolivia's urban elite, particularly in regard to work ethics and their abilities to self-organize. Second, the center will serve as a museum, at the insistence of the community, to present their culture to the outside in terms that they themselves decide. Third, the center will serve as a powerful physical symbol of community unity replacing earlier buildings associated with the hacienda complex and a little-used church. Fourth, the center will permit the community to control tourism on the island: tourists will have a safe place to sleep and interact with the community on the latters' own terms, and community members will be able to present their culture in a manner that elicits pride and dignity as they define it. Fifth, the center will serve as a negotiating tool with large tour companies who can develop contractual relationships with the community for future tourist-community relationships. Finally, as tourism continues to increase, the community should be able to maintain some control over the process. The degree to which the community directly benefits from tourism is the degree to which the community will protect the cultural and natural resources that attract those tourists.

The second case concerns a legal land dispute on the Island of Wasini in Kenya. The Island of Wasini is located several hundred meters off the southern Kenyan coast in Kwale district. It is inhabited by two communities: the Wavumba of Wasini village and the Wachifundi of Mukwiro village. Both communities belong to the large community of Swahili peoples of the East African coast. Archaeological data collected from the island suggest that the island has been inhabited since the thirteenth century A.D. Oral tradition collected by Kusimba suggests that present peoples migrated to the island in the eighteenth century from Vumba Kuu on the mainland following an epidemic and constant attacks by mainland communities.

Kusimba's primary research has been to understand the development of complex Swahili polities of the East African Coast between A.D. 700 and 1750. This research has involved the integration of historical, anthropological, ethnoarchaeological, and archaeometallurgical approaches to understand the role of indigenous economic and technological production in the development of urban polities in the region. While collecting oral traditions Kusimba became aware that many Swahili peoples were angry at the way in which the anthropologists and historians had presented their cultural history. Many of them bitterly complained, arguing that their falsified culture and identity had negatively influenced government policy against Swahili, especially Muslim Swahili. They argued that current destruction of Swahili sites and monuments and systematic appropriation of Swahili lands, underinvestment in human power, and ethnic and religious discrimination of the Swahili in Kenya could only be understood in those terms. These problems created a dilemma at several levels. Kusimba wrote a critique of the manner in which anthropologists and historians had written the history of the Swahili peoples arguing that the falsified history of the Swahilis, presenting them as descendants of Asian colonists, had caused irreversible damage to the community's perception of itself in relation to other Kenyans. More importantly, such a history, which questions the legitimacy of Swahilis as true Africans, had provided the political tools for the Kenya government to appropriate the Swahilis most important means of subsistence and survival: their land (Kusimba 1996). The paper that Kusimba published focused on several cases of appropriation of Swahili lands by government officials. Central to this was the land case that was pending in the High Court of Kenya involving Abdulrahman Saggaf Alwy and others versus the attorney general and others. Abdulrahman and other legitimate heirs of Wasini Island had been removed from the island in 1965 when the government instituted a land adjudication program. They had sued the government in 1969 and their case had not been heard by 1992 when Kusimba first met the plaintiff. As expected, many colleagues both in Kenya and abroad criticized Kusimba for being to "pro-Swahili." A draft of this paper with its detailed documentation on the question to the Wasini Island case was given to the plaintiff who made the copy available to the judicial authorities through his lawyer. In July this year, a verdict favorable to the plaintiffs was made by the High Court in Mombasa based in part on the information provided to the justices by the paper.

These two cases illustrate that when archaeologists engage in community action they can both empower local communities and at the same time reverse processes that lead to the erosion of local identity and its past. In one case, the position of the archaeologist as intermediary between a community and an urban elite permitted the development of a cultural institution that strengthened the community's standing in the country as a whole. In the other case, the archaeological and historical data were used directly by an individual to obtain a just legal judgment against more powerful adversaries.

In both instances, the advocacy activity of the archaeologist was parallel to the scientific research. The database was not compromised, and if anything, the collection and interpretation of those data were strengthened by the active participation by the archaeologists in the lives of the community in which they worked.

May 1996

Afterword:
Who Was Arthur C. Parker, Anyway?

David Hurst Thomas

This volume is a terrific idea, and I thank the editors for asking me to be a part of it. I've enjoyed reading the Working Together pieces over the years. A number of these papers are already mini-classics, and I had somehow missed (or forgotten) some of the others. It is good to have everything in one place. I'd bet that several of these Working Together columns will end up being critical in helping to reinvent a workable archaeology for the twenty-first century. Good job, SAA!

The Society for American Archaeology did another good thing in establishing the Arthur C. Parker/Native American Scholarship Fund. Although involved in the early stages of creating this fund, I have no idea who thought of naming the Indian scholarship fund after Parker. Given the recent tensions between archaeologists and Indians, many are surprised at the irony: Who knew that the first president of the Society for American Archaeology was a Seneca?

Like many contemporary archaeologists, I had never heard of Arthur Parker before the scholarship fund was named after him. Parker belonged to a history that I did not know. Over the past decade, I've learned more about the history of American archaeology—particularly with respect to Native American people. In the rest of my comments, I will take a brief look at the career of Arthur Parker, one of the leading Indian intellectuals of his day.

To be sure, Parker deserves to be memorialized in the SAA's Native American Scholarship Fund. But does Arthur C. Parker—Indian intellectual-turned archaeologist—have any relevance to American archaeology in the twenty-first century?

"At Home on Either Side of the Buckskin Curtain"

Like other Indian intellectuals of his time, Arthur C. Parker (1881–1955) wore many hats, some of them feathered. He was a folklorist, ethnologist, writer of children's books, historian, museum director, advocate for Indian rights, and American archaeologist of the first order.

Parker's generation of Native Americans defined new ways of interacting with the non-Indian world. "They saw avenues open before them for an Indian discovery of non-Indian America," writes Frederick Hoxie (1992:972), for launching their "own voyages of exploration. Those voyages, in turn, would help both tribal communities and the larger public define a path leading form the 'ancient way' to the twentieth century."

Like his fellow travelers, Parker's generation set the terms for a new encounter and reversed a 400-year history of Indians being defined as "discovered" objects. For the first time, a number of influential Indians took hold of their own imagery and turned it around for their own benefit.

Parker was born in western New York in 1881 on the Cattaraugus Reservation of the Seneca Nation. His great uncle was Ely S. Parker—Iroquois leader, engineer, military secretary to General Grant during the Civil War, and Lewis Henry Morgan's highly respected collaborator on League of the Ho-de-no-sau-nee. Arthur Parker's maternal grandmother was a white New Englander whose Congregationalist family helped establish the local mission school. Despite his distinguished Seneca Iroquois ancestry, the rule of matrilineal descent prohibited Parker from enrolling as a member of the Seneca Nation (although later in time, Parker became an adopted member of the Bear Clan and assigned the name Gawasowaneh, which means "Big Snowsnake." He grew up in a household that proudly mingled Indian and white values, where portraits of distinguished Seneca ancestors in Indian dress hung next to those of white New Englanders.

Local Indian beadwork and arrowheads decorated the bookshelves, crammed with Devonian-age fossils from the rocky cliffs of Cattaraugus Creek—all collected from those secret places where Seneca elders told Parker the Little People lived. He learned to hunt with bow and arrow and expressed an early interest in the natural history of the reservation. Parker spoke Seneca as a second language. Indian friends and relatives would spend long hours in the parlor, telling young Arthur the tribal stories and passed along the rich oral tradition of the Senecas.

When he was 11, his parents moved to White Plains, an affluent suburb of New York City, and his life turned upside down. Young Parker missed his Cattaraugus homeland but he pursued his childhood interest in natural history as best he could, spending considerable time at the American Museum of Natural History, only an hour's train ride away. Put off by the antiquated exhibits, he wangled his way behind the scenes, entering a world of "spicy dust and mothballs, but mostly of mystery and greatness" (Hertzberg 1979:52). The curatorial staff befriended Parker and patiently identified his collections of artifacts, fossils, and birds' eggs.

"In the early nineties," Parker recalled, "I was permitted to examine the skeletal material at the American Museum of Natural History, to discuss the 'bones' with . . . Hrdliçka and finally to have some systematic guidance from Professor F. W. Putnam" (Thomas 1955:4). Although he studied for the ministry after graduating from public high school, Parker kept up his contacts with curators at the American Museum, particularly Frederic Ward Putnam, one of America's most influential anthropologists. Archaeologist Mark Harrington, one of "Putnam's boys," invited the 14-year-old Parker to join him on a dig at Long Island's Oyster Bay in 1903. Later that summer, they worked together digging on the Cattaraugus Reservation, an arrangement that worked well for both. Harrington's new assistant provided him access to the reservation, and Parker was proud to be returning home in his new role of fledgling museum archaeologist. This early dig experience convinced him to undertake a career in archaeology. This decision came at a fateful time, when museum-based anthropology faced competition from a more "academic," more "scientific" brand of anthropology being taught in the large universities. Aware of this shift, Parker deliberately chose the museum world, selecting the genial and outgoing Putnam as mentor over the "awesome," but icy Professor Boas at Columbia.

In 1904, Parker joined the New York state government as an ethnologist attached to the state library. The next year, he became the first State Archaeologist, affiliated with the New York State Museum in Albany. Digging at the Ripley site, an Erie Indian village and mortuary site in Chautauqua County, Parker excavated and analyzed dozens of human burials in 1906. His final report on the excavations has been called a "landmark in the history of American archaeology" (Hertzberger 1979:57)—the first time an archaeologist had interpreted his excavation findings based on firsthand knowledge of local Indian life.

Parker became a leading museologist—he literally invented the term—arguing that museums are "the university of the common man" (Ritchie 1956:294). Parker went on to become director of the Rochester Institute of Science and New York State Indian Commissioner (1919–1920). In 1935, Parker was elected the first president of the Society for American Archaeology (SAA), the premier professional archaeological organization in North America.

Putnam believed strongly that anthropology must be brought to a wider audience. He served as the head of the anthropology section at the Columbian Exposition in Chicago (1893) and, while professor of American archaeology and ethnology at Harvard, he was also a curator at New York's American Museum of Natural History. Putnam was the essence of a "museum man," a builder of institutions, who thought of museums as the proper training ground for young anthropologists—a vigorous but informal education.

Parker's Vision for Native America

Having survived their predicted extinction, Indians of Parker's generation began exploring non-Indian America on their own, applying their "ancient ways" to fresh pursuits including art, politics, medicine, the law, sports, and even anthropology. They began to create their own reality, defining pathways distinct from those mainstream American images that had nearly destroyed them.

For his part, Parker tried to span the social and racial gulfs between early twentieth-century Indians and non-Indians through his own brand of museum-based anthropology. But there was a larger problem: If anthropologists like Franz Boas and Alfred Kroeber were correct—and learned culture mattered more than racial heritage—then what happens to a minority, Indian or otherwise, when their cultural behavior is modified? Are assimilated Indians still Indian?

Indianness to Parker still mattered and he felt it important to transmit this knowledge to white America. He transformed himself into a tribal storyteller, somebody whose knowledge of the past provided a unique twist on the present. Stepping beyond tribal distinctiveness, he drew upon a body of pan-Indian knowledge to counteract negative stereotypes and imagery. Parker emphasized the positives in conventional Indian symbolism to defend native people from early twentieth-century attacks by educators, missionaries, bureaucrats, land-grabbers—and anthropologists like Lewis Henry Morgan and Alice Fletcher, who argued for the destruction of "tribalism."

Parker became active on the political front, joining with the upper crust of self-made Indian intellectuals to establish the Society of American Indians (SAI) in 1911. The SAI advocated a national rather than tribal agenda, promoting self-help, personal enterprise, education, and the breakup of the reservation system as essential to Indian success in America. He campaigned for a national American Indian Day and joined SAI leaders in criticizing Indians who went "back to the blanket," slipping back into a traditional culture the SAI saw as "clannish" and regressive. Parker spoke for the SAI leadership when he wrote that:

> the true aim of educational effort should not be to make the Indian a white man, but simply a man normal to his environment . . . No nation can afford to permit any person or body of people within it to exist in a condition at variance with the ideals of that nation . . . the Indian should accustom himself to the culture that engulfs him . . . developing the great ideals of his race for the good of the greater race, which means all mankind" (quoted in Hertzberg 1971:63).

The Society of American Indians was heavily influenced by the anthropological ideas of the day. Parker and several other founding members were trained professional anthropologists, and a number of non-Indian ethnographers joined the SAI as non-voting members. Although Boas had begun his two-pronged campaigns against racial determinism and unilineal evolution by this time, his message was not picked up by SAI, whose leaders were steeped in Morgan's theories of social evolution. Sounding every inch the social Darwinist he was, Sherman Coolidge, founding president of the SAI, argued that "we have reached a time when the white people are pretty well educated to the fact that the Indian can be civilized, can be Christianized, can be a good man" (quoted in Hertzberg 1971:65; see also Hanson 1997).

Ironically, Parker fought the inequities of anti-Indian racism with his own brand of scientific racialism. This was a time when many saw America as struggling to maintain its identity in the face of large numbers of European immigrants. The melting pot concept was seen as critical in breaking down the new cultural diversity and converting the new immigrants into productive, hard-working American citizens.

Carrying over the doctrines of racial determinism that still dominated anthropology in the early twentieth century, Parker helped incorporate this perspective into the platform of the SAI. Racial consciousness formed for Parker the rationale for a national, pan-Indian identity. He wrote:

> Today there is a growing consciousness of race existence. Today as perhaps never before all men of the aboriginal peoples feel themselves members of the red race or of aboriginal ancestry. No man should seek to destroy the special genius that race ancestry gives him. The God of nations did not give races distinctive racial endowments and characteristics for naught. And now, with a coming race-consciousness the American Indian seeks to go even further and say, 'I am not a red man only, I am an American in the truest sense, and a brother man to all human kind' (quoted in Hertzberg 1971:141).

Parker not-so-discreetly played off his own authentic Indianness against what he saw as the rootlessness of "imported Americans," races he characterized as ignorant and artificial. Parker's racialist views reflected the growing concern that immigrants were devaluing and diluting the American spirit. If these unlettered immigrant newcomers were ever to help America, Parker argued, a week of camping and "living like an Indian" under the tutelage of real Indian counselors might be just what they needed.

Problems with the Melting Pot

As it turned out, Parker's vision for the American Indian did not prevail. At the fifth annual meeting of the SAI, Carlos Montezuma, a Yavapai Apache, took the podium and delivered a different message. Targeting Parker's moderate assimilationist position, Montezuma's speech was provocatively titled, "Let My People Go." He ridiculed Parker's National Indian Day proposal and attacked the SAI's middle-of-the-road positions, arguing that the preeminent pan-Indian organization had disintegrated into "the mere routine of shaking hands, appointing committees, listening to papers" (quoted in Thomas et al. 1993:378). Railing against the heavy-handed BIA regulations, Montezuma asked: "The only way to adjust wrong is to abolish it, and the only reform is to let my people go. After freeing the Indian from the shackles of government supervision, what is the Indian going to do: Leave that with the Indian, and it is none of your business." Montezuma established his own newspaper *Wassaja* (which would, decades later, label anthropologists a "vulture culture").

Montezuma's radical views carried the day over Parker's melting-pot moderation. In 1923, an elite panel known as the "Committee of 100" convened to help reformulate on federal Indian policy, including anthropologists Frederick Hodge, Alfred Kroeber, Clark Wissler—and Arthur C. Parker. Although their report still supported assimilation, it also called for greater sensitivity to Indian customs and urged Congress to protect tribal land. The federal government followed up three years later by commissioning the respected and nonpolitical Brookings Institute to undertake a thorough study of Indian policy. Its 1928 report, commonly called the Meriam Report, was highly critical of previous government policy, urging that tribal governments be formally incorporated, that Indian boarding schools be closed, and that federal policy be redirected to promote cultural pluralism in lieu of assimilation.

During this period, Boas and Kroeber personally advised John Collier, commissioner of the Bureau of Indian Affairs to reinforce tribal authority and adopt a Boasian-style sense of cultural relativism at all levels. Collier agreed and the resulting Indian Reorganization Act of 1934 formally signaled the shift away from the melting pot toward the modern concept of tribal sovereignty. While sometimes imperfect, the new tribal constitutions provided for self-government by Indian residents on the reservations, prohibited further breakup of Indian land and provided for land consolidation programs by tribal councils.

"The Indian New Deal wasn't perfect," writes John Echo-Hawk, director of the Native American Rights Fund, "but its results were fundamentally beneficial for Indian people. The Indian Reorganization Act reversed the direction of American Indian policy" (quoted in Limerick 1987:209). The pattern of history changed from the erosion of Indian sovereignty to its restoration and revival. Although there were reversals during the tribal terminations of the 1950s, seven decades of federal Indian policy have effectively slammed the door on the melting pot politics so ardently advocated by Arthur Parker and his fellow Indian activists in the early twentieth century.

Shifting Anthropological Theory

A reservation-raised Seneca and savvy government bureaucrat, Parker maintained strong ties to the scientific establishment throughout his life. He was educated in an anthropological tradition that stressed the importance of recording Seneca culture and language before it disappeared.

Parker saw no conflict between his Seneca heritage and his responsibilities as a professional anthropologist. He used his influence as state archaeologist to help various Indian causes, and excavated to help clear up disputed land titles. Drawing upon his expertise in physical anthropology, he often assisted homicide police. In one case, he determined that bones recovered by the police were not those of a murder victim but of an Iroquois leader who had been buried two centuries before. "We have been able to defend the Iroquois from harmful influence and notify them of impending legislation," Parker wrote (quoted in Thomas 1955:8). "That a museum of archaeology should do this is most fitting and demonstrates that we are capable of acting as an intermediary not only between the Indians of today and their past history, but between the Indian and the whiteman of today." Parker was committed to preserving native language, mode of thought, belief systems, and native institutions. He prided himself on interpreting Seneca life from an insider's perspective—telling the world something of value that it otherwise would not know.

Many late-nineteenth-century archaeologists—including Adolph Bandelier, Frank Cushing, Jesse Walter Fewkes, Victor and Cosmos Mindeleff, and Gustaf Nordenskiold—agreed with Parker about the importance of relating Native American oral tradition to the archaeological record. As part of their archaeological research, they collected Indian traditions to help understand chronology, site function, and cultural affiliation of the sites they were studying. In 1900, Fewkes (1900:579) noted that "This work . . . can best be done under guidance of the Indians by an ethno-archaeologist, who can bring as a preparation for his work an intimate knowledge of the present life of the Hopi villagers." These investigators saw themselves as operating with an appropriately scientific framework, attempted to begin with an "ethnographic" known, working their way back into an archaeological "unknown." But it was exactly this "insider's" perspective that would attract the wrath of Boas and his students.

In 1898, while still at the American Museum of Natural History, Boas had published a programmatic paper outlining his visions of structuring future anthropological research. Broadly defining American anthropology as "the science of man," Boas identified three specific areas of inquiry: physical anthropology (the study of the variability in human form), linguistics (exploring the range of human languages), and ethnology (discovering the laws governing the activities of the human mind, and reconstructing the history of human culture and civilization). As he noted at the time, "these subjects are not taken up by any other branch of science, and in developing them anthropology fills a vacant place in the system of sciences" (Boas 1899:93). Although Boas would modify this definition several times during the next 40 years—he later annexed archaeology as a fourth branch of anthropology—the 1898 paper defined the modern structure of the field.

For the first time, Boas specifically defined the subject matter of anthropology in terms of three key variables—biology, language, and culture. "Race" was no longer the sole determinant of cultural behavior. In fact, in the Boasian scheme, none of anthropology's three variables could be assumed to be primary: Each varied independently. Boas insisted that different approaches were required to study each branch of anthropology, and that each involved quite separate kinds of historical processes. This marked a significant departure from the evolutionary anthropology of Cushing, Fletcher, Morgan, and Powell.

Boas argued that cultural development was so complex and had taken so many diverse paths that there could have been no progressive evolution in the human past. The world's most complex forms of social organization were sometimes associated with the very simplest kinds of technology (as among the historic period Australian aborigines). Boas also maintained that human institutions such as slavery, private property, and state-level government are associated with an amazing array of related sociocultural features. He saw each culture as unique. No sweeping cross-cultural generalizations were possible. This doctrine of cultural relativism questioned the existence of any universal standards by which to judge either the degree of cultural development or the intrinsic worth of different cultures. Boas and his students attacked the generalized evolutionary themes of Fletcher, Morgan, and Powell as ethnocentric, ahistorical, and ultimately unverifiable.

Arthur Parker—a Christian, a Mason, and a progressive liberal—took these changes in anthropological theory very personally. After all, Parker saw himself and the other "acculturated" Indians of the his era as having ascended to the higher rungs of the evolutionary ladder. According to Hazel Hertzberger (1979:55), "There was certainly no other budding American anthropologist to whom the rejection of Morgan and of cultural evolution could be so deeply personal and familial an affair, nor, perhaps, one who equated anthropology so closely with preserving the fame of the 'Indian race'."

Boas attempted to raise anthropological standards to a level that would satisfy even a hard scientist, instilling in his students a sense of scientific professionalism. "From physics Boas brought into anthropology a sense of definiteness of problem, of exact rigor or methods, and of highly critical objectivity," Kroeber (1935:540) wrote. "These qualities have remained with him unimpaired, and his imparting them to anthropology remains his fundamental and unshakable contribution to our discipline." As Don Fowler (in press) has put it, Boas made "a conscious attempt to 'mystify' science as the objective search for Truth, and see scientists as infallible, dispassionate knowledge-makers."

Boas argued that ethnographic data must be carefully framed into objective and rigorous categories that would eventually lead to the discovery of scientific laws and principles. By these guidelines, ethnographic evidence must be collected objectively and precisely. Hypotheses must be formulated explicitly and tested against independent data. This framework, grounded in Enlightenment science, was designed to ensure that conclusions were objective and true: If two scientifically trained ethnographers observed similar events under similar conditions, they should be able to record, objectively, exactly the same data. Although these objectives were grounded in the methods of Samuel Morton and Lewis Henry Morgan, Boas faulted their anthropological techniques and theoretical assumptions. Scientists must observe and describe aspects of a culture that even those participating in that culture do not know.

This is why Boas and his students belittled those trying to approximate an "insider's" perspective on Indian life, and nowhere does the Boasian vision for a dispassionate "science of man" emerge more clearly than with respect to native oral tradition. In a testy critique, Robert Lowie savagely criticized the reliance on oral history. "Native 'history' is not history in our sense," he argued (1915:599), "any more than the fact, even if true, of my neighbor's cat having kittens is history; and as for tribal differences, what criteria have we for estimating them solely on the basis of the traditions? From the traditions themselves nothing can be deduced." Then, in a monumental fit of pique, Lowie threw down the gauntlet: "I cannot attach to oral traditions any historical value whatsoever under any conditions whatsoever." In his address as retiring president of the American Folk-Lore Society, delivered in December 1916, Lowie continued the theme, suggesting that any scientists believing that Indian oral traditions had valid "historical value" are like "circle-squarers and inventors of perpetual-motion machines, who are still found besieging the portals of learned institutions."

Lowie "utterly denied" that primitive people possess a historical sense or perspective. "The psychologist does not ask his victim for his reaction-time," he argued (1917:163), "but subjects him to experimental conditions that render the required determination possible. The paleontologist does not interrogate calculating circus-horses to ascertain their phylogeny. How can the historian beguile himself into the belief that he need only question the natives of a tribe to get at its history?" Although "primitive history" might retain some ethnographic interest for study as such, Lowie argued that anthropological evidence obtained "objectively" would always be superior to tribal hearsay.

This assault on Indian oral tradition carried the day, and anthropologists across the country chimed in to support Lowie's views. In 1917, Alfred Kroeber wrote that "The habitual attitude of the Zuni, then, is ahistorical . . . That now and then he may preserve fragments of a knowledge of the past that approximates what we consider history, is not to be doubted. But it is equally certain that such recollection is casual and contrary to the usual temper of his mind."

Archaeologists were swayed by what the cultural anthropologists said. Also in 1917, while on leave from his Pecos excavations and awaiting assignment to Officer Training School, Alfred Kidder moved to the First Mesa at Hopi. "I learned a great deal about Hopi archaeology," wrote Kidder (quoted in Givens 1992:59–60), "and among other things discovered that Lowie was quite right. Lowie [said] 'Under no circumstances will I ever believe any historical tradition told me by the Hopi' . . . When someone like Fewkes began pestering them, and asking them leading questions, they, of course, had to say something, so they just made these things up out of the whole cloth. I don't believe there is any truth to any of that stuff. This history of the development of the Hopi towns has to be worked out archaeologically . . . " Archaeologist F. W. Hodge (in Lowie 1917:165), among many others, agreed with Kroeber's earlier assessment: "Zuni traditional accounts of events which occurred over three centuries ago are not worthy of consideration as historical or scientific evidence."

While admitting that primitive astronomy and natural history might occasionally coincide with "our equivalent branches of learning," Lowie insisted (1917:163) that "in history, as everywhere else, our duty is to determine the facts objectively; if primitive notions tally with ours, so much the better for them, not for ours." Boas and his students were advocating a hard-lined, physics-based view of science, and this impartial-objective-outsider's perspective won out. The "insider's truth" approach to anthropology was discredited for decades.

# # #

So it was that, during the early twentieth century, a chasm began to separate American anthropologists from the Indian people they wanted to study. As anthropologists became increasingly concerned with establishing an objective science of mankind, many Indian people expressed their concerns about preserving their own specific tribal histories, customs, and traditions. Mainstream anthropology came to view "insider" anthropologists like Cushing as something of an embarrassing joke—dressed up like an Indian and trying to penetrate the Zuni mind. Although Arthur Parker was a professionally-trained anthropologist, his anthropological contributions were marginalized because he affected an "insider's perspective" rather than the strict empiricism advocated by Boas and his students. This is why twentieth-century anthropology came to view American Indian perspectives on their own past as basically irrelevant. And, for their part, Indians became increasingly wary of throwing in their lot with anthropologists.

Modern Indians pursuing a career in archaeology still experience some of the challenges that faced Arthur Parker a century ago. Although Parker has been called the "most distinguished American Indian savant of his generation" (Fenton 1968:2) and his Indianness served him well in his rise in the New York State government, he still found himself caught in the middle: spokesman for Indian people while a practicing museum professional and working anthropologist. Like Parker, today's Native American archaeologists will experience manifold allegiances, torn between professional and traditional loyalties. Also like Parker, some will experience hostile reactions from both scientific and tribal communities.

But there are now signs that in the twenty-first century, American archaeology might be more welcoming to native people. Like many of the archaeologists contributing to this volume, I was trained under the old, pre-NAGPRA rules, which invested archaeologists with the primary authority to protect, excavate, curate, and interpret the archaeological record. But in 1990, NAGPRA broke professional archaeology's long-standing monopoly on the ancient American past, and contemporary Native Americans now have a legally defined stake in the archaeological record of their ancestors. Over the past decade, archaeology has become only one of the multiple stewards of America's remote past.

Many of the Working Together columns document the progress of native people as they become active participants in an American archaeology that is trying to reinvent itself for the twenty-first century.

Notes: The ideas expressed in this chapter are developed in considerably more detail in Thomas (2000, especially chapters 7, 8, 10, and 18). The expression "At home on either side of the buckskin curtain" comes from Fenton (1968:2).

References Cited

Allison, J.
  1996 Cisco's Ko'an: Educating Archaeologists about Indigenous Peoples' Self-determination in the Land Use Planning Process for Cultural Resources. *SAA Bulletin* 14(1):14–15, 26.

Aldenderfer, M.
  1993 Editor's Corner. *SAA Bulletin* 11(2):3.
  1998 "Let a Hundred Flowers Bloom, the Problems of Weeds, Birds, and Crabgrass Notwithstanding." Theory in American Archaeology. *Cota Zero* 14:53–60.

American Anthropological Association
  1998 Code of Ethics of the American Anthropological Association, Approved, June 1998. *Anthropology Newsletter* 39(6):19–20.

Anyon, R
  1995 Letters to the Editor. *SAA Bulletin* 13(5):4.

Anyon, R., T. J. Ferguson, L. Jackson, L. Lane, and P. Vicenti
  1997 Native American Oral Traditions and Archaeology: Issues of Structure, Relevance, and Respect. In *Native Americans and Archaeologists: Stepping Stones to Common Ground*, edited by N. Swidler, K. E. Dongoske, R. Anyon, and A. S. Downer, pp. 77–87. AltaMira Press, Walnut Creek, California.

Arbogast, W. R., F. D. Tierson, and A. Naranjo
  1996 *A Prehistoric Burial at 5EP2200, El Paso County*, Colorado. Report prepared for the City of Colorado Springs.

Bahr, D. M., J, Smith, W. S. Allison, and J. Hayden
  1994 *The Short, Swift Time of Gods on Earth: The Hohokam Chronicles*. University of California Press, Berkeley.

Barnes, W. C.
  1941 *Apaches and Longhorns: The Reminiscences of Will C. Barnes*. Edited by F. C. Lockwood. Ward Ritchie Press, Los Angeles.

Baugh, T. G., and S. Makseyn-Kelley
  1992 *People of the Stars: Pawnee Heritage and the Smithsonian Institution*. Report on file, Repatriation Office, National Museum of Natural History, Smithsonian Institution, Washington, D.C.

Billeck, W. T., and J. Urcid
  1995 *Assessment of the Cultural Affiliation of the Steed-Kisker Phase for Evaluation by the National Museum of Natural History Native American Review Committee*. Report on file, Repatriation Office, National Museum of Natural History, Smithsonian Institution, Washington, D.C.

Binford, L. R.
  1962 Archaeology as Anthropology. *American Antiquity* 28:217–225.

Boas, F.
  1899 Advances in Methods of Teaching. *Science* n.s. 9:93–96.

Bray, T., and T. W. Killion
  1994 *Reckoning with the Dead: The Larson Bay Repatriation and the Smithsonian Institution.* Smithsonian Institution Press, Washington, D.C.

Brumfiel, E. M.
  1994 Making History in Xaltocan. *SAA Bulletin* 12(4):4–7, 15.

Carlson, K. M., P. Molloy, and T. W. Killion
  1997 *Determining the Biological Affiliation of Human Remains: An Assessment of Available Techniques.* Report on file, Repatriation Office, National Museum of Natural History, Smithsonian Institution, Washington, D.C.

Clark, G. A.
  1991 Introduction. In *Perspectives on the Past: Theoretical Biases in Mediterranean Hunter-Gatherer Research,* edited by G. A. Clark, pp. 1–21. University of Pennsylvania Press, Philadelphia.
  1992 Continuity or Replacement? Putting Modern Human Origins in an Evolutionary Context. In *The Middle Paleolithic: Adaptation, Behavior and Variability,* edited by H. Dibble and P. Mellars, pp. 183–205. University of Pennsylvania Museum, Piladelphia.
  1993 Paradigms in Science and Archaeology. *Journal of Archaeological Research* 1(3):203–234.
  1996 NAGPRA and the Demon-Haunted World. *SAA Bulletin* 14(5):3; 15(2):4.
  1997a Through a Glass Darkly: Conceptual Issues in Modern Human Origins Research. In *Conceptual Issues in Modern Human Origins Research,* edited by G. A. Clark and C. Willermet, pp. 60–76. Aldine de Gruyter, New York.
  1997b Race from the Perspective of Western Science. *Anthropology Newsletter* 38(7): 54.
  1997c Pernicious Vanities. *Anthropology Newsletter* 38(7):54,56.
  1998 Fixin' Racism. *Anthropology Newsletter* 39(3):7.
  1998 NAGPRA, the Conflict between Science and Religion, and the Political Consequences. *SAA Bulletin* 16(5):22, 24.
  1999a NAGPRA, Science, and the Demon-Haunted World. *Skeptical Inquirer* 23(3):44–48.
  1999b Modern Human Origins—Highly Visible, Curiously Intangible. *Science* 283:2029–2032.

Clark, G. A., and C. M. Barton
  1997 Rediscovering Darwin. In *Rediscovering Darwin: Evolutionary Theory and Archeological Explanation,* edited by C. Barton and G. A. Clark, pp. 309–319. Archeological Papers No. 7. American Anthropological Association, Arlington, Virginia.

Condori, C.
  1989 *Conflict in the Archaeology of Living Traditions.* Unwin Hyman, London.

Conkey, M. W., and J. D. Spector
  1984 Archaeology and the Study of Gender. In *Advances in Archaeological Method and Theory* 7:1–38.

D'Andrade, R.
  1995 Moral Models in Anthropology. *Current Anthropology* 36:399–408.

DeBarrios, P.
  1993 Native Americans and Archaeologists Working Together toward Common Goals in California. *SAA Bulletin* 11(3):6–7.

Deloria, V. Jr.
  1992 Indians, Archaeologists, and the Future. *American Antiquity* 57:595–598.

Dongoske, K.
  1995 Letter to the Editor. *SAA Bulletin* 13(2):7.

Dongoske, K. T. J. Ferguson, and L. Jenkins
  1993 Understanding the Past through Hopi Oral History. *Native Peoples Magazine* 6(2):24–31

Dongoske, K., M. Yeatts, T. J. Ferguson, and L. Jenkins
  1995 Historic Preservation and Native American Sites. *SAA Bulletin* 13(4):13.

Dongoske, K., M. Yeatts, R. Anyon, and T. J. Ferguson
  1997 Archaeological Cultures and Cultural Affiliation: Hopi and Zuni Perspectives in the American Southwest. *American Antiquity* 62:600–608.

Doyel, D.
  1982 Medicine Men, Ethnic Significance, and Cultural Resource Management. *American Antiquity* 47:634–642.

Echo-Hawk, R.
  1993 Exploring Ancient Worlds. *SAA Bulletin* 11(4):5–6.
  1997 Forging a New Ancient History for Native America. In *Native Americans and Archaeologists: Stepping Stones to Common Ground*, edited by N. Swidler, K. E. Dongoske, R. Anyon, and A. S. Downer, pp. 88–102. AltaMira Press, Walnut Creek, California.

Eggan, F.
  1967 From History to Myth: A Hopi Example. In *Studies in Southwestern Ethnolinguistic*, edited by D. Hymes, pp. 33–53. Mouton, The Hague.

Fenton, W. N.
  1968 Introduction. In *Parker on the Iroquois* by Arthur C. Parker. Syracuse University Press, Syracuse.

Ferguson, T. J.
  1996 Native Americans and the Practice of Archaeology. *Annual Review of Anthropology* 25:63–79.

Fewkes, J. W.
  1900 Tusayan Migration Traditions. In *Nineteenth Annual Report of the Bureau of American Ethnology for the Years 1897–1898*, Pt. 2:573–634. Government Printing Office, Washington, D.C.

Flannery, K. V.
  1967 Cultural History Versus Cultural Process: A Debate in American Archaeology. *Scientific American* 217(August):119–122.

Fowler, D.
  In press. *A Laboratory for Anthropology: Science and Romanticism in the American Southwest, 1846–1930*.

Gero, J. M.
1991 Who Experienced What in Prehistory? A Narrative Explanation from Queyash, Peru. In *New Directions in Archaeology: The Processual/Post-Processual Debate,* edited by R. Preucel, Southern Illinois University Press, Carbondale.

Gero, J. M., D. Lacy, and M. L. Blakey (editors)
1983 *The Socio-Politics of Archaeology.* University of Massachusetts, Amherst.

Givens, D. R.
1992 *Alfred Vincent Kidder and the Development of Americanist Archaeology.* University of New Mexico Press, Albuquerque.

González-Blanco Garrido, S.
1988 *Tlahuac Prehispánico.* Miguel Angel Porrúa, México, D.F.

Gould, S. J.
1977 Eternal Metaphors of Paleontology. In *Patterns of Evolution, as Illustrated by the Fossil Record,* edited by A. Hallam, pp. 1–26. Elsevier, Amsterdam.

Hall, R. L.
1997 *An Archaeology of the Soul: North American Indian Belief and Ritual.* University of Illinois Press, Urbana.

Hanson, R. R.
1997 Ethnicity and the Looking Glass: The Dialectics of National Indian Policy. *American Indian Quarterly* 21(2):195–208.

Hertzberg, H. W.
1971 *The Search for an American Indian Identity.* Syracuse University Press, Syracuse.
1979 Nationality, Anthropology, and Pan-Indianism in the Life of Arthur C. Parker (Seneca). *Proceedings of the American Philosophical Society* 123:47–72.

Hodder, I.
1984 Archaeology in 1984. *Antiquity* 58:25–32.

Holen, S. R,. and J. K. Peterson (editors)
1995 *The Stabaco Site: A Mid-Eighteenth Century Skidi Pawnee Town on the Loup River, Nebraska Archaeological Survey,* Technical Report 95–101, University of Nebraska State Museum.

Hoxie, F. E.
1992 Exploring a Cultural Borderland: Native American Journeys of Discovery in the Early Twentieth Century. *The American Journal of History* 79(3). Discovering America: A Special Issue (December):969–995.

Johnson, E.
1973 Professional Responsibilities and the American Indian. *American Antiquity* 38:129–130.

Jones, D. G., and R. J. Harris
1997 Contending for the Dead. *Nature* 386:15–16.

Kaplan, A.
1964 *The Conduct of Inquiry.* Chandler, San Francisco.

Kelley, K. B., and H. Francis
   1994   *Navajo Sacred Places*. Indiana University Press, Bloomington.

Killion, T. W., S. Brown, and J. S. Speaker
   1992   *Naevahoo'ohtseme: Cheyenne Repatriation*. Report on file, Repatriation Office, National Museum of Natural History, Smithsonian Institution, Washington, D.C.

King, T. F.
   1996   More on TCPs and Section 106. *SAA Bulletin* 14(1):13.

Kohl, P.
   1990   *Discussion, Histories of "People without History": Papers in Honor of Eric R. Wolf*. American Anthropological Association 89th Annual Meeting, New Orleans.

Kroeber, A. L.
   1917   Zuñi Kin and Clan. *Anthropological Papers of the American Museum of Natural History* 18(2):39–204.
   1935   History and Science in Anthropology. *American Anthropologist* 37:539-569.

Kusimba, C. M.
   1996   Kenya's Destruction of Swahili Cultural Heritage. In *Plundering Africa's Past*, edited by R. MacIntosh and P. Schmidt. Indiana University Press, Bloomington.

Limerick, P. N.
   1987   *The Legacy of Conquest: The Unbroken Past of the American West*. W. W. Norton, New York.

Lipe, W. D.
   1974   A Conservation Model for American Archaeology. *Kiva* 39:213–245.

Lowie, R. H.
   1913   Review of The Omaha Tribe by Alice Fletcher and Francis La Flesche. *Science* 37:910–915, 912.
   1915   Oral Tradition and History. *American Anthropologist* 17:597–599.
   1917   Oral Tradition and History. *The Journal of American Folk-Lore* 30(116):161–167.

Lynott, M. J.
   1997   Ethical Principles and Archaeological Practice: Development of an Ethics Policy. *American Antiquity* 62:589–599.

Lynott, M. J., and A. Wylie (editors)
   1995   *Ethics in American Archaeology: Challenges for the 1990s*. Special Report. Society for American Archaeology, Washington, D.C.

Mann, B. A., and J. L. Fields
   1997   A Sign in the Sky: Dating the League of the Haudenosaunee. *American Indian Culture and Research Journal* 21(2):105–163.

McCann, B.
   1988   The National Socialist Perversion of Archaeology. *World Archaeological Bulletin* 2:51–54.

McGuire, R.
1992   Archaeology and the First Americans. *American Anthropologist* 94:816–836.

McKeown, C. T.
1995   Overview of the Native American Graves Protection and Repatriation Act. In *The Native American Graves Protection and Repatriation Act of 1990: Compliance Workshop Proceedings*, p. 15. Haskell Indian Nations University.

Mauro, T.
1997   Bones of Contention. *Preservation,* January/February:22.

Meighan, C. W.
1996   *The American Committee for the Preservation of Archaeological Collections Newsletter*, November. Whittier, California.

Miller, E.
1995   *Refuse to be Ill: European Contact and Aboriginal Health in Northeastern Nebraska*. Unpublished Ph.D. dissertation, Department of Anthropology, Arizona State University, Tempe.

Minthorn, P.
1997   Archaeology of the Dammed. *Common Ground* 2(1):34–39.

Molloy, P., P. E. Minthorn, and G. P. Aronsen
1996   *Inventory and Assessment of Human Remains Identified as Nez Perce in the National Museum of Natural History*. Report on file, Repatriation Office, National Museum of Natural History, Smithsonian Institution, Washington, D.C.

Molnar, S.
1998   *Human Variation: Races, Types and Ethnic Groups*. Prentice-Hall, Upper Saddle River, New Jersey.

Morell, V.
1995   Who Owns the Past? *Science* 268:1424–1426.

Mudar, K., K. Nelson, S. Speaker, R. Scott, S. Street, and E. Miller
1996   *Inventory and Assessment of Human Remains and Associated Funery Objects from Northeast Norton Sound, Bering Straits Native Corporation, Alaska in the National Museum of Natural History*. Report on file, Repatriation Office, National Museum of Natural History, Smithsonian Institution, Washington, D.C.

Na Iwi O Na Kupuna O Mokapu v. Dalton, 894 F. Supp. 1397 (D. Hawaii 1995).

Naranjo, T.
1995   Thoughts on Migration by Santa Clara Pueblo. *Journal of Anthropological Archaeology* 14:247–250.

National Park Service
1997   Wooden Figure Remains at Center of Dispute. *Common Ground* 2(1):64.

Noble, V.
1993   Letter to the Editor. *SAA Bulletin* 11(5):3–4.

Pendergast, D., and C. Meighan
1959   Folk Traditions as Historical Fact: A Paiute Example. *Journal of American Folklore* 72(284):128–133.

Phillips, D. A. Jr.
  1996 More on TCPs and Section 106. *SAA Bulletin* 14(1):13.

Riding In, J.
  1992 *Report Verifying the Identity of Six Pawnee Scout Crania Held at the Smithsonian Institution and National Museum of Health and Medicine: Part II.* Report on file, Native American Rights Fund, Boulder, Colorado.

Ritchie, W. A.
  1956 Arthur Caswell Parker—1881–1955. *American Anthropologist* 21:293–295.

Rose, J., T. Green, and V. Green
  1996 NAGPRA is Forever: Osteology and the Repatriation of Skeletons. *Annual Review of Anthropology* 25:81–103.

Sagan, C.
  1996 *The Demon-Haunted World: Science as a Candle in the Dark.* Ballantine Books, New York.

Sagan, C., and A. Druyan
  1992 *Shadows of Forgotten Ancestors.* Random House, New York.

Samuel, G.
  1993 *Civilized Shamans: Buddhism in Tibetan Societies.* Smithsonian Institution Press, Washington, D.C.

Schwab, D.
  1993 Continuing Cooperation between Archaeologists and Native Americans in Montana. *SAA Bulletin* 11(5):5–6.

Scheper-Hughes, N.
  1995 The Primacy of the Ethical. *Current Anthropology* 35:409–420.

Sebastian, L.
  1995a Letters to the Editor. *SAA Bulletin* 13(3):3.
  1995b Historic Preservation and Native American Sites. *SAA Bulletin* 13(4):13.

Shanks, M., and C. Tilley
  1987 *Reconstructing Archaeology: Theory and Practice.* Cambridge University Press, Cambridge.

Shaul, D. L., and J. H. Hill
  1998 Tepimans, Yumans, and Other Hohokam. *American Antiquity* 63:375–396.

Smythe, C.
  1998 *Wounded Knee Case.* Ongoing Consultation, Repatriation Office, National Museum of Natural History, Smithsonian Institution, Washington, D.C.

Society for American Archaeology
  1999 Poster Session 7—Archaeological Constituencies: Native Americans and Other Publics.

Speaker, J. S., B. S. Byrd, J. W. Verano, and G. Stromberg
  1994 *Inventory and Assessment of Human Remains Potentially Related to the Apache and Yavapai Tribes in the National Museum of Natural History.* Report on file, Repatriation Office, National Museum of Natural History, Smithsonian Institution, Washington, D.C.

Spector, J. D.
1993 *What This Awl Means: Feminist Archaeology at a Wahpeton Dakota Village*. Minnesota Historical Society Press, St. Paul.

Steinacher, T. L., J. R. Bozell, G. F. Carlson, and J. Ludwickson
1991 *Nebraska State Historical Society Position Statement: Section B*. Report on file, Repatriation Office, National Museum of Natural History, Smithsonian Institution, Washington, D.C.

Stumpf, G.
1993 Arizona's Approach to Native American–Archaeologist Relations. *SAA Bulletin* 11(3):15.

Svaldi, D.
1989 *Sand Creek and the Rhetoric of Extermination: A Case Study in Indian-White Relations*. University Press of America, Lanham, Maryland.

Swidler, N., K.E. Dongoske, R. Anyon, and A. S. Downer
1997 *Native Americans and Archaeologists: Stepping Stones to Common Ground*. AltaMira Press, Walnut Creek, California.

Teague, L. S.
1993 Prehistory and the Traditions of the O'Odham and Hopi. *Kiva* 58(4): 435–454.

Terrell, J.
1990 Storytelling and Prehistory. *Archaeological Method and Theory* 2:1–29.

Thomas, D. H., J. Miller, R. White, P. Nabokov, and P. J. Deloria
1993 *The Native Americans*. Turner Publishing, Atlanta.

Thomas, D. H.
2000 *Skull Wars: Kennewick Man, Archaeology, and the Battle for Native American Identity*. New York: Basic Books, New York.

Thomas, W. S.
1955 Arthur Caswell Parker: 1881–1955. *Rochester History* 17(3):1–30.

Thornton, R.
1990 *The Cherokees: A Population History*. University of Nebraska Press, Lincoln.

Trigger, B. G.
1980 Archaeology and the Image of the American Indian. *American Antiquity* 45:662–676.
1984 Alternative Archaeologies: Nationalist, Colonialist, Imperialist. *Man* 19:355–370.

Trope, J., and W. Echo-Hawk
1992 The Native American Graves Protection and Repatriation Act: Background and Legislative History. *Arizona State Law Journal* 24(1):35–78, pp. 47–52.

Tsosie, R.
1997 Indigenous Rights and Archaeology. In *Native Americans and Archaeologists: Stepping Stones to Common Ground*, edited by N. Swidler, K. Dongoske, R. Anyon, and A. Downer, pp. 64–76. AltaMira Press, Walnut Creek, California.

Vansina, J.
1985   *Oral Tradition as History.* University of Wisconsin Press, Madison.

Varela Morales, M., and P. Varela Morales
La Cotorra: Revista Histórica Cómica Política. Nextlalpa, México.

Watkins, J.
1998   Native Americans, Western Science, and NAGPRA. *SAA Bulletin* 16(5):23, 25.

Watkins, J., L. Goldstein, K. Vitelli, and L. Jenkins
1995   Accountability: Responsibilities of Archaeologists to Other Interest Groups. In *Ethics in American Archaeology: Challenges for the 1990s,* edited by M. Lynott and A. Wylie, pp. 33–37. Society for American Archaeology, Washington, D.C.

White Deer, G.
1998   From Specimens to SAA speakers: Evolution by Federal Mandate. *SAA Bulletin* 16(3):6–8.

Whiteley, P. M.
1988   *Deliberate Acts: Changing Hopi Culture through the Oraibi Split.* University of Arizona Press, Tucson.

Willey, G. R., and P. Phillips
1958   *Methods and Theory in American Archeology.* University of Chicago Press, Chicago.

Wiget, A.
1982   Truth and the Hopi: An Historiographic Study of Documented Oral Tradition Concerning the Coming of the Spanish. *Ethnohistory* 29:181–199.

Williams, B. F.
1989   A Class Act: Anthropology and the Race to Nation Across Ethnic Terrain. *Annual Review of Anthropology* 18:429–439.

Yellowhorn, E.
1996 Indians, Archaeology, and the Changing World. *Native Studies Review* 11:23–50.

Zimmerman, L.
1989 Made Radical by Mine Own. In *Conflict in the Archaeology of Living Traditions,* edited by R. Layton, pp. 60–67. Unwin Hyman, London.

Contributors

Mark Aldenderfer, editor of the *SAA Bulletin*, is professor in the Department of Anthropology at the University of California-Santa Barbara.

Roger Anyon is with Heritage Resources Management Consultants in Tuscson, Arizona.

Colleen Beck is associate research professor and interim director of the Quaternary Sciences Center at the Desert Research Institute in Las Vegas, Nevada.

Elizabeth M. Brumfiel is professor in the Department of Anthropology and Sociology at Albion College in Albion, Michigan.

James E. Bruseth is director of the Archaeology Division, Texas Historical Commission, in Austin, Texas.

Cecile E. Carter serves on the Cultural Committee of the Caddo Tribe of Oklahoma.

G. A. Clark is professor in the Department of Anthropology, Arizona State University, in Tempe, Arizona

Janet Cohen is with the Navajo Nation Historic Preservation Department.

James E. Corbin is professor and coordinator of the anthropology program at Stephen F. Austin University in Nacogdoches, Texas.

Amy Dansie is an anthropologist at the Nevada State Museum in Carson City, Nevada.

Kurt E. Dongoske, associate editor for the Working Together column in the *SAA Bulletin*, is tribal archaeologist with the Hopi Cultural Preservation Office in Kykotsmovi, Arizona.

Roger C. Echo-Hawk is at the Denver Art Museum.

T. J. Ferguson is with Heritage Resources Management Consultants in Tucson, Arizona.

Robert Furlow is environmental scientist in the Environment, Safety, and Health Division, for the U.S. Department of Energy, Nevada Operations Office, Las Vegas.

Loretta Jackson is program manager for the Hualapai Office of Cultural Resources in Peach Springs, Arizona.

Robert Kelly is professor of anthropology in the Department of Anthropology at the University of Wyoming in Laramie.

Thomas W. Killion works in the Repatriation Office at the Smithsonian Institution National Museum of Natural History in Washington, D.C.

Rose Kluth is program director for the Leech Lake Heritage Sites Program at Cass Lake, Minnesota.

Rick Knecht is director of the Museum of the Aleutians in Unalaska, Alaska.

Chapurukha M. Kusimba is assistant curator of African Prehistory in the Department of Anthropology of the Field Museum, Chicago.

Leigh J. Kuwanwisiwma is with the Hopi Cultural Preservation Office in Kykotsmovi, Arizona.

Lillie Lane is a Navajo cultural specialist with the Traditional Cultural Program of the Navajo Nation Historic Preservation Department.

Randall H. McGuire is a professor in the Department of Anthropology at the State University of New York-Binghamton.

Bonnie McKee is a board member of The Archaeological Conservancy in Albuquerque, New Mexico.

Barbara J. Mills is associate professor in the Department of Anthropology at the University of Arizona.

Paula Molloy works in the Repatriation Office at the Smithsonian Institution National Museum of Natural History in Washington, D.C.

George P. Nicholas is lecturer and archaeology program director of the Secwepemc Cultural Education Society/Simon Fraser University Program in Kamloops, British Columbia.

Michael E. Smith is professor in the Department of Anthropology, State University of New York-Albany.

Janet D. Spector is associate professor in the Department of Anthropology at the University of Minnesota-Twin Cities.

Charles Stanish is professor in the Department of Anthropology at the University of California-Los Angeles.

Karen E. Stothert is a research associate at the Center for Archaeological Research, University of Texas-San Antonio, an investigator for the Museo Antropológico, Banco Central del Ecuador (Guayaquil), and honorary lifetime president of the Fundación Museo Los Amantes de Sumpa.

Nina Swidler is with the Navajo Nation Historic Preservation Department.

David Hurst Thomas is curator of anthropology at the American Museum of Natural History in New York.

Davina TwoBears is completing her dissertation in Tomah, Wisconsin.

Joe Watkins is agency archaeologist, Bureau of Indian Affairs-Anadarko Agency in Oklahoma.

John R. Welch serves as the historic preservation officer for the White Mountain Apache tribe and archaeologist for the Fort Apache Agency, Bureau of Indian Affairs.

Gary White Deer is current president of Keepers of the Treasures and director of the Native American Indian Association in Nashville.

Alison Wylie is a professor of philosophy at Washington University in St. Louis.

Mike Yeatts is with the Hopi Cultural Preservation Office.

M. Nieves Zedeño is at the Bureau of Applied Research in Anthropology, University of Arizona, Tucson.